Bless Me Too, My Father

Bless Me Too, My Father

Living by Choice, Not by Default

KATIE FUNK WIEBE

Foreword by Ruth Brunk Stoltzfus

HERALD PRESS
Scottdale, Pennsylvania
Waterloo, Ontario

LIBRARY OF CONGRESS
Library of Congress Cataloging-in-Publication Data
Wiebe, Katie Funk
   Bless me too, my Father / Katie Funk Wiebe ; introduction by Ruth
Brunk Stoltzfus.
   p.   cm.
   ISBN 0-8361-3472-9 (pbk.)
   1. Wiebe, Katie Funk.   2. Mennonites—Kansas—Hillsboro-
-Biography.   3. Hillsboro (Kans.)—Biography.   4. Middle age.
5. Aged.   I. Title.
BX8143.W43A3   1988
289.7'3—dc19
[B]   88-2997
                                                       CIP

The paper used in this publication is recycled and meets the
minimum requirements of American National Standard for
Information Sciences—Permanence of Paper for Printed Library
Materials, ANSI Z39.48-1984.

Except as otherwise indicated, Scripture quotations are from the *Holy
Bible: New International Version.* Copyright © 1973, 1978, 1984 by the
International Bible Society. Used by permission of Zondervan Bible
Publishers.

BLESS ME TOO MY FATHER
Copyright © 1988 by Herald Press, Scottdale, Pa. 15683
   Published simultaneously in Canada by Herald Press,
   Waterloo, Ont. N2L 6H7. All rights reserved.
Library of Congress Catalog Card Number: 88-2997
International Standard Book Number: 0-8361-3472-9
Printed in the United States of America
Design by Gwen Stamm

94 93 92 91   10 9 8 7 6 5 4 3

*To my four adult children,
who each helped me to choose a fuller life
as we grew more mature together.*

Contents

Foreword

Bless Me Too, My Father, is hard to put down. The week's newsmagazine can be read later or never. It is more important and more interesting to read about Katie Funk Wiebe's experiences—her inner searchings, aspirations, faith-struggles, growth, changes, and the continual "reaching" that characterizes her years.

As the author bares her soul, readers will identify with her. They will see themselves on her pages as she tells, for example, of the times she felt (as an adult) that she was "the last person to be chosen on the team." Or when she experienced loneliness that hung on "like a low-grade infection." She is frank about her fears, her pains (including those as a bruised parent), and her struggles. She dwells on them long enough for reflection and narration (storytelling), then goes on to application and action, blessing us with her insights.

A key idea in the book is to "develop a lifelong plan for growing." Author Wiebe set that goal for herself at the time she needed to retool for a vocation—when she was left a young widow with four small children and no Social Security benefits. Again, in her "beginning fifties" when the last of her four children left home, she grew in new directions as she decided her adulthood would be free, not cramped according to expectations around her.

In her words, "I opted to be free to be myself, to be creative, to use my gifts, to explain my life, to share, to love, to live deeply, to endure, to fail if need be."

As a self-starter still vigorous at middle age, she decided her task was to reevaluate and renew her life. "I would have to find out for myself," she says, "whether a middle-aged mother of four young adult children—a late professional in a church college, who was looking for ministry in a constituency that preferred its women in the traditional mode—could encounter new truth." She listed her goals for putting together the pieces of her life and wrote below, "I press on to take hold of that for which Christ Jesus took hold of me..." (Phil. 3:12).

Reading and study shaped her faith, also church hymns, sermons, family, friends, "but especially fellowship at special times around the Lord's table with other believers," she writes. "When other life options looked attractive, I recall saying 'Yes' to Christ and his truth at a communion service.

"Prayer remains a difficult assignment for me, and I believe also for many computer-age Christians," she says. "I have problems in other areas, but I want to keep reaching."

We resonate with her words: "I would have to dig for spiritual food," and in search for a good method of Bible study. She says it changed her life to study the Bible "with several translations, a concordance, Bible dictionaries, handbooks, commentaries—and much patience. I keep notes. I sort, reject, synthesize.

"I felt misled," she says, referring to those translators and interpreters of the past who manipulated certain Scriptures to discriminate against women and support male dominance. "I felt left out" in reaction to the lack of inclusive language.

The author speaks out courageously on active social concern saying, "Nonviolent love is action-oriented, not silent passivity." She writes of "hazards to the faith-life": misinterpretations, misassumptions, culture change, and the like. "When I think I understand all of this, God breaks through in a new way. Then at another time, he comes to me in clear words of Scripture, the creed, or a hymn, or a prayer. I'm never quite sure where I will meet him next—only that my anchor of faith is what I have thought through about him and with him and live out in my life."

She mentions "new interpretations of passages dealing with worldly amusements, divorce and remarriage, abortion, human sexuality, the role of women," and wisely advises that "error in interpretation is lessened if it is hammered out within the community of faith in prayer and humility rather than only by individuals. The greatest danger of faith becoming hazardous to the faith-life occurs when there is no discerning community to provide the checks and balances to our interpretation."

When to change? When to refuse change? What changes are justified when the culture changes? What changes are inconsistent with the Bible and never justified? The author agrees that these are important questions, I am sure.

Through the years I have had the pleasure of personal contacts with Katie Funk Wiebe as we traveled at times to speak in the other's home state, or on occasion by letter or phone call. I have been enriched by her books and her columns in church papers. She is a cherished person of warmth and wisdom. I think of her as filling Robert Maynard Hutchin's idea of an educated person as one who can (1) read critically, (2) think independently, and (3) enter good-naturedly in the controversies of her time. Add that to Katie's love for God, his Word, his Son, and you have an educated, dedicated servant of the Lord.

We can rejoice in her commitment to writing as a Christian calling. It would be our loss to be without her words on forgiveness, loneliness, suffering, widowhood, servanthood and mutual submission, mentoring, creativity, writing, storytelling, celebration, rethinking one's own theology, war, violence, peace, women in the church, prejudice, choices, decisions, aging, growing, changing.

We can be glad she kept doing some hard thinking contrary to the passive role expected of women. "My church had excused me from rigorous thinking," she says. Rigorous thinking on many different issues is what gifted, courageous Katie Funk Wiebe has done, and we can be grateful that such a woman has given us the benefits of it in *Bless Me Too, My Father.*

This book is for men and women interested in being creative and contributing individuals in all stages of adulthood, not "shunted to the siding like an uncoupled car," as author Wiebe puts it. It is for women with pent-up gifts that need to come out for use in the church as the Bible teaches, and for fulfillment as a legitimate by-product. It is for young and old who want to keep growing and changing in their life of faith.

Ruth Brunk Stoltzfus
Harrisonburg, Virginia

Author's Preface

I write books for myself. When I cannot find the exact book I need I write it, for writing pushes one into being. My book *Alone: A Widow's Search for Joy* was such a book. At the time of its publication few books had been written for the widowed. By sharing my experiences I hoped to clarify some aspects of widowhood for myself and also to help other widowed people find the freedom to discuss their experience and to move on.

Now a decade later, I have written about the next step in the journey. I had never expected mature adulthood, especially after the children left home, to be quite as demanding and needing so much change. At first, once again I feared I was an oddity. About this time I read two writings, one by an author, whose name I regretfully cannot recall, who described middle Americans as being theologically formed. Now in a swiftly changing culture, they are struggling with the process of aging because they are unable to change their minds about how life is to be lived with God. As a result they limit their inner growth—and their well-being.

The second writing was by psychologist Paul Tournier, who said that to continue growing, to live "a meaningful autumn," older persons must free themselves from the thought-patterns of adulthood. Didn't Tournier mean letting go of youthful thought-patterns? No, he meant adult thought-patterns. Just as youth have to free themselves from childish ways to achieve young adulthood, and young adults must free themselves from youthful ways to move into adulthood, so mature persons must free themselves from adult thought-patterns before moving into the latter phases of life. Life is a matter of constantly saying good-bye and hello.

At the time I wasn't planning many major changes, but one small family and vocational crisis after another forced me to reexamine my situation. In addition, in about fifteen years I knew I would be of traditional retirement age. What then? If I wanted to be a different person then, change in attitudes would have to begin now. And some of the biggest changes would have to be in my theology, for that affected every other aspect of life.

This book is therefore about change, especially theological change and choices in the middle years, which vary from person to person, beginning as early as age forty for some and as late as fifty or sixty for others. The computer has made us pay attention to the fact that we must constantly choose if we don't want to use default programming. Each year in this informational age, I seem to be pushed into making more choices: whether to mentor a gradeschool writing student, to buy more hospital insurance, to donate to a charity, to get my watch repaired or buy a new one, to subscribe to a new magazine, to write a letter to an editor to air my concerns regarding a political matter, to read a new book release, and many more. But as a person past age sixty, I additionally face many other more extended decisions that will have more lasting effects. Because they are not as immediate, I tend to decide by default. And then I am the loser.

Because I am a single woman, and a professional one at that, this book will be about change as a woman, but I do not consider it a woman's book. Learning the art of living is the same for all people. And these are arts we need to share. After we have lived our life, why should we hang onto it? I offer my story as an example of the process of living as a middle adult, not because I have done it better, but because at this moment I have freedom to speak about it.

Katie Funk Wiebe
June 1, 1987

Acknowledgements

Some of the material presented here has appeared as parts of talks and articles. Chapters 2, 8, 14, and parts of 5, 6 and 8 appeared in *Today's Christian Woman*, Chapter 15 in *With Magazine*, and sections of others in *Christian Living, Christian Leader* and *Gospel Herald*. The major part of Chapter 13, "Spading Up Words," appeared as "The Barriers Are Not Real" in *The Ethnic Woman: Problems, Protests, Lifestyle* edited by Edith Blicksilver. Reprinted by permission of Kendall/Hunt Publishing Company, © 1978.

Esau said to his father, "Do you have only one blessing, my father? Bless me too, my father!" Then Esau wept aloud.

—Genesis 27:38

CHAPTER 1

Bless me too, my Father!

*Revise where you have become stodgy
spiritually and you will find it goes back to a
point where there was something you knew
you should do but you didn't do.*

—Oswald Chambers

In the family room, I found James' prized goldfish dead at the bottom of the tank. The small fish lay there, limp and distorted. I felt sad. Not for the fish. But for the fact that what is alive must die. And that I was moving into the last major phase of my life.

I had crawled past fifty with reluctance. "Sixty, here I come," I had whimpered to myself.

Now James had left home for college. After debating the matter for several weeks, one Sunday afternoon he had come home to tell me he had found a comfortable niche for himself in one of the residence halls. He had decided to move into the dormitory, he said. Move out of his room at home. It was time.

I was alone. Truly alone this time.

My husband's death fourteen years before had brought one kind of aloneness to my life. Because of our family's move from Canada seven weeks before his death, I had been left with four young children to support without the benefit of social security payments. After a few years of office work in an editorial office,

I had returned to school with the goal of teaching at the college level. I had often felt alone and lonely during this time, but hadn't had time to deal with the matter in the relentless round of activities. My present aloneness refused to be set aside as summarily.

James, the last of my four children, had now left home to make it on his own. My strange feelings and reactions dismayed me. I had felt confident I could handle this midlife adjustment, in fact, had looked forward to living alone to forge ahead with my own plans. I found myself wandering about the house, from room to room, straightening pictures and books and wiping away imagined dust, looking for something to engage my interest. In stores, I, who always swept past anything not on my list of things-to-buy, caught myself glancing over magazine stands for something interesting to read. I woke up at night with a terrible fear of both newness and oldness. I was sleeping too much. Teaching had lost its fascination for me. I was watching too much television. It was easy to do nothing as I flopped from couch to chair. I cautiously observed my friends to find out who else was feeling old and deserted.

I plunged my hand into the cold water of the fish tank to bring the small blob of dead flesh to the surface, fully intending to drop it into the garbage disposal. Instead I threw it out the door. Dust to dust.

Living alone would require many adjustments. Eating, for example. I had bought groceries again this week as if I had not just one young adult eating with me but a whole football team. Freudian shopping slip? It would be easy to avoid meeting people, for who needed me? Whom did I need? Anyone? As long as I remained very quiet, said nothing, did nothing, went nowhere, I could remain secluded. It would also be easy to forget God, for what did he know about middle-aged widows with too many groceries in their pantry? He leaned toward the ones with empty cruses of oil.

The intensity of my own waylessness perplexed me. The

year had been difficult beyond measure. The evaluation of my teaching at the college had not gone well. A critic seemed to pop up from behind every door. When I was a poverty-stricken widow with four small children struggling to survive, I had received more generous sympathy and help in many areas than I probably deserved. Or was it that people felt more comfortable stooping to help an obviously financially needy person than accepting ideas and opinions from someone who now wanted to be treated as an equal? After I had regained some inner strength following my husband's death, returned to school to earn a degree so I could teach, and began to offer my views on various subjects, particularly on the role of women in church and society, a gust of cold wind headed my direction.

"When the way forks, when the expanse of desert lies in front without a beaten pathway—stand still," wrote F. B. Meyer. *Here I am, Lord, standing still, not sure which direction to turn.* At times I felt like a strong lion, ready to charge in and conquer. More often like a newborn kitten whose eyes had not yet opened.

In a few weeks I would be fifty-two—which seemed like the end of something instead of the beginning of a new life, the way I wanted it to be. At this age people thought of retiring, of pulling back, of counting grandchildren, and planning last big trips.

Obviously I had run at least half the course of my life, but now I couldn't find the energy to run the other half. Could I at this age break out of the fences built around me which I had reinforced with the nails of grudges and hurts and begin anew? Did I have the courage to seriously consider that I could change myself, my lifestyle, my vocation?

At what point does growth stop for some adults and why? I noticed that numerous middle-aged parents lived through their children as if their own lives had inexplicably stopped. Life continued for them through this extension of themselves; they never reached for new frontiers. At family reunions, instead of explaining what growth, what change had taken place in themselves, they brought out their "brag-books" and records of their children's accomplishments. They seemed to have lost (or was it misplaced or even simply discontinued?) hope for growth for themselves while outwardly displaying a bright facade of courage and joy. Often I longed for friends to drop the facade (the loud bravado and much talking about children's accomplishments) so I could see the color and condition of their inner self to find out if it matched mine.

I longed for something, not quite sure what, but at least a release from this waylessness. I wanted to know blessedness, the way the Old Testament sons had blessings pronounced upon them by their fathers. Words that weren't just nice words, but that imparted spiritual grace. "Jacob blessed his sons, every one he blessed"—not one was left without a blessing. But what about his daughters? What had they felt? Was I an unblessed daughter of Jacob? Had his daughters ever pleaded with him the way Jacob's brother Esau pleaded with Isaac, their father, "Bless me too, my father!"

Alternately I felt at peace, troubled; at ease, tense; assured, yet perplexed. I knew that in the eyes of some people I had taken a step toward greater freedom in Christ by returning to school and shifting to teaching, but I also knew that not all my wheels were aligned in that direction.

I pondered the issues. I was under tension and not sure why. Was it the problems with my aging car—the ugliest thing' on the block, someone joked. Or that people were beginning to call me a writer when I saw myself only as a dabbler? Or was it because of family tensions caused by the estrangement of Joanna, my oldest daughter, who had found her way from the family hearth into the hippie movement? Or that I found myself sympathizing more and more with biblical feminists when I longed to hang onto a more traditional conservative theology that would keep me safe, secure, and uncriticized?

I missed my four children desperately while at the same time wishing that now as young adults, they'd work at their problems by themselves. I found it enervating to process all of their difficulties with them. Yet can a parent ever really be free of children? Would one want to be? I pondered the matter. Perhaps there is no such thing as true freedom—only a stoic independence from the circumstances of life parading as freedom accompanied by a vague confidence that God is in control and knows the small hell his children are going through.

What was I looking for? The answer came one day as I thought through my earlier life. I was looking for the core that was myself—not what others thought I should be. That seemed certain. When I asked friends for advice, the most common response was "Be yourself."

Who was myself? Once there'd been a young woman who had been open to life, ready to risk, free to wave banners, and mount soapboxes, confident of her skills. When had I lost her? And why? How did she get caught in patterns of living that robbed her of joyousness? Could she be found again? The image of myself at age sixteen in my bright blue beret with a fifteen-inch pheasant feather waving jauntily in the breeze challenged me not to forget her.

That winter and the next I pondered these concerns. I was going through a transition. Middle-age crisis? Not exactly. Yet I was on a catapult I was trying to get off before it hurled me to unknown destinations. But if I eluded it, I might never again have another chance to find that young girl with the feather in her cap.

As I reflected, I recognized I was caught in a combination of systems of thought and patterns of living that were destroying my joy. I had been cooperating with these systems in my destruction because it seemed the thing to do. A Christian woman accepted submissively what life brought, what the church taught, even if this approach seemed restricted and cramped.

I could identify some of the restraints—the pressure to keep my lament at any stage in life to myself, to keep in line with tradition, to avoid risk, to take life seriously, almost glumly. Not being an authority on anything, especially in the church and its institutions, yet wanting very much to be found faithful to God's truth, I had yielded to these loud, yet unspoken, demands. When as a widow with four children, I had finally decided to find a new course of action, I had at times lashed out with anger at life's inequities. As a single woman, I felt victimized, powerless.

My eyesight had been too sharp. I sensed that now. Everywhere I found people dividing into three groups—persons with clout, those without it, and those trying to move from one group to the other. And I said so.

One evening as I watched the Watergate film on television, I felt overwhelmed by the total corruption in government, a corruption that seemed to taint too many other areas of life. Did purity of motive exist anywhere? The film vividly showed men of apparent integrity caught in the ugliness of clawing for power and position at any price. To achieve authoritative control seemed more important than providing good leadership.

Were the authority patterns in the church any different? There, too, I found people in control classifying other people, particularly minorities and women, setting them aside like an unneeded tool because they were not part of the traditional ecclesiastical power bloc. Usually it was an unconscious act, never done maliciously. Suggestions for change were responded to with "This is the biblical pattern. We've always done it this way, and it wouldn't work if we tried it another." Again and again I heard that change must come slowly because of the fallout if it happens too quickly.

After a church service, I often could not recall one idea to take home with me other than that we had learned a new song, that the pastor had worked diligently through his three-point sermon outline, and that then we had gone home to our own private realities. Fleetingly I considered changing churches.

Then, at least selling the house we had lived in for many years, because the large yard was becoming too burdensome. Too much grass in summer and too much snow in winter. I considered leaving the community. Traitorous thoughts, each one.

At the time I was receiving invitations to speak on being a widow, the topic of my last book. Yet what did I have to say now about widowhood or anything else? The experience and the book were behind me, yet I was expected to keep up the appearances and feelings of a widow, to remain a professional widow though I was trying to achieve a new identity as a single professional woman.

But if I didn't accept these assignments, would I join the many middle-aged women and men without portfolio, whose children were gone or going? Their services were not zealously sought or wanted in the church structures. I watched some slipping in and out, peering at church life plaintively, as if looking in from the outside, silent. Did they feel like failures? Or rejects?

Had my past few years been a failure as a mother, a teacher, a person? If so, what should I do with my failures? Years ago flopped cake became pudding, a poorly knit sweater was unraveled and reknit. Writing rejection slips could be hidden in a folder or dropped in the wastepaper basket. I had often felt both frustration and pity for parents who buried their "unsuccessful" children by sliding over them in conversation, in Christmas letters, in photographs. But to bury these "failures" also meant burying dreams they might have had for these children. If I wanted to resurrect my dreams for my own life, I would also have to dig up my failures—all of them and deal with them one by one before I could begin the living out of the dreams.

To begin again would mean recalling events and people I wanted to forget—and dealing with them before I was free to forget. And it would mean embracing the whole of life, not just a small part, in a new way. "Life is a strong drink, meant to be drunk deeply, without being watered down," writes George F. Simons in *Journal for Life*. I was thirsty for another swallow of that strong drink at age fifty-two.

I read of a little man who was looking for his house key under a streetlight. "Where did you lose it?" asked a passerby. "Over by the bushes," he replied. "Why are you looking for it here?" "There's more light here," he responded. Yes, like him, I liked doing things where they were easiest—but I would have to go back into the dark and retrace my way or resign my teaching position, quit writing, quit being me.

I would have to choose my way, a frightening thought. I had always been one to say that I allowed God to choose my way. I was submissive to him. His will was my will. Yet that approach clearly allowed me to drift if need be. Now though he might direct, I had to choose. I had to take the first step.

The Jews in Babylonian exile blamed their unpleasant situation on heredity and environment: "Our parents are to blame." The prophet Ezekiel refused this explanation. Though their situation might have been caused by their parents' sins, they were responsible for their response to the present situation. They had to accept responsibility for being far from the temple, from their homes, and familiar surroundings. Their suffering in exile was an opportunity to repent and to become partners with God once again in a serious faith covenant, or lose his blessing in their lives. This moment of distress was my opportunity for renewal also.

The summer before I took a sabbatical leave from the college my task seemed clearer—to reevaluate my life. Simons talks about two birds of prey in our lives, two devouring needs—productivity and belonging. Between them a personal spiritual life is picked to pieces. The last decade had been overly busy going to school to earn a degree so I could teach, while supporting and nurturing four active youngsters, each now moving in his or her own direction. I had had no time in this period of over-productivity in many areas to find a corner I could call my own.

Simon suggests we need to say "Aha!" to an inner experience that matches a creedal statement. I wanted to be able to do that. No one tells us enough about the time in life from about forty-five to sixty-five and on, when we are still vigorous, or that these "Aha!" experiences are still possible for mature adults. I would have to find out for myself whether a middle-aged mother of four young adult children—a late professional in a church college, who was looking for ministry in a constituency that preferred its women in the traditional mode—could encounter new truth.

I was reminded of the words of Lillian Hellman that encourages people to use the wisdom that comes with age. "Some people learn early; some, never." Wisdom to her is fitting things together—"people, knowledge, books, aims, all one knows and all one feels; fitting together as many pieces as you can." Before the fitting together I wanted to do would have to come a tearing down and a giving up of prized attitudes and beliefs. And then the sorting, choosing, and fitting.

I had been conditioned to believe that God led by visions, signs, fleeces, but then also pushed his child into the preferred way with a firm hand. Now like Mary who sat at Jesus' feet and of whom he said, "Mary has chosen the better part," I would have to choose between the good and the better, not just between right and wrong—without a fleece, but with the help of the Holy Spirit. To not choose was to be a drifter, to live by default, like a prostitute, a call girl, who answers any and all calls. Prostitution on a spiritual level could take place if I answered every call and demand made upon me by church, family, community, school, friends, lifestyles, ideology, and theology without discernment.

One evening before I went to bed I wrote down some goals for putting together the pieces of my life which had been invaded once again by fear of physical and mechanical breakdowns, by bureaucratic decrees, by a lack of purpose coupled with boredom, and with what seemed like huge fissures in my theology through which new ideas were trickling in but not being caught and clarified. I had been taught to think defensively regarding theological matters, and to bristle when someone disagreed with my inherited interpretation of the Word. Now I would have to take the offensive theologically and to figure out what I believed about what mattered. I might have to change my mind.

I wrote in my journal:

1. Review my theology
2. Plan for spiritual growth
3. Diet and exercise (I was gaining weight)
4. Learn to speak in public
5. Find out more about grass roots women
6. Learn to be more open to people
7. Relax more—sleep better
8. Learn hospitality

A little later I added the following:

9. Improve writing and teaching skills.
10. Learn to travel alone.

Beneath it I wrote Philippians 3:12-13: "I press on to take hold of that for which Christ Jesus took hold of me. . . . Forgetting what is behind and straining toward what is ahead, I press on toward the goal to win the prize for which God has called me heavenward in Christ Jesus."

My plan broke down into several categories: to add knowledge, to add experience and skills, to add relationships, to add spiritual strength. I felt like an adolescent—finding an identity independent of children.

But I had a tiny hold on my waylessness.

CHAPTER 2

Joy for the journey

*It takes courage to be, to accept not only the
determinants of one's circumstances but the
possibility of modifying the situation so as to
allow still greater freedom.*

—Morris Inch

By the time I was twenty-one, I could perform adequately
two of the three skills my immigrant father insisted every
woman needed to survive: bake bread, darn socks, and milk a
cow. I could not milk even though I was an adult, married, and
pregnant, the main reason being I had never had the opportunity. My father wasn't a farmer, but a storekeeper.

Yet practical skills in living seemed necessary for adult life.

Then one morning my neighbor called me a child.

Morning sickness had squashed me flat during the first
weeks of pregnancy. The honeymoon was barely over. When
the morning alarm rang, I clung to my bed like a prisoner
about to be taken to the gallows until my husband brought me
some warm bland food to soothe my anguished insides.

One morning, my neighbor, a newcomer from Slavic
Europe, who couldn't speak much English as yet, knocked on
the door to return an item she had borrowed. She entered at
my husband's loud "Come in" to see him carrying the tray to
the bedroom. She chuckled.

No physical work daunted this woman. She could shove furniture around like a house mover, tramp to the shopping center and lug home large sacks of groceries like a busboy, and chop wood for their coal and wood range like a lumberjack.

She followed her chuckle with a statement I could hear and understand in the back bedroom: "*In Amerika, Frauen wie Kinder.*" (In America, women are like children.)

I winced. I wanted to shout, "No, we're not. You just don't understand what it's like to dump your insides into a basin every morning," until I remembered she had given birth to three children, had migrated to a strange country, had undergone many hardships during the war in Europe, and could still smile at the day.

Her words jabbed again and again after she left, while I waited for the oatmeal to calm my stomach. What she had said about my kind was true. Morning sickness wasn't the real issue; she had been watching me and other neighbor women. I had to admit sometimes some of us were childish, wanting to be treated like children as we demanded, coaxed, wheedled, and edged ourselves out of adult responsibilities.

Like most young women, I had been eager to rush time, eager to begin the thrills of adulthood. I had never seriously considered what it took to be an adult in an adult relationship. I had simply assumed that when you were old enough, you took on the grown-up qualities needed for grown-up tasks, like marriage.

I had assumed adults were completed persons, like a piece of knitting bound off, never to fray again. Yet here I was frayed by morning sickness, frayed by the fact I had to live far from my parents, frayed by small cooking disasters, and absolutely unraveled when my husband and I got into an argument. None of this was supposed to happen to adults, I thought.

Like most other young women of my generation, while I was growing up I had never seen myself beyond the age of nineteen or twenty. Then a knight in shining armor (over his slacks and sports shirt, of course) would gallop down the gravel road past our wooden fence, sweep me off my size 8½ spectator pumps, and ride off with me into the golden sunset. If he had no horse, a bicycle or car would do.

The dream ended abruptly at that point every time. After the brilliant sunset scene, I had no further plans. What was going to happen after twenty-one didn't really matter. Marriage was moonlight and roses, forever and forever, rang out my hallelujah chorus.

What was I going to be doing when I was forty? Who cared? Probably what my mother was doing at forty—looking after the family. What was I going to be doing at fifty? At sixty? That mattered even less. Probably what my stout little grandmother with her long black dress and lace apron was doing at fifty and sixty—sitting by her window, knitting, and contentedly enjoying the people walking by. Sixty was too far into the future to even speculate. The glamor of being twenty-one when I could wear high heels and lipstick without a parent commenting, "Not so bright," was enough dream to satisfy.

Perhaps the sharp break off in the thinking about adult life of young women like me in the late 1940s and 50s was that it simply did not entice. It looked dull, drab, uninviting. Youth were idolized in popular movies, advertisements, and music. Youth were the hope of the new society being built on the war ruins. Youth was a glorious time of opportunity. Youth were the only ones who knew how to enjoy life. Adults could learn from them about the way to face life joyfully and vigorously, not youth from adults.

During this period, the church accepted what society said about young people. Church leaders shunted us into the "rich, invigorating experiences" of camps, retreats, and youth fellowships, where we were expected to make the BIG decisions of life: accept Christ as Savior, select a mate, choose a vocation, become independent of parents, and make our own way in life. We solemnly threw logs into the campfire, while declaring our goals (which usually included a fervent, if silent, "Please, Lord, a nice boyfriend this year also"). We walked down aisles to altars to make new commitments. We volunteered for all kinds of mission and evangelistic activities that adults believed in but didn't participate in. We accepted the adult directive that youth was the best time of life.

It seemed natural, therefore, to assume that adulthood, after the honeymoon was over, meant settling into drab routines of raising children, making a living, guarding the budget, and vicariously enjoying life by watching, emulating, and imitating the sneakered and jeaned crowd.

Expectations of adulthood were limited, because adulthood seemed to be a restrictive rather than freeing experience. Although adults talked a lot about spiritual growth, the term was limited to disciplining oneself to prayer, reading the Bible regularly, going to church, giving to Christian causes, and avoiding evil companions, places, and activities. Relational virtues like love and peace were mentioned often, but not how they fitted into the total Christian experience. Perhaps I just didn't catch on—yet these qualities seemed to be a thing apart—like the dressing dolloped on the salad at one's pleasure, not the main ingredients. While you were young, you guarded against deliberate sinning in certain specific areas (drinking, dancing, smoking, premarital sex); after that you moved into safe, secure waters with few temptations of the flesh.

Yes, twenty-one was the magic number at which life culminated on a grand high, especially if you married. At that moment the product—a grown-up person—emerged, and the assembly line carried her along, adding little or nothing to her character until she was old, worn out, and ready to be filed away in a small room in a home for the elderly. Beyond twenty-one the road was long, broad, and boring, with little to challenge it, and little to enjoy except memories of moonlit nights on the beach.

Here I was in my beginning fifties forced to rethink once

again what the adult life was about. The synonym for adulthood was obviously not maturity, for it was possible to have two sets of children in the house at the same time—loudly quarreling children and angry parents. Change and upheaval was obviously not restricted to youth. Grown-ups also majored in them.

"I never expected to have to make so many big changes in middle age," a friend confessed. She spoke of her "funny" feelings for about a year and a half when she changed jobs, two children left home, they made a house move, and finally, her husband became ill with hepatitis, and she had to take over in all areas. On top of that, she was experiencing embarrassing hot flashes. No one had told her adult life would be full of bumps and bruises—even though she knew her children would eventually move out of the big house, that physical changes accompany aging, that vocational changes could come after fifty. And no one had told me.

Advances in sanitation, nutrition, and medical care have, of course, increased the life expectancy of adults but also the demands on them. Women, who at one time thought their lives were nearly over when the children left home, now find they may have from twenty to thirty good years ahead, some of them possibly alone, for husbands frequently die first because they are often older and have a shorter life expectancy.

Such changes in longevity have caused psychologists to declare we need a new understanding of adulthood, defining it not as a period of stability, but as a series of changes and crises. Some of these, like menopause and death of parents, can be predicted, but others like the death of a child, change in vocation, or sudden testing of life views, may be unexpected, yet are common.

In my groping to understand my situation I turned to Scripture. I found these changes in adult life paralleled there. However, the Bible doesn't read like a front-page news article with all the details in the lead paragraph. Consequently, we see characters such as the aging Simeon or the starry-eyed David through a rosy filter and not like the flesh-and-blood, sometimes middle-aged and older, persons they really were.

I checked Bible story after Bible story for age clues of characters and concluded many were talking about adult life and types of choices adults make. Christ's follower Mary was not an adolescent tossing campfire logs into the fire when she poured perfume on Jesus' feet and wiped them with her hair. Mary and her sister Martha, according to some scholars, were middle-aged sisters, the latter a widow, when they struggled with disbelief at their brother Lazarus' death. Elizabeth, wife of Zechariah, and Sarah, wife of the patriarch Abraham, faced the trauma of birth after their menses had ceased. Was it all joy for these elderly matrons to rush out to the sand dune to throw up despite their elation at knowing their longed-for child would be born?

Hagar, mother of the young man Ishmael, was no teenager when she had a near failure of faith when Abraham turned her out into the desert. Likewise the man at the pool of Bethsaida, handicapped for thirty-eight years, and the apostle Paul, were adults when they were challenged to change their whole approach to life. Paul had to change his views about Gentiles and about other matters dear to his Jewish heart—even about women. He eventually acknowledged them as fellow kingdom workers.

All these stories were about adults facing change, particularly the kind of change required when confronted with the claims of Christ.

The sorting that I did that year of self-searching revealed that Christian adultness was more than taking time to read the Bible, pray, and go to church. It had to do with gaining confidence in myself as a person whom God loved. It had to do with realizing that because I shared in the gifts of the Spirit to the body of Christ, I had something to offer the Christian community. It had something to do with learning to confront and

also to relate to others, including the members of my family
and those I worked with. It had a lot to do with being responsible for my own sin, salvation, and service, and with learning to
make decisions. It had to do with development of Christian
character, with holiness, with the virtues of joy, love, and
peace, with learning to forgive and be forgiven, and with becoming a caring person even as others had cared for me. And
especially, it had to do with learning to confront fear, with its
many disguises that surfaced everywhere with the agility of a
ghost in a country churchyard.

Whenever I sat back to listen to people talking, I heard fear-
language mixed with their fun-talk—fear of catching a cold, of
becoming sick, particularly with cancer, of never having a date,
of guests popping in without warning and finding a messy
house, of children misbehaving, of finding one gray hair—and
then two, of no children coming home for Christmas, of all the
children coming home for Christmas, of becoming pregnant
after forty, of not having enough time, and especially, of facing
old age alone and physically handicapped.

A neighbor and I had discussed the accidental death of a
young mother of three in our community. She insisted the
death was God's will. I demurred, and offered her a book in
which the author pointed out God is not the author of evil; his
will is whole families, not broken ones. He allows such events
as illness and death to happen; he doesn't will them. She
refused the book, for "If I read it, I might have to change my
mind."

I had retreated into silence, but inside I had taunted her:
"You poor thing—afraid to read a book about something
you've made up your mind about." That evening as I had
rehashed the conversation with a friend, embellishing it with
proper intonations and background effects, I was interrupted
by a phone call requesting me to lead the devotional period at
the next women's meeting. I heard myself saying a firm "No"
because I was afraid. Marilee had her fears about new ideas,

but I also had a bountiful supply of them stowed away. I was afraid to speak before a group of people because I might not sound spiritually sophisticated. I was afraid my prayer might sound anemic. I wasn't even going to allow myself the opportunity of finding out whether I could pull words together in such a way that they might draw people together in worship before God. I was a member of the band of the fearful as much as Marilee. My hypocrisy condemned me.

Somehow, handling fear in a fearful age had to be fitted into my puzzle. I knew Paul's words to his young friend Timothy held the key: "God hath not given us the spirit of fear, but of power, and of love, and of a sound mind" (2 Timothy 1:7, KJV). Years ago I had begun a kind of manifesto, or personal statement, about what I was learning about growing up after twenty-one. I needed to revive this document before I could work on my new goals.

My first assertion, the kingpin on which the others hung, in this writing done years ago when the children were small, was fairly simple.

• *My life belongs to God in Christ Jesus. I am committed to the truth of the Word of God, and as much as possible I want to honor him with my life by the strength of the Spirit.*

I have to live that life. No one else can live it for me. Nor can I merely think my life. I must live it in relationship to others, testing truth, making mistakes, sometimes succeeding.

I may be tempted to let other people run my life, to determine how I wash dishes or dust, what I read, and whom I spend time with. I may be tempted to hide behind other people, especially men, and let them do the serious thinking about the Christian life while I coast. I may be tempted to go into a holding pattern until I have more time to be a Christian—until the children are out of diapers, or out of school, or until a fairy godmother exchanges my balky washing machine for a new one—but excuses don't work.

Life expects something of me now—in the midst of night

feedings, when husband forgets to bring home milk for sup-
per—not just in the future when life will move more evenly. I
must have my own thoughts and viewpoints. I can't live on
borrowed ideas anymore than I can live on borrowed faith. Dis-
cipleship is for all God's children, not just a select few.

Now at this new juncture I could add: Discipleship is for the
married, for widows, for the divorced, for singles, for adults
who need to find their way again. When I come before God, he
is not going to ask me whether I have served too many quick
casseroles to my family or whether I have polished the floors
regularly. He will ask whether I have been his disciple.

• *Because life comes in sections or stages, there's no point in*
pushing the one I'm presently in. This statement was added
when I had finished with the spilled-milk, dripping-noses stage
of childcare. But I wrote it down for future reference when I
might again feel the frustration of wanting to be any age but
the one I was in.

Dr. Marion Hilliard, popular Canadian writer of several
decades ago, wrote, "Women have a definite physical cycle
and need to move in step with life on a grander rhythmical
scale as well." After getting an education, a woman will
possibly work for a while before and after marriage, if she mar-
ries. When the babies arrive, she should consider seriously
switching gears for a time, unless her husband becomes the
primary nurturer. When the children need less of her attention,
there will again be opportunity to change the focus of her attention. To fight time at each stage of life, whether it is
adolescence, young adulthood, middle age, or retirement, only
compounds the frustration, was her advice.

As a young mother of four, I was frustrated at times to the
point of despair by the daily 24-hour close encounter with
persons under three feet and a husband frequently absent in
church work. Like the children of Israel who craved the leeks
and garlic of Egypt, I longed intensely for the good times with
adults left behind in the office.

So my word to myself then was, "*Relax, take life in sections. Time is your ally, not your enemy, intent on turning you into a crone. Although it may seem there is never enough time, there is always time enough for what God wants of you.*" Life at any time is God's gift, I told myself. He expects a mature response in all circumstances, including those which are the result of your decisions.

Obviously I had chosen to marry and to have children. Then why resist this period of life because it didn't include the rewards of the next one—grown-up children? Sometimes the main task in life for a woman is going to school, at another it's working outside the home or taking care of children, at another it may be volunteer work in church and community, and at another simply being quiet. It's most important to move in rhythm with each period of life, like two ice skaters, not like two cats tied together. The heavily mascaraed teenager in a slit skirt, the young mother screaming at her children in the supermarket, and the middle-aged woman in tight jeans and tighter T-shirt all reveal only one thing—dissatisfaction.

At any point of change, crisis, or decision we can choose our attitude toward the matter. We can become bitter, angry, and self-pitying, or we can move ahead with acceptance and openness that God can work in our lives regardless of the circumstances. Just as sin can enter a life at a point of decision, so God can also meet us here. Decisions of any kind are times of growth.

These were my earlier thoughts. I had thought they were good ones when I wrote them. All right, why was I now resisting the natural leaving of my children? Why not embrace this opportunity to grow in new directions? Why not take advantage of my singleness? That was a scary thought, but worth hanging onto. This age, too, could have its splendors, I reminded myself.

Earlier, as I had faced the need to retool for a vocation following my husband's death, I had included another point to

my manifesto: *Develop a lifelong plan for growing.* I had had
to remind myself that I might have to let the school bells ring
for me a long time. After I returned to school, my traffic patterns to the university didn't stop for some time.

Growth, however, is not limited to new knowledge, or to
learning new skills, like word processing. Christ's invitation to
life is actually an invitation to join the community of persons
who reject immature patterns of living and who are growing
into an awareness of their powers and accepting responsibility
for them. That's where I had been sidetracked. My high level
of discomfort now wasn't a setback, but a step forward, a nudge
from God to keep moving.

One definition of maturity is to bring one's powers to full
realization, to know oneself to the extent that you know what
you can do. A seed cannot reproduce or use its powers of re-
production until it is ripe. Christians are not fully mature (the
word used in Matthew 5:48 is "perfect") until they know what
their talents and gifts are and develop them. Mature behavior
means making oneself responsible for all one can be, rejecting
immature images of living promoted by a secular society and
which hold one to sub-Christian and sometimes subhuman living.

Hugging the safe place because it meant less risk of falling
flat on my face wasn't the thing to do, I told myself repeatedly.
I thought I had worked my way through the matter of choosing
my attitude toward life during the years following my husband's death and my return to the professional world, but now
I had to go through the process again. And that was okay also.

I looked closely at myself in a three-sided inner mirror, at
what I could and couldn't do, at what I thought God wanted of
me. For each person the next step will be different, but for me
the challenge had begun—finding joy for the journey at a new
stage in life. Sixty, here I come.

CHAPTER 3

Passage to India

Forgiving turns off the videotape of pained memory. Forgiving sets you free. Forgiving is the only way to stop the cycle of unfair pain turning in your memory.

—Lewis B. Smedes

"Do you like India?" the young dark-haired girl in the sari asked.

"Yes, very much."

"I'm glad," she replied. After returning to India from England, where she had been studying for several years while her father was in medical school, she had found it hard to adjust. But now it was her country again.

About a year after I had made my list of goals for the next years, I applied for and received a sabbatical leave from my teaching position. With the first royalties from my book *Alone: A Widow's Search for Joy* I headed for the East during the fall semester. For six weeks the country of India, of which I had read much as a child, was mine as well as belonging to my young questioner. I was enjoying it and learning from it, unaware that it would become a pivotal experience for me as I looked ahead to the next decade.

Often I stood by the roadside and watched India's masses move by. At other times, when in a car, bus, or train, I moved past them. But always there were people, on foot, on cycles, on carts, and a few on cars and buses moving along to market or to the fields.

One day I caught something about India that should have been apparent at the beginning: India is a land of contrasts. On the one hand, there is much beauty and richness. I saw magnificent forts, temples, palaces, and beautiful homes with luxuries that matched anything America could produce. I shopped in a large emporium far beyond my expectations. I watched a wedding at which five thousand guests were served an elaborate meal with stewards and hostesses and lights and flowers in abundance. I talked to many well-educated people, each of which seemed to be able to quote Shakespeare better than any American college student.

But India is also a land of burdens and burden-bearers. The very land itself seemed burdened with too many people. They crowded the cities, the rich living in grand mansions and the poor in the *bustees* (cell-like shacks), often built against a wall or a building or on the street.

The roadways were burdened by this massive population. Frequently my friends and I joked that the road belonged to whoever was on it first. Dogs refused to move for cars. Herds of goats crossed the bridge slowly while the car waited. A farmer spread his grain on the road to dry, and pedestrians and cars moved around. Passing through a railway station became an exercise in agility, as we dodged passengers sleeping on the platform or perched protectively on their goods.

All vehicles bore heavier burdens than their makers intended for them. Buses roared past, crammed full, with additional passengers sitting on the outside luggage rack or clinging to doors and windows.

Rickshas, one of the main means of transportation, came in several varieties—motorized, cycle or coolie-drawn. But sometimes they had no load limit. If another person could pile in, the coolie was expected to manage. The cart-pullers, one of the lowest castes, skin darkened, their faces lined with quiet desperation, strained under their heavy loads. I looked at the ropelike veins bulging on their legs and the sweat pouring down their foreheads. Life expectancy for them would not be much beyond forty or forty-five.

Always the load seemed heavier than what one would normally expect that piece of equipment, animal, or person to bear. Water buffalos, camels, and donkeys plodded along, urged by a driver. Where were the trucks?

Men and women did the work of big earth-moving machinery to build roads. They squatted by the hour, breaking rocks for gravel, and then the women, erect, graceful, carried it to the road site in baskets on their heads. The tarring was done by heating small trays of tar over fires and smoothing it with hand trowels. Where were the big earth-movers?

Mothers carried gleaming waterpots on their head or shoulder, with perhaps a baby strapped to their back and a few children tugging at their skirts. Men struggled under huge loads balanced on a stick across their shoulders so large the bearer couldn't be seen.

And the children of India. In the United States some expectant mothers worry whether they will know how to hold their new baby. In India I saw little children, some as young as three or four, with a youngster strapped to their back or clinging to their side. I saw children burdened with finding food, sorting through sweepings from the street to pick a few kernels of wheat, or gathering cow dung in a low basket, hoisting it to their heads to carry away. Children carried the burdens of adults.

Burdens.

But I too was burdened. My journal in the fall of 1977 before I left for this six-week study tour of India carries many entries about my burdens. Of particular concern to me was my oldest daughter, Joanna, caught in the radical student movement of the times. Our severe clashes over this issue widened the gap between us. I hated the anger and humiliation I felt. I hated my helplessness in trying to convince her there were better ways of living free than footloose and without visible means of support.

I went to India, wanting to forget my burdens. Yet can one ever truly forget a difficult past in such a way that it is remembered with joy? I recall a woman visiting me. She resented that her mother-in-law had robbed her marriage of its best years by dominating her husband's decisions. Whatever her mother-in-law thought she didn't need, she did without. And her husband acquiesced. She couldn't get rid of her burdensome memory now that both husband and mother-in-law were dead.

We get rid of clothing or articles we don't want by discarding them. The used-clothing store, the garbage can, are willing receivers. It is not as easy to drop from thought or family a member in whom one has invested a major part of one's life. Yet hadn't Joanna dropped us? Her restless wandering continued for several years. Did she want to be part of the family if she seldom came home? When she did, it was with friends I found hard to welcome warmly with their strange clothing, hairstyles, mannerisms, and most galling—an apparent freedom to flout tradition. Her ceremonial hugs came as from a cold marble statue.

At family reunions, as we laughed and conversed our way through a bountiful meal, I found myself wondering where she was and why. Why wasn't she with us? Was she eating enough? Warm enough? And remembering I loved her? Had I told her that, or was my message of rejection stronger?

Then when it seemed she had completed one stage in her search for freedom, she moved hell-bent into another as terrifying and embarrassing to me. Always there was the fear of what might come next. In between I made stabs at love, at forgiveness, at showing the kind of compassion Christ would show but without the turnaround I wanted to see in her. My open and frantic desperation was a shabby bribe demanding she change her behavior so I would feel better.

Like a running sore, the healing never came. From time to time it opened up, emitting pus, blood, and plasma. Where had I failed? How could I make amends?

June 15, 1948, the morning of Joanna's birth, began with contractions about 5:30 a.m. in the one-room house we were living in temporarily across the tracks in the small community where my husband was teaching a short-term adult high school. I had been too soon pregnant to suit me. And too sick with nausea almost the entire nine months. Always short of money. Marriage on a shoestring hadn't daunted us when we had made our plans for life together. I had only one decent dress the entire nine months to cover my growing bulk. I was too ignorant about what was happening to my body during pregnancy and what would happen during birth. Such matters were too little discussed even with doctors. Yet with delight and wonderment I made nightgowns, diapers, and other clothing, and knitted little sweaters, trying to complete the list in the mother-and-child book as to what a newborn should have. A new life. Part of us would be part of our lives. We waited for the miracle of birth.

Early one June morning, after timing the contractions for several hours, we departed for the hospital about thirty miles away. Walter left me there to get back to teaching history and English. Why hadn't he stayed? No particular reason. I said I'd be okay. Anyway, husbands didn't stay when women were occupied with a normal body function. And the doctor said it would take a long time. First babies always did. All the novels I had read said that husbands were only a nuisance at birth and therefore were ushered out by the women in charge. Walter's own mother had given birth to twelve children in their home, my mother to five. Furthermore, I was in a hospital where I expected consideration and dignity.

So I began one of the longest days in my life, feeling more and more alone with each passing hour, terrified by pain I did not understand the purpose of and feeling rejected by the indifference and callousness of nurses and doctors who dropped in occasionally for a cursory examination to see how I was progressing. They had other things to do than comfort about-to-become-mothers. When I finally could stand the pain burrowing into my lower back no longer, I cried and moaned, only to be told by the nurse to shut up. I drank and drank. Of the birth I had no memory—only that I didn't care to see the beautiful healthy baby girl when she was born—the birth had cost too much lonely pain.

The ensuing hospital experience was also traumatic—fifteen beds in the sunroom, side by side, with no privacy. The crowning indignity was not to be given a bedpan "because it wasn't time for a pan," standard hospital procedure at the time. I had been unable to relieve myself at the previous bedpan hour four hours earlier. So I wet the bed—corner to corner. I wanted to hide in shame. I was feeling less and less human as nurses examined bottom sides and cracked nipples, picked out stitches, and offered heat lamps and balm to aid healing.

And then Walter slept through the first visiting period.

Why did that memory surface now when I was thinking of leaving for India?

There had been some difficulty simply getting to India. American church women had been invited to send delegates to an Indian women's church conference, the first of its kind, yet I could not interest my church leaders to give me encouragement for this trip, much less financial help. One told me they were fearful of another denomination's theology being inadequate or watering ours down. They could not bless me.

The issue seemed to be whether women should come together for fellowship and sharing information. What was the continuation program planned after this conference? Was it sufficiently evangelical to receive their endorsement? What was the value of bringing "chickens" together for a conference, quipped someone in my presence.

So reluctantly I decided to go without official endorsement. Yet I admit I longed for either a big church official or a little church official to bless me, even from a distance, for something as risky as a voyage to India, my first overseas trip.

Memories of other hurts I had received caused by criticism, particularly through getting caught in the power plays of ecclesiastical politics which sometimes judge persons like pawns in a chess game, came to mind. The history of institutions is always a history of triumphs, glorious ones, but also of wounds—sometimes cleared from the record by calling them "personality conflicts." And I nurtured the hurts. I allowed them to move in deeper.

I could not escape the self-inflicted wounds—self-contempt, self-denigration, and self-disappointment because of my failure to trust God in this matter and my readiness to give in to despair, anger, and worry.

I carried the burden of wounds that I thought I had long forgotten but that were ripped open by the claws of memory when I tried to find justice. The result was bitterness, self-pity, and, clearly, a loss of effectiveness.

My goal in traveling to India was to attend the women's church conference, I told friends. The issue of a blessing I put aside. Other matters I hoped time would take care of. Deep down I knew I was searching for evidence of the power of the gospel. Did Christ's gospel bring peace and healing to those who trusted in it? If I saw it in a foreign culture, I would have greater faith, I assured myself.

The women's conference went well, as four hundred Mennonite women from all parts of India worshiped together for several days. I found meeting Indian Christians an enrichment I had longed for.

At an all-Indian evangelical Christian communications seminar, at which the conferees were primarily nationals, I, as an American observer, sat toward the back. The daily speaker spoke on the theology of communications. I was unprepared for his words. I had no defenses up, so I was caught by the full impact of the Spirit of Christ as he spoke about the healing of memories through power applied directly by prayer to the wound. Then the wounded person can forgive, see things in a new light, and be healed of past hurts.

I listened carefully. Maybe I would hear something that would be helpful.

He explained how woundedness separates us from other people and from Christ. Because we block the image of Jesus Christ in our lives as long as the wound is open and throbbing, the memory of that hurt separates us from other people and from Christ. The right reason for asking for forgiveness is not just to ease psychic pain.

He was yanking at the scab on my wound.

But the healing of memories is not just a psychological process, he said. It takes more than finding the cause of the hurt and talking it out. Wounds are not cured by tears. "Salt tears preserve the memory," he said. Nor does healing come by rededication to Christ. It occurs only if we can see the past with a new attitude, with the eyes of Christ, and give up our right to get even. Hurt opens us up to other people or closes us to other people and to God. There is no in-between stage.

I was taking notes, but they were being written on my heart. My concern in my relationship with Joanna had been myself, and how her behavior affected me and my reputation. How much had I been concerned about her?

"Draw a circle," he said, "and draw a line through it vertically and label the line 'hurt.' In the center place the initials of the person who has hurt you."

Mentally I was following his instructions.

"Ask yourself, 'Lord, what do you think of this person?' Listen for the answer. If God loves this person, will love fight love?"

God loves Joanna. The word was clear.

"Replace the hurt with love, with unconditional forgiveness, regardless of the act. No 'if,' " the speaker said. He was cutting asunder bone and marrow with the delicate knife of a neurosurgeon to get at the cancer.

"Hurt always controls us; we never control it. Hurts keep us awake at night and hound us during the day. And behind each hurt is always a person. We hurt because of people—what they did or didn't do."

I was the sinner. I had always focused on Joanna as the guilty one. I wept as I saw myself clearly in my relationship to her, our firstborn, the child conceived out of the passion of early days of marriage.

She had been a creative, aggressive child—never content to sit on my lap so I could cuddle her, or to play with a doll. She grabbed for every new experience, pushing me far beyond what I could handle easily as a new parent. She moved through school more quickly than was advisable because her early teachers found it difficult to challenge her mental and creative capabilities. So mathematics went unlearned in the grade she passed over, while works of the imagination caught her up with the force of a hurricane. She wrote and wrote in her journals—I, who later taught and encouraged journaling—couldn't understand her need to pour her heart out on paper.

Whatever was new in clothing and hair styles—jeans with flies, mini-skirts, beehive hairdos—she tried, and then either claimed or discarded. No asking of permission. I might come home to a bathtub with jeans weighted down to bleach them or to a brilliantly designed poster she had created for her room. The girls' bedroom was repainted as often and as brightly as she was able to convince her sisters it needed a facelift.

The death of her father at age fourteen broke whatever bond we had had. She lost her confidant. She couldn't handle the many platitudes about the death of a young father people offered us. I felt her slipping from me even more by the time boyfriends became important. So I dedicated her to God. She was his child. Let him look after her.

Only dimly did I sense it was my way of handling recalcitrant behavior. I, as an adult, and a recent single parent because of my husband's death, was working my way through many new issues I never expected to face as a homemaker in church and society at the same time as she was moving through a difficult teenage rebellion. Ideas I tested in writing, she experimented with practically until they lay lifeless before her or invited her to move beyond them to greater freedom. I wished she would choose a more conservative lifestyle even though I was looking for a freer one for myself.

Then came college and university and a headlong plunge into a a circle of friends I found even more difficult to accept. She was the sinner. I was the saint. She was the problem. I had the answers.

Why didn't we talk more when she was in university? When she headed for Costa Rica? After she returned from Guatemala, where she had been lost for several weeks after the earthquake? I don't know. The narrow bridge had broken with the heavy weight of condemnation.

One disaster after another occurred in our relationship, with me seeing myself always standing on the edge of the pit reaching for her hand—never crawling into it with her. She needed money, I sent it. She needed a temporary place to stay, I gave it. But these were handouts. What I truly wanted to give, I didn't have.

A person with a boil is hesitant to have anyone come close. Yet unless the hidden pus escapes, the boil continues to hurt, the speaker at the India conference said. "If we do not submit, God may bring us someone who tests us even more. Or we can have it our own way and God sets us aside." He wants us to develop joy in the midst of pain, peace and confidence in the midst of confusion, submission in the midst of heavy-handed authority.

I was the sinner. The problem was mine. I couldn't escape the verdict.

The speaker's next step toward healing was even more difficult: Thank God for the memory that has been hurting, yet be aware that God works with us at our speed in learning this lesson of thankfulness. He never pushes us harder than we can cope. Thankfulness opens us to new sensitivities about people who are also hurting. It may be the only way some of us will ever learn compassion.

This was his message to this group of Indian leaders searching for the best way to fulfill their ministry in a Christian community where colonialism, imperialism, and their own complex caste system had left behind serious wounds, running with pus, in the jostling for power, position, and influence. Yet he was saying that growth can come by the healing of memories. Everyone wants the spirit of Pentecost, but no one wants to go over Calvary to get there. Blessing can come out of tragedy. Peace and joy come out of pain. Peace is joy resting. Joy is peace dancing.

I walked over Calvary. I said, "Forgive me, Lord."

Then the moderator, an Indian national leader, asked me to pray. I was stunned. Didn't he know women in America in my denomination weren't asked to pray and bless a congregation at the close of big conferences? This was a tribute given to the most respected and experienced leader present—not to the lesser parts of the body of Christ. But I went forward and I prayed—but I don't know what I said. But when I returned to my chair, my friend reached for my hand. Silent tears flooded her eyes. She had sensed the touch of the Spirit. I had blessed her.

The mending of my relationship with my daughter was not a dramatic overnight affair, but a lengthy one. I had to remind myself constantly that I had forgiven her. The past was the past. Slowly the bridge would have to be rebuilt. Forgiveness had to be acted out in each encounter. Over the next years we made more mistakes. For a long time we alluded only with great pain and discomfort to certain aspects of our life together.

On one particularly trying occasion when her financial situation had forced her into a corner, after much agonized but hurried thought, I took out a fairly large personal loan at the bank and sent it to her, not as a handout but as a symbol of my love. Her membership in our family was more important than the monetary rewards of my labor.

Our family was being rebuilt. Slowly, step by step. Often with more pain. But we were a family again.

Recently when Joanna and her family were visiting, I heard her in the basement rummaging in her trunk, left behind for storage. Suddenly she appeared jubilantly before us waving her jean-cloth hippie skirt, covered with multitudinous patches. "I think I can get rid of this now," she said. "No," I advised her, "keep it. Keep it as a reminder—something to laugh about years from now. "

We laughed together.

India may be a land of burdens, but it became a place to lift them. A place of grace. A place of blessing. A unexpected way to get back on track.

CHAPTER 4

I know you and I love you

We grow quite old before we get the opportunity to prove the truth of our armchair convictions.

—Aggie Klassen

During the next years I met dozens of parents carrying the same unnecessary burden of pain and guilt I had carried too long. In a home, on a plane, over coffee, I heard them say: "We stagger under the load. How long, O Lord, how long?" The stories were different, but all had a similar pattern. A child had gone astray. They blamed themselves.

Both parents were probably on the phone the evening their son told them he was living with a girlfriend. "I wished Jerry had hit me with a baseball bat instead of with these words," said one father. The wife said she had felt hot and cold at once and didn't know how to respond. They had suspected something when a female voice sometimes answered their calls.

Their son wanted to bring his live-in home with him the next weekend. They slept little that night. Only the next evening could they even begin talking about it. Not fully. Not about the hurt, guilt, shame, and remorse. But they talked a little—about their son and his once vibrant faith. Someone had once called him the next Billy Graham, for he could really preach.

Why their family? Hadn't they brought up their kids in the way they should go? Family devotions, vacations, letters, phone calls, presents, affirmations—they had done it all with joyful love. She hadn't been employed outside the home until the children were in high school because of their needs.

Toward the end of the week they had the courage to phone their son to tell him they would prefer to visit him at the university rather than having him come home with "her." A first meeting might be easier on neutral territory.

Sunday morning the mother decided she didn't feel up to attending the Bible study hour with its emphasis on personal sharing. So she and her husband visited another congregation. They found themselves slowly withdrawing from congregational life under the weight of the betrayal of their faith and values, a common reaction to such rejection by a child.

The pain did not let up, even after they met "her" and found her to be a gentle, refined young woman, as nervous about meeting them as they were about meeting her and their son.

The pain hung on like an angry cat that had jumped onto their backs; its claws dug in deeply. In the morning when they awoke, it was with them. All day it burdened their lives. In the evening as they read their Bibles and prayed for grace to respond as Christ expected them, their prayers for love and wisdom fell to the ground like lead-filled shoes. No release.

How did one separate sin from the sinner? How could they show love and forgiveness without condoning what they believed to be wrong? Were they too conservative in the matters of sexual behavior?

What would the church think of them? Should they drop their church work—his deacon work, her weekly Bible study ministry? Their son was still a church member. Should they bring up his behavior so he could be disciplined?

It wasn't fair to be thrown without warning into a situation where their entire way of life, their faith, and their family solidarity were called into question. They felt like failures.

Both of them had grown up with a tradition of reticence about discussing family problems with other people. What happened within the walls of the home stayed within those walls. Even there, you didn't talk about the joys of love or the pain of hate and anger. These emotions were expressed in actions only. Though they had been trying to be more open and communicative about their faith life in keeping with the current spirit in the Christian community, they found themselves falling back on the old ways of keeping everything under cover.

At Christmas they usually wrote a family letter in which they included a sprightly upbeat paragraph about each child's accomplishments during the year. This year they left the letter until too late, so only cards were sent with a brief note of greeting.

The fear was always with them that their son might come without warning and bring his girlfriend with him, expecting to sleep together. As long as he was single, they could say, "You sleep here and your girlfriend over there." What if they had children? What then? Would the children call them Grandma and Grandpa?

And this matter of writing letters. Should they include the live-in companion in the salutation? Should they send a wedding present if there had been no wedding? Uncle George, family genealogist, would have to figure out how to deal with this live-in arrangement that had no specific dates—only vague beginnings and abrupt endings, stages, or eras.

By the time they were ready to tell their closest friends, their son came home one weekend with another woman, a tall brunette, obviously pregnant. The other one had moved out and opted for the single life. They felt suffocated under this new avalanche of grief.

This short scenario, a mild compilation of what numerous parents are experiencing, does not end here. Family love and family hurt has no clean cutoff points. I could have added adultery, divorce and remarriage, childcustody battles, wife and child abuse, drug involvement, encounters with the law, and many others to this story.

Parents struggle intensely to know the power of the gospel so that their children will remain both a lifetime member of their family and of God's family. One of the end results of the experience is always an intense lesson in recognizing their humanity—how much they dislike being controlled or rejected by children—and how much they need God's mercy and grace.

I like to read about the prodigal son. His father (and mother?) could celebrate the son's return because they had forgiven freely. Earlier they had mourned his absence and that his contribution to the family well-being was lacking. They had also mourned the merciless power of sin that had robbed them of joy and the benefits of a full relationship with them.

Mourning is painful, even this kind. It hurts. Can it have any purpose in our lives, we ask. One woman told me about her runaway daughter. For no apparent reason, she left and for five years was never heard from. Each time a young woman was mentioned in the news—a body found, an arrest made for violation with the law, an accident—the mother kept her ears tuned to newscasts until information about the young woman's identity was released. She ached intensely for some knowledge of her daughter.

The most usual approach to the pain of loss is to try to figure out how to get rid of it. We want to escape pain before finding out why we have it. We want to take something, anything, to deaden the hurt. So some people turn to pills and alcohol rather than allow pain to do its work.

Pain has been given to us for a special purpose—to let us know the body is not well. Physical pain asks the question: What is wrong with my body? Pain tells us clearly that the cut finger or the broken toe belongs to us and needs attention. Spiritual and emotional pain asks the same question and makes the same statement.

Dr. Paul Brand, missionary to lepers in India, after a long train ride, thought he might have leprosy, for when he pricked himself in the heel with a needle, he felt no pain. He had told others that leprosy was not readily contagious, and now he feared he had contracted the dread disease himself. In the morning, when he tried the needle test again, he yelled out in pain. The relief of experiencing pain was staggering, he writes. He fell to his knees to praise God for pain. He had apparently numbed a nerve during the long ride and therefore had felt no response the night before. Thereafter, when he cut a finger, turned an ankle, or even suffered from nausea as a reaction to mushroom poisoning, his response was "Thanks, God, for the pain."

Pain is necessary for survival. It is an indication of life, not death. Lepers lose fingers and toes, mostly through injury, because they feel no pain when they pick up a hot pan or cut a finger. In the early days of Dr. Brand's ministry in India, the missionaries gave the lepers cats to protect their extremities from being eaten by the rats, for they could feel no pain.

Pain in the family or the community of God asks a question: What is wrong? The pain I was feeling told me something was terribly wrong. The person who never feels physical pain is a robot—not a whole person. The person who never feels emotional and spiritual pain is also not a whole person. And therefore will also lose body members.

Yet how does healing and comfort come for pain caused by a break in relationships? Through an act of the will. Through an act of faith. Through giving and receiving forgiveness.

If the story of the prodigal son is taken at a human level, the father had every right to be unforgiving. Their son had squandered his hard-earned money and had besmirched his name. Yet Jesus said the father forgave. The son's sin of rejection needed forgiveness. But not all sins need forgiveness, writes Lewis B. Smedes in *Forgive and Forget*. Sometimes all we need is a generous nature to ignore the slights and annoyances that come our way and to rejoice with those who succeed at something we were trying to achieve.

I recall one minister telling me how in his first pastorate, one of his more conservative members was extremely upset by his gold wedding band, which flashed as he waved his hands when he spoke. She told him so. That kind of slight does not need forgiveness, according to Smedes, only a generous spirit.

False guilt also does not need forgiveness. Yet guilt which comes as a result of judgment and criticism of us by others who advocate a false lifestyle may be as painful to us as true guilt, which comes from the judgment of God. Mass media advertising burdens us with guilt we should never carry—water spots on glasses, static electricity in our clothes, limp greasy hair. Who hasn't seen grown-ups in abject humiliation because their housekeeping, lawn upkeep, and attire didn't match the neighbor's? Is their guilt any different from that of mothers in India who once felt guilty if they didn't let a handicapped child die or if they gave birth to twins?

The film *Tootsie* showed me how this false guilt so easily becomes a woman's burden. The main male character, played by Dustin Hoffman, doesn't show up for supper at his girlfriend's house, so when he finally arrives, they have words. He apologizes for his late arrival, and then she apologizes for having expected him to come, though coming to her place was his idea. She carried false guilt created by a society which says a woman should bear the responsibility when things go wrong or a relationship goes sour.

Our society has many small children plagued by false guilt because they fear they may have caused their parents to divorce. Young children may also feel guilty for having done something in their innocence and ignorance they did not fully understand. A young man told me how he had laughed when his small brother died, making his parents very upset with him. He carried the guilt of that laugh for years and didn't know how to get rid of it.

Another woman mentioned that when the sister she had longed for was born, she had smothered her with kisses and hugs. Later on, when she was charged with daily care of the active toddler, the little sister became a downright nuisance. One day the older sister quite matter-of-factly took back all the kisses she had given her sister, sucking them from the little girl's cheeks toward herself. Soon after, the little sister died and the older one carried the burden of her action as a small child into adulthood until a friend helped her see she was carrying an unnecessary load.

I see some parents groaning under false guilt for a child's wrong life decisions, blaming themselves, even though they wouldn't think of crediting themselves for all the child's right decisions.

Smedes says there are hurts that need forgiveness: acts of disloyalty and betrayal, such as adultery, which is disloyalty to a promise, parents' failure to attend a child's graduation that they promised to attend, friends who take their business elsewhere, a person who gossips a friend's secret all over the community, the worker who puts a fellow worker down.

Someone has said that three of the most difficult things in life are to say, "I'm sorry," "I forgive you," and "You may have my place of power. I'll step down." After my own lengthy experience of learning to forgive, I realize that in the Christian community forgiveness is much needed, much taught in general terms, but little practiced. We don't know how to forgive.

We are taught God's love, but we don't quite believe it is true. Many of us have grown up never learning practical forgiveness. Some Catholics are saying they are ahead of us—they confess their sins daily. We sometimes don't know what to do with them, so we add new ones to the load daily.

I don't know what people have been doing with an unforgiving spirit. Some battle it out. Others retreat to long periods of silence and anger, until they can talk comfortably again. Others believe that human nature can't be changed, and that time heals all, so endure it. Others smooth things over with words and gifts, with mothers being the greatest smoothers-over to avoid conflict from surfacing. I recall one home in which all communication between the father and children had broken down. Instead, the mother carried messages from child to father and vice versa in their presence, smoothing over the conflict, so it wouldn't erupt in angry outbursts.

Others go about reconciliation the wrong way. An incident I would like to forget happened when I was attending Bible college. Our dean of women was not to our liking. She had come from across the border. We found her approach strange and judged her unspiritual because her religious language did not match ours. We wouldn't let her come close to us. So, during a day of fasting and prayer, under conviction for our harsh attitude, each of us (about twenty girls) went one by one to ask her forgiveness. I have often wondered since what a steady parade of girls telling our gray-haired dean of women they didn't like her did to her morale. She never stayed at the institution.

There are several reasons we don't forgive. We, in the church with a long tradition of good names, worry more about our own reputation than reconciliation with the offender. The child, maybe a spouse or friend, has hurt us. Our concern is for ourselves, for the hurt we are feeling and the accompanying anger, frustration, and mistrust. What will people think of me now that he or she has done this? They will see me as a rotten parent, a horrible wife, a terrible neighbor, or a difficult worker. It wasn't my fault. People must be made to see I'm not to blame.

So we try to keep the whole dirty business as far from us as possible by condemning and trying to extricate ourselves—or by saying nothing. We hope no one will ask. We want to shove the matter into a dark hole where no one will see it—and it won't bother us.

And forgiveness is impossible.

Another reason we don't forgive is that we have a strong sense of right and wrong, especially if we have been brought up in the Christian community. We know what sin is—we learned it from childhood on up—drugs, including drinking and smoking, premarital sex, adultery, gambling—you know the list.

As I continued to study the Scriptures I found that Christ's main concern was righteousness, or right living, meaning right relationships between persons and between persons and God. "Love one another even as I have loved you," taught Jesus.

When hurt by someone, however, we stir up our own sense of righteousness to say, "I can't condone the sin of that person," and then wonder why oneness eludes us. Our idea of righteousness means sinlessness in the other person, but not in ourselves.

As I gradually felt freer to speak about my experiences with my daughter, others shared theirs. I heard about parents who had never given them a fair break, an early teacher who didn't understand, a harsh and judgmental church leader, a too-critical son or daughter—all leading to a wounded spirit. Couples wondered why something once so beautiful as their love, beautifully choreographed at the wedding, had become so ugly and hurtful. Without forgiveness, relationships break. Divorce is the final act of saying to someone, "I don't trust you any-more."

At one time I, too, had demanded what I was now hearing others say: "They should pay for their mistake. They'll never learn otherwise," or "Aren't we letting them off by forgiving them, condoning the sin?"

Hate is our only weapon to keep hurting the other person, says Smedes. Because revenge is not nice these days, we use this powerful weapon, which has the characteristic of turning on the user. When we don't forgive, we bind ourselves to that other person and destroy ourselves.

Forgiveness releases us from bondage to that other person. We're free. We don't need to rehearse revenge speeches anymore. Scores may never be evened out, but the slate is cleared. In Smede's words, "It stops the cycle of unfair pain." The hurting can stop. You and the other person can start over again. Reconciliation can take place.

On the cross Jesus said, "Father, forgive them, for they know not what they are doing"—a blanket pardon for whatever in us causes our relationhips with others to break. We can have forgiveness. We can be forgiven.

The aim of a forgiving person is to keep relationships together—to hold together—to be a peacemaker that Christ might be glorified. One syndicated columnist advises her readers, "Don't waste yourself on the person who has hurt you. Get rid of the jerk." Sometimes such advice may be necessary. I don't deny it. But not always. God's word is "Forgive, release that person. Forgive as I forgive. Don't bind him or her with your anger."

Forgiveness, as I see it, is a combination of judgment and grace. As a child I memorized John 1:14: "The Word was made flesh, and dwelt among us, (and we beheld his glory, the glory of the only begotten of the Father,) full of grace and truth." This abstract terminology never made sense to me until one day a minister explained it. Grace, which always precedes truth, means, "I love you, daughter, son, husband, wife, father, or mother." Truth means, "I know you in your weakness and your strength. I see you as a person whom God loves. I see you as a person who needs to know this love. I love you and I know you."

That is forgiveness. There may be more hurts and forgiving ahead, but it is time to start over, to claim our right to stop hurting. The final goal of forgiveness is not just getting rid of the hurt, but reconciliation. It releases us from the past, heals the present, and makes the future a possibility of joy.

Dietrich Bonhoeffer, the German theologian, writes that we

have forgiven when the carrying of the other's burden becomes a joy, or when we can look back with joy on what was pain. Dag Hammerskold states we forgive when we release the other person and take on ourselves the consequences of the other person's actions, when we suffer with them what it is they have done.

While in Nepal I heard of a young Christian nurse who modeled this kind of forgiving spirit. Over tea and sweets her friend told us of the cruelty of the nurse's father to her in childhood. When she became a Christian, he beat her and locked her up. Later, when he became ill, she asked for time off to go home "to lavish her love on him" even though he had treated her badly. She led him to Christ because of her loving care. When a Norwegian friend Ruth came to see her and the sick father, she suggested a time of prayer with the family behind closed doors. The father said, "No, leave the door open. Let everybody know what is going on." He had nothing to hide.

When I had nothing to hide, I found I could also lift other people's burdens. And bless them.

CHAPTER 5

Stretching doesn't always hurt

*If you have ever had the vision of God, you
may try as you like to be satisfied on a lower
level, but God will never let you.*

—Oswald Chambers

About two years after I had made my list of goals, I found
myself in Europe on a church history tour. The children were
all young adults. I was finally able to indulge some of my love
of travel and new experiences. We visited castles and ca-
thedrals, windmills, dykes, and canals. And museums. Lots of
them.

One day our tour group followed our guide up winding stairs
of an ancient castle to what once had been the grand dining
salon. In the stone floor near the head of the table I saw a
grated opening in which the castleowner's prized prisoners
were confined under constant observation. He could throw a
scrap of food to the caged human below him if he so desired—
or withhold it also, if that was his wish.

In an even larger room we came upon a collection of torture
instruments of the Middle Ages—handcuffs, balls and chains,
spiked collars and belts, tongue pinchers, stocks for gossips, and
a guillotine. I stood for a long time before the infamous rack, a
device on which the unfortunate captives were bound and then

stretched by means of winches until they died. I had read about racks years ago as a child. I wondered about the many people who died as the torturer slowly, deliberately, tightened the ropes to make the pain more excruciating.

Life is always a stretching, I surmised, as I contemplated the wooden rack before me. Sometimes God allows us to experience painful stretching, not so we'll die, but to grow. Every new experience, new encounter with a thing or person, can stretch us toward life and greater freedom and joy. To grow means to stretch—to become more involved with people, ideas, and especially the truth of God. The apostle Paul's conversion was his greatest stretching experience, for he had to decide whether he was actually for God or against him when he persecuted Christians.

In Jesus' time, the Jews were concerned mostly with keeping themselves the same size throughout life. They clung to their familiar interpretation of the law. They didn't want it changed. The lawyer who had asked Jesus, "Who is my neighbor?" really was asking, "How can I keep from being stretched, from having to change my way of life? Who do I *not* need to be a neighbor to? How narrow, how small, can I keep myself and not sin?"

Jesus told the Jewish teacher the story of the good Samaritan, a person the Jews collectively agreed they did not need to help. But the expert of the law responded, in effect, "I like myself the way I am," and refused to accept Jesus' invitation to be stretched. He refused to change his view of how God works in our world. He refused to change his theology.

Working at theology had been the first item on my list. Not that I hadn't been aware of the need to do theology. Two major events, among many smaller ones over a period of years, had jolted me into theological awareness about fifteen years earlier. The first was the sudden death of my husband after fifteen years of marriage. No other event has forced me to change patterns of living and thinking so suddenly, so rapidly, so violently.

Often I felt like a small ship caught in the white water of a heavy sea.

The second event was the equally sudden death of a young father in our community who quit taking insulin because he, his family, and friends believed God had healed his diabetic condition. They were convinced the Bible taught that healing was in the atonement.

At the time I compared the young man's death with my husband's death and the deaths of persons who die of old age, accidentally, or of cancer or other disease. The man's friends had prayed for healing; I and my family had prayed for healing. But death had come anyway to both men.

Had none of us had enough faith? When did our "good" faith become "bad" faith? Were any of these prayers we said time and time again prayers of faith? Was my faith a weak dabbling in spiritual power? Was their faith a presumptuous forcing of God to the test?

Such questions tumbled about in my mind for some time, never finding a resting spot. They were theological questions, for they were questions about the nature of God in the face of human suffering. Does God respond to human prayer? Does "walking with God" mean tiptoeing through the tulips of life, hoping he's somewhere within calling distance but never quite sure? Or does it mean demanding he act to prove he is who he says he is? When nothing happens, when there are no clear answers to prayer, must a Christian resort to semantics to get out of the bind by declaring to the world, "God healed my husband. He raised him higher!"

It was one thing to cling to an interpretation of Scripture that I believed to be true, while knowing many other believers regarded it as one of many possible interpretations. It was another matter to hold to an interpretation I believed to be the only true one to find it collapsing when tested. A lot of folk theology, sometimes referred to as religious platitudes, floats about in the Christian community. Some has to do with healing, much with guidance and with answers to prayer.

Against this strong folk theology stands the weight of the scientific community. One side says, "Have faith to be healed." Science says, "Given these health conditions, the prospect of complete recovery is very small." Folk theology says, "Expect a miracle." Science says, "Given the influence of environment and heredity over many years on this person's behavior patterns, hope for change is slim." The frequent result is that the person who is taught one idea (God always answers prayer as specifically as we ask in faith) and who then encounters the darkness of no answer, or what seems like the very absence of God, experiences serious internal war: "This is what I've been taught to believe; this is what I'm experiencing. Where is truth?" Job and the psalmists were troubled by these same questions several thousand years ago.

But now I was telling myself once again: Do theology. Because I was human, I had questions about my faith, yet I also knew these questions should not throw me into a tizzy even when they did. Doubt did not mean unbelief. Doubt was only the weeds in the garden that needed to be eradicated.

To theologize is to have courage to shape faith by looking honestly for answers to God-questions. To theologize means to travel together with the patriarch Abraham on his lonely pilgrimage from Ur of the Chaldees to the Promised Land. To theologize means to agonize with Hannah, second wife of Elkanah, who desperately wanted a child and could not understand why God didn't give her one. To theologize means to keep company with Mary and Martha, who were troubled that their friend Jesus, who loved their brother Lazarus, didn't show up when they sent the message he was sick and needed his friend's help.

As I stood before that medieval instrument of torture, I concluded I had been doing theology all my Christian life, only calling it adjusting, or growing.

I grew up in a small immigrant community in northern

Saskatchewan, a secure little place in the middle of nowhere. While growing up, I sorted what I believed in the manner of children. What my parents believed was right and true. What everyone else believed was wrong. We were on the inside of truth and all others on the outside.

Years later I met a former grade school classmate, now a priest and professor in a Catholic college, who told me he too had thought in his formative years that his family was the only one with Christian truth, the only home in which parents taught biblical principles and prayed with their children. He had been surprised as an adult to learn that there had been other families, like ours, in that community that also had cherished Christian truth during the years when we were all snot-nosed youngsters hanging around the skating rink.

I liked my little world of religious ideas and didn't expect it to become much bigger. But when I went to work in the city after high school, I attended Inter-Varsity Christian Fellowship meetings. I listened to young people of many denominations saying, "I too believe in God and Jesus Christ as Savior." I gulped hard. But I was willing to admit my small branch of the church didn't have a corner on truth, but that these Presbyterians, Baptists, Lutherans, and others also worshiped Christ as Savior. So one day I took courage to reach out and draw them into the family of God. The stretching didn't hurt a bit.

But I still had unspoken reservations for years about other kinds of Christians, particularly the ones who wore the funny little white net prayer coverings and those who always prayed silently. My more vocal brand of Christianity had it over these strange beings. Someday in glory I and my kind were going to sit on God's patio and have a special barbecue with him because we did things right.

Then one day I interviewed a woman for an article related to her work in the church. She wore a white gauze devotional covering. At the end of the interview, she turned to me gently and said, "I am so glad to know there are Christians in your church too." I felt stunned. She felt the same way about me that I felt about her.

God said to me, "Now you know. Reach out and draw her in. God is no respecter of persons. Whoever calls upon the name of the Lord shall be saved." So I cautiously reached out and drew in another group of Christians—and they drew me toward them.

I was doing theology and didn't know it. I was making the gospel operative in my life. But there was more to do.

As a child I had had little contact with people of other races. We learned the chorus about "Jesus loves the little children of the world, red and yellow, black and white," but never applied it to the Indians who inhabited a reservation near our community. We expected them to keep their place.

I recall the college student who told me she had heard as a child that if you touched a person of a different skin color, you broke out in a rash. I can recall more vividly the first time I sat beside a black man. It was in a limousine from the airport to a hotel in Chicago. And he was a big man, dwarfing me. In the five-mile journey to the hotel, I tried to sort through all I had heard and felt about prejudice. I didn't like all of it.

Then one year my husband, who was studying at Syracuse University, roomed with a Formosan and a Nigerian. No rashes came of that experience. Only good things. To learn to know persons as individuals rather than only as a member of a group or category eliminates prejudice. If God was no respecter of persons of other races, why should I be one?

As a church we keep people out of the family of God by our attitudes. Many more people can crowd around Christ if we make him the center instead of first drawing the size of the circle and then placing ourselves and Christ in it. I stretched and included other races in the family of God.

But updating my theology had to include more than racial prejudice. I was ready to sit with Job, with the psalmists, with these others. I was ready to work through why some scriptural injunctions are emphasized though others are considered minor teachings. Why other teachings, once considered extremely important, have been almost phased out of circulation. Why still others not mentioned in Scripture, except by vague implication, take on the importance of the net under the high-wire acrobats. And why Christians can hold opposing views on the same subjects.

Let's take an example. You're in a small-group meeting.

"Do you have some items for praise and prayer?" asks the group leader.

"My mother's health is low—she has cancer."

"Our missionaries need a visa to return."

"My son found the sweater he lost last week."

The underlying theology here is that whatever your need, God supplies the answer. Having a problem with spouse, child, or friend? Christ will remove the problem. Having difficulties on the job? Christ will find you a better one. Short of cash? God supplies. Feeling guilty about this morning's cutting remark? He forgives.

Fairly simple. How Christ becomes the answer to life's endless problems, swift disappointments, and ill-nourished dreams isn't explained. And that's what most of us want to know. How does spiritual truth become living reality? What did the psalmist mean when he said, "Delight yourself in the Lord and he will give you the desires of your heart," or when Jesus said, "But seek first his kingdom and his righteousness, and all these things will be given to you as well"?

Over the years we tend to compile a lot of neatly packaged answers about how God reveals himself and relates to his children. The back of my Scofield Reference Bible had all kinds of scribblings stating, "If you meet God's conditions, he will fulfill his promise." It was sort of like getting God in a headlock.

I had worked hard at meeting the conditions. I was sure divine guidance always came as clearly as the STOP sign at the end of the street. God had a blueprint for my life, which included all important details like vocation, husband, children, where I should live, and what I should do and wear. My job was to figure out the details, like going on a treasure hunt.

All I had to do was look up the issue in the Bible and wait for God's signal. One friend told me that during her divorce she was so desperate for some sign from God, she had audibly begged for a note from God in her young son's presence. When he woke early and didn't find one, he wrote her a note to keep her from being too disappointed.

Like her, most of us are not plagued with an unwillingness to be shown the way. We long to know it so we can do it. I hungered for it. I felt, however, as if I'd been placed in a monstrous maze in some cruel fun center, and unless I found the one path out, I'd be wandering in its *cul de sacs* until eternity. To decide arbitrarily which turn to make in the jungle of paths was to shift to God's Plan B for me even though I didn't know what Plan A was. I frequently felt caught in a catch-22 as I listened to other Christians calmly and coolly discuss prayer requests, as if they were ordering the Sunday roast, while I was anxiously hoping God would just shove me in the right general direction because I was too terrified to take any step alone.

I could see no STOP or GO signs, only a brackish fog. If Christ wasn't the answer, was my spiritual state the problem? I hated to admit that was a convenient way of easing out of the difficulty and one I had used before in a pinch.

A young friend whose boyfriend had discarded her like yesterday's tossed salad spent several days in sincere prayer, convinced God would answer by sending him back to her. His return was her need, therefore her request. Hadn't God promised to give his children the delights of their hearts if they trusted in him? She was trusting.

When the young man abruptly married someone else, she dropped her Bible and her faith in the wastepaper basket, terming them unworkable in today's society and moved in a different direction. She was unable to reconcile the warring forces inside her which said, on the one hand, God is a loving and prayer-answering God, and, on the other, in this situation he didn't really care for her. And she refused to do theology.

Some people may not take such drastic action as soon. Some become dismayed, a little depressed, grasping for clues to the full life that always seems beyond them, but slog on. Others pay pew service to organized religion, for it provides them with certain social benefits, but dismiss the possibility of Christ remaining the Lord of life. The risks of getting hurt are too great if one trusts. What if the system broke down again at a crucial moment, like the final seconds of a close football game, when the player fails to kick the ball between the posts for the needed points?

In my young adult years, I had gleaned an understanding of God that had shaped my outlook on life, its values, hopes, and ambitions. Part of that early perception was that God was my personal friend, but also my personal messenger boy, at my beck and call whenever I got into a mess. What God did between times didn't really concern me. He knew the number of hairs on my head and saw the sparrow fall.

At the time I hadn't yet faced many big questions of life, such as suffering, sin, and evil in my life and in that of others. Therefore I didn't find it presumptuous to nudge God occasionally to keep proving to me that he was God. After all, he loved me, didn't he?

Then after a period of years my theology began tripping me up. I ran into problem after problem with what I said I believed about God and with what was happening despite that belief. I was also finding out that as long as I stayed comfortably close to my own small group of friends, where everyone understood the teachings of the Bible and used faith language the same way I did, I could get along reasonably well, especially if I avoided making many faith decisions.

My thinking about God, inherited and self-developed, was

creating inner turmoil. I had been theologizing, but somewhere some misinformation had crept in and was slowly dislodging my joyful faith in God. I had to sort through matters more clearly, or bow out. I refused to do the latter. I opted for the former. I believed in God and in his Son Jesus Christ as Savior of humankind. To deny Christ and turn back, as some disciples did during his lifetime, would mean losing not only the investment of years but the only solid rock in my life.

I moved to the position that the Christian walk is a school. No one begins with a graduate degree. Just as the first encounter with calculus doesn't necessarily mean perennial defeat, so unsuccessful tests of life are not failures of God or of us. I decided to learn more about theology so I could better understand how God relates to all of humanity, but especially to me.

CHAPTER 6

What? Me a theologian!

*Theology is too important to be entrusted to
the seminaries alone.*

—Jim Wallis

"What? Me a theologian!" My friend could never see herself
in that role. The term brought up nightmares of walls of books,
heavy discussions, and grim encounters. "I just read my Bible,
pray, and do what I think is right. Theology's not my thing,"
she had said.

She dismissed with a flick of her hand my suggestion that
she was making a theological judgment about her unambitious
neighbor when she related his lack of financial success to his
lack of commitment to God. Yet she echoed my thinking about
theology before I began my search when I, too, believed
theology was for preachers in black suits and professors in
academic garb, and that I could excuse myself from doing
theology because I was neither.

Yet I felt pushed to find out more about what I believed and
why because so much of life for the Christian depends on one's
theology. We live according to our theology. As I studied and
sorted, I gradually came up with certain principles:

No. 1: *Theology is for everyone.* At first I didn't believe it, but the more I studied the Bible, the more obvious it became to me that theology is not something restricted to or reserved for leaders. Some aspects of this queen of sciences require highly trained and penetrating scholarship, yet other aspects are not always a function of vast and detailed learning. The task of theology is to root believers firmly in the Christian life by thinking through God's word for their own lives as it relates to their particular context.

No. 2: *Theology is not only a lot of informal opinions or a set of formal propositions.* What a mouthful! I could hardly get myself to write it down. Yes, theology does contain propositional truth, or statements of doctrine synthesized from scriptural teaching. A common error for the beginning lay theologian is to confuse theology and doctrine, although they do overlap. Doctrine is usually considered the straightforward teaching of the Bible on any subject—salvation, for example. Statements of faith usually have to do with doctrine. Doctrine remains fairly steadfast.

Theology is an attempt to understand those doctrines and relate them to practical life. Some people equate doctrine and theology. They set them side by side, like a couple of bowling pins, and substitute one for the other as if they were synonymous. They take a statement like "God is love," and an interpretation of this statement, "A loving God gives me everything I want," and punch them into their mental computer as if they were the same statement. Sometimes the two statements may overlap in meaning. When they don't mean the same thing and one thinks they should, he or she has a problem.

To say "Christ is the answer" is an attempt at theology—undeveloped theology, but theology, nevertheless. So is the statement "Prayer changes things." These are attempts to translate scriptural truth into language and symbols all can understand.

When theologies are highly developed, they are referred to

as systematic theologies. But our personal informal system is also a theology, even though it may not be well organized or even thought through. It has been brought together over the years from religious training and traditions at home and church, and from daily experiences, reading, and reflection.

We keep adding bits of information about God to our fund of knowledge about him, testing new ideas in the next situation that requires a faith response. These testing situations are usually personal or family changes and crises, like illness or death, or success or failure on the job, with a spouse, a friend, or a child. The crisis may be caused by the loss of a lifelong dream or a treasured possession or friend. It may be precipitated by a newspaper article dealing with the United States' right to sell military arms to a third-world country. Our response in any of these situations is based on the assumptions about God we have internalized over the years rather than upon creedal statements we have memorized.

While sitting in our padded pews on a Sunday morning, everything the minister says, the liturgy, the hymns, may make much sense, but when we hit the job on Monday morning, or even before that, when we get home from the service and decide what we will be doing in the afternoon—watch television, visit a sick neighbor, write letters, go on a picnic, or do the laundry and hoe the garden—our true theology goes to work.

Despite our generous words about what we believe about God as being all-powerful, all-knowing, all-loving, all-merciful, we respond fairly consistently to the system of beliefs we have uncritically incorporated in our worldview over the years. Persons who have learned to think about God as a harsh, legalistic judge, will feel guilty if they haven't fulfilled his minimum requirements of daily Bible reading, prayer, and other behaviors. Their guilt refuses to release them from their duty to a twenty-minutes-a-day-God.

After the death of my husband, and again after the death of the young father with diabetes, I asked myself where I had gotten the idea that God could be my personal cosmic errand boy, hopping to do my bidding whenever I clasped my hands in prayer. Why did I believe for years I was so special with God, he would never allow me or my family to have any serious problems? One woman I read about watched the spring floods edging closer to her home. "I just knew God wouldn't let that water come into our house," she said. But it came. When the floodwaters entered my life, rather than my house, to my surprise I found God was there as I sopped up tears rather than floors.

I began my informal study of how God reveals himself by attempting to separate what I thought I should believe from what I knew to be reality in my life regarding divine leading. It was like separating sugar from flour in the cake batter. But by identifying my convictions, both strong and weak, and tracking down scriptural principles, I knew I would have greater confidence and courage to move ahead.

I laid out before me the Scripture passages dealing with God's will, such as Proverbs 3:6: "In all thy ways acknowledge him, and he shall direct thy paths," and accounts of God's leading in the lives of Bible characters and contemporary Christians. I read books on the subject—they piled up on my shelves. I listened to the experiences of friends.

To presume to know exactly how God can and should lead his children means we are relying almost exclusively on loyalties developed and language gleaned from the Christian community and subsequently stored, frequently for years without enough review. A little theology makes itself visible here and there in our daily experience and we grab for it. Alice and Bill say the Gideon fleece method of guidance works for them whenever they need guidance and cite proof in the check that came unexpectedly in the mail the next day after they laid out their fleece. We cache that bit of information away for possible future use. The pastor says parents shouldn't blame themselves for their children's moral failures; everyone is personally responsible to God. That makes sense. We squirrel that bit of truth away for the time when we face that mountain pass with our own children. George Mueller prayed for food to feed his many orphans and God answered his need. Why not for me?

The first positive statement I could make to myself about divine guidance was fairly simple: God reveals himself to his children, not always in the same way, but he does guide. But before I could go on, I had to rethink my view of the nature of God. From various sources, certainly not from the Bible, I had accepted that people moved about in a mechanistic world in predetermined paths, like wound-up toys, and not as free moral beings. When the sovereign God spoke, we reacted, not acted. But I would have denied to the death that I believed this. This study in itself took me down many other paths of research.

No.3: *Theology can change.* I tried hard to reject this idea but finally had to give in. That theology can change, should possibly change when one enters a different culture, is difficult for the person who has been taught that God is a changeless God, a "rock of ages." "They're changing the Bible. What is left for me believe?" older Christians lament as they hear about new interpretations of passages dealing with worldly amusements, divorce and remarriage, abortion, human sexuality, and the role of women.

Their pain is real, acute. They look for a place to lodge their questions. They aren't cynical or even judgmental—just looking for an answer, or at least a listener. From time to time they re-convince themselves that Christianity must be all right or it wouldn't have lasted so long and enlisted so many intelligent followers. They accept that the church for all its failures and problems represents something good and true. Still, they have questions, often arising from experiences which are too uncomfortable and embarrassing to discuss openly. Some feel pressured to say they believe certain things about the Bible, yet deep inside they know they don't. They long not for more facts, more doctrine, more propositions, but help in relating belief to experience. Some of them, members of the church for forty to fifty years, die convinced their confusion and floundering was their own fault. The real problem is that they never learned to change their mind.

They refused to admit that the package of theological learning they wrapped up and tied carefully twenty or more years ago no longer fits the current culture. They have become familiar and comfortable with one theology—a theology of salvation, missions and evangelism, stewardship, and church loyalty—and are now forced to consider additional theologies related to environmental change, technology, leisure time, human sexuality, social concerns, and nuclear buildup. The earlier theology was a good theology, a workable one. Bewildered and uneasy with the urge to keep in step, some become defensive and resentful. Every spokesperson for change becomes the enemy, determined to liberalize and undermine their faith. So they dig in for battle like those who opposed Galileo when he offered the view that the planets rotated around the sun instead of around the earth.

Anyone who has been through the experience of having to change his or her mind knows that until things are fastened down once again and formulated into a system of belief, life is a turmoil and God seems to have drifted off somewhere to the periphery.

I grew up in a conservative denomination in which believing women wore long hair and no makeup. I sensed a strong mandate to wear a hat to church as a prayer covering. I felt as perplexed as these older people do today when I first worshiped with a congregation in which head coverings were a bother, makeup acceptable, and hair could be any length. Even movies were acceptable. For a time, I, too, asked, "Are all values relative? Is everything not fastened down by edict being swept out from under me?"

I grew calmer when I realized that the basic beliefs of the Bible hadn't changed. God was still on his throne even though some people might have different customs than I had. Sin still had power to destroy. Salvation was still an open invitation, redemption still occurring. Divine truth was not at stake, only some interpretations of it. This new congregation and I were living in two different theological worlds. I was clinging to the view that a changeless God could not support cultural change and that all these new experiences were a drift toward worldliness and relativism.

Yet God remains immutable. Anything people say about him doesn't change him. His attributes remain the same, but his changelessness doesn't deter him from being active in history, even stirring up a little change. Culture changes, and forms or methods of conveying truth change. A depersonalized society of the sixties and seventies required the small-group movement to meet the intimacy needs of people alienated from one another by increasing institutionalization, mobility, individualism, and privatism. At present a greater awareness of social injustice in our global community demands more concern on the part of the Christian. At stake is only a willingness to learn more about God, not less, even though to change one's thinking can be compared to cutting off one's little finger. It hurts as much.

No. 4: *Theology can be subject to human error.* It may seem that I am saying the Word of God is in error, but I'm not. Because theology is the human interpretation of what the Bible says (which we hope is always under the perfect guidance of the Spirit), and because human thinking is imperfect, theology may be an imperfect interpretation of Scripture. Not only is God much greater than his revelation of himself in Scripture, but also much greater than our limited efforts to codify him and nail him down to something we can understand and handle.

When parents say calmly at the death of their child, sick with leukemia, "God needed her more than we did," the words may comfort, but the theology behind them may be erroneous. Does God need a child? Does he whimsically select a child here or there because he wants more children in heaven with him?

Here are two other extreme examples of erroneous theology, one from history, one from the experience of a friend. During the Reformation period, a group of believers of the radical left wing accepted as truth that Christ taught that his followers should become as little children. So they took off their clothing and played with toys all day. Startling? Certainly. Even amusing. But obviously an incorrect interpretation of the Bible, for Jesus was speaking metaphorically and these people took the Word literally.

Another one: Jana's husband spent hours and hours reading the Bible. One day he abruptly left her and their two young children because God had told him that if he didn't hate his wife and children he could not be Christ's disciple (Luke 14:26). A perplexed and disturbed Jana considered her alternatives: welfare or find baby-sitting services for her toddlers and employment for herself. Her husband's literal interpretation of Scripture had destroyed their family.

Extreme examples of misinterpretation of Scripture are easy to spot from the perspective of time and distance. In 1591, when Eufame Maclaine hired a midwife to provide her with medicinal relief from the pain of childbirth, her twin infants were taken from her and she was burned at the stake. The first obstetricians to use anesthesia were attacked for acting contrary to the divine injunction that "in sorrow shall she bring forth," not in absence of pain. Their theology was suspect by the orthodox.

The less extreme examples, however, cause the perplexity and confusion today, because once we latch onto an interpretation of Scripture, we cling to it with the tenacity of the new super-glue and will do almost anything to protect that view from harm. Birth control, abortion, the role of women in ministry, divorce and remarriage, homosexuality, and other issues are putting some people through a wringer of confusion. It is equally perplexing for some to know that some persons see the approach of television evangelists as simplistic and so much hype. Others swear by them. One group of persons promotes social justice. Another group wants their name removed from subscription lists when too much is said about Christ being on the side of the poor and the oppressed. Some Christians shut their mind off when the preacher thunders away with a hellfire and brimstone message. Others can't handle the suggestion that the Sermon on the Mount might have serious implications for believers today. The serious devotional life seems anachronistic, dating back to medieval times, to those working to meet desperate physical needs of the poor. Yet, on the other hand, those deeply involved in evangelism think protesting against nuclear armament is a disgrace to the name of Christ.

Who's right? Who's wrong? Which is bad theology? All? None?

To bring the varying views together seems as futile as planning to have tea with a tiger in the rose garden. In the Middle Ages, the state church imprisoned, tortured, and put to death its theological opponents. Today Christians are more likely to resort to arrogance and disdain for those they think live in a benighted state of liberalism or conservatism. The putdown, "I am appalled that anyone could believe such nonsense!" followed by social ostracism is the common modern equivalent of the medieval rack.

No. 5: *Another road correction I had to make was to resist theologizing beyond the revelation of Scripture.* Scripture can't be forced to mean what we want it to mean because we like that meaning.

I have heard some people offering the simplistic formula, "Let go and let God!" for every critical situation. I backed off from that one for a better look. The Christian life is a meaningful relationship between a personal God and the person who chooses to follow him, based on trust. It is an intelligent relationship, but not one restricted to Mensa members. Even the mentally handicapped can know this relationship. It does not involve a mechanical approach to Scripture or a magical one. To use Scripture like some magic chant or amulet, or to wrest meaning from its words that is not there leads to error. The Spirit uses the meaning of the whole Bible to guide and strengthen.

Once a well-meaning friend told me how to get quick and sure guidance on such matters as whether to take a long, expensive trip or to change jobs. All one had to do was to keep reading the Bible until one came to a verse with wording that fitted the situation, like "Go now unto the city . . ." or "They went not," and then follow this instruction precisely. A variation of this popular theology is to open one's Bible at random, count down seven verses (the perfect number) and use that verse as the plan of action to locate a lost pair of scissors or an earring or to find a new job.

I doubt whether God intended us to use Scripture in this manner, for it treats Scripture like a horoscope and pulls verses out of context. The purpose of relating to God in Christ Jesus is a holy life that glorifies him. The Scriptures direct us explicitly with regard to honesty, love, and forgiveness. For situations involving these principles we need no special guidance. To be honest or corrupt, to love or to be fearful, to forgive or to hate should never be an issue.

To use Scripture like a Chinese fortune cookie can lead to massive confusion. What if you were searching for guidance and came to the verse, "The Lord will also bring you every kind of sickness and disaster"? Would this be a warning? Would the words "the harvest is plentiful" be promise of a 60-bushel-per-acre crop?

Too often when perplexed I resisted having to struggle through the pain of deciding a matter based only on prayer, circumstances, personal judgment, and my understanding of the principles of Scripture. I preferred a master-puppet relationship in which God pulled the strings and I jumped into action. I thought there would be fewer mistakes and less agony that way. I was wrong.

The Spirit of Christ uses the meaning of the whole Bible to guide and empower. To use Scripture like a gimmick or to take from it meaning that is not there in its verbal and cultural contexts leads to disappointment and approximates the mechanical view of the sacraments accepted in pre-Reformation period, a view the Reformers gave their lives to change.

After the death of my husband I gingerly began to theologize about faith and healing. I wrote that "healing faith is not brought into existence by earnestness or presumption. We can't force ourselves by sheer will power or intellectual strength of scriptural knowledge to achieve healing. It isn't something appropriated in desperation. Boldly asserting words of faith doesn't bring about healing any more than being sure one will win the sweepstakes. In seeking guidance for life events, like change of vocation, we may mistake our own zeal or earnestness for the faith needed for healing. To differentiate between faith and presumption is sometimes difficult."

This was a small "Here I stand" statement to myself, a little island of security I had located temporarily. I knew other footholds would also appear as I needed and looked for them.

No. 6: *Theologies have their fads, like Paris fashions, only they move a little more slowly.* Os Guinness describes some theologians as "theological fashion models" in both the liberal and conservative mode. When I was young, the pop theology of the time was the "I am nothing" brand, which encouraged believers to become "broken and empty" vessels for the Lord. We were urged to resist any kind of pride through appearance, performance, action, and word, for fear we might rob God of his glory. Pride was the Big Sin, the only sin.

I recall being so terrified about *not* being "nothing" for God, I had no confidence to do anything—play the piano, speak publicly, or teach a Sunday school class for fear I might not be assuming the proper humble posture. I remember stumbling through assignments. Failure always seemed a more appropriate result than success, for then no one could accuse me of pride.

One day I had an Aha! experience: God does not expect me to be an invertebrate, an empty husk, a shell, slouching along in the hidden cracks of life. What glory does that give him? If he loves me, I can love myself also. His invasion of my life does not wipe out my personality, but enhances it. His love means I can reach out to others with joy and freedom. And this happened after I was forty!

Another prominent theology then as now is the "faith" type, which glories in revealing that life has no underpinnings but faith—sort of like wearing hose without garters. This theology is highly subjective, highly enthusiastic, reveling in Jesus-hugs and lots of God-and-Jesus-words, intent on risking as much as possible to let the world know, "Look, folks, no hands!" Some have referred to it as "an instant contentless spirituality." Jesus is "neat," "exciting," and not much more. Adherents are pressured to have a neat experience of him.

I do not deny miracles of faith in response to prayer, but the "neat Jesus" theology, when taken to the extreme, releases a person from responsibility to think and act. Turning a problem over to God, small or large, does not mean sitting back and doing nothing, or waiting for him to move, but choosing, sometimes under tension, and then accepting that decision as God's will, knowing God has promised to be with the person committed to him. For me to be able to state this was overcoming a big hurdle in a many-hurdled race.

No. 7: *We are each accountable for what we believe.* Where do we get our authority for the interpretation of Scriptures? Who decides theology? Who establishes whether the Bible teaches birth control or abortion and similar controversial questions not directly spoken to in Scripture? The answer is, of course, that we all do. Bible scholars, theologians, and church leaders work at it, but so should everyone else who believes in the Bible. Error in interpretation is lessened if it is hammered out within the community of faith in prayer and humility rather than only by individuals.

The greatest danger of faith becoming hazardous to the faith life occurs when there is no discerning community to provide the checks and balances to our interpretation. I've heard people say, "My Bible says. . . ." However, there's no such thing as "My Bible" and "Your Bible." There's only our Bible, the Word of God given to all. To incarnate that Word in daily life is a task for all of us together—in small groups, in congregations, in denominations. Together we must discover what God is saying to our generation about his Word and the world.

While God assuredly speaks to the individual, interpretations of difficult passages should be tested by the community of faith under the guidance of the Holy Spirit. Others should have a chance to say to us and we to them, "What you're saying about the way God guides is truth for all of us." Each should be willing to say to the other person, "Though God doesn't seem to be speaking to me in that way, I'll go along with you until more of us come to another understanding."

No. 8: A belief system, even if well worked out with all the fat trimmed off, is worth little unless it is used to find an entrance into the world of work, school, leisure, family, and church life. *Theology must be related to experience.* To retreat with dogmas and doctrines into a private world is to ape the monks of the Middle Ages. To package our belief system beautifully with words and offer it as a sure-answer formula for life, but without the gift of self, is to become a faith-huckster. To be concerned only with honing the propositions of doctrine to a razorlike sharpness and then to spend our energies protecting them from assault and change, as the Pharisees did, produces many words, but no living Word.

Now I could summarize: Theology is an informal but somewhat systematic reflection on God, his love and purposes for humankind, and on the Scriptures in their entirety, not on isolated verses. A true theology is a growing, living statement of convictions arising out of interaction with the Bible, tradition, and the new realities of daily life. A true theology creates a new history, though it must be tested by history. A true theology is more than quoting the Bible. It is more than saying, "This is what the Bible meant." It also says, "This is what the Bible means today." It is a process of discerning and exposing the gods of our time to glorify God.

I could say with confidence that whatever theology I developed would never require me to lie to myself, to rationalize, or to believe nonsense, nor to come before a critical decision with trembling, fearing God might cast me on my own resources. God's gifts are confidence, self-esteem, and power with humility, not craven fear (2 Timothy 1:7).

To theologize is an invitation for God to enter my life with truth through his Spirit to direct my thinking and lead me to greater certainty about him. If I make a mistake, God's economy has room for forgiveness. As Mary chose to sit at Jesus' feet, to anoint him before the crucifixion, to come to the cross and the empty tomb, so I must choose. Theology always comes out of personal struggle, like a butterfly bursting its bonds to the freedom of beauty.

The goal of theology is not first of all to become a theologian, but a saint, and a Christlike saint at that. It is not an attempt to destroy the Bible but to understand it. It is not first an academic discipline, but a confession: "I've worked this concept through, now here I stand. What comes next?" Doing theology means I cannot expect the Bible to speak to every issue of twentieth-century times, for the Bible is not a science textbook. But I can expect God to give sufficient guidance for life, salvation, and calling.

We do theology to recapture faith in times of uncertainty. At times we see dimly; other times more clearly how our story fits together with purpose. This story is made more significant when we can see it in relation to God's story in Christ Jesus. Theology is a life-giving discipline, like prayer and meditation.

As I have shared my faith-struggles over the years, and sometimes there have been many of them, I have longed to say, "Friend, here use this recipe. Take two cups of this and one cup of that. I assure you it will work. God always responds to that approach." Each of us tends to analyze and systematize what we do not fully understand or control. I love my grocery lists and things-to-do lists, for they give me a sense of power and control. I'd like to be able to do the same for my inner life.

Yet having established all these footholds, I have to admit that the coming of God remains a mystery. Job once demanded an answer of God and received none other than that God was God and Job was human. I can talk about hazards to the faith-life, misinterpretations, misassumptions, culture change, and so forth. Yet when I think I understand all of this, God breaks through in a new way—in a moment of silence in the early dawn, a line of a hymn, the look of a happy child, the anguish of a lonely friend, an article about women and children in a third-world country, the look of forgiveness at a harsh word, the warm clasp of a friend.

Then, at another time, when I look for God in experience, he comes to me in the clear words of Scripture, the creed, or a hymn, or a prayer. I am never quite sure where I will meet him next—only that my anchor of faith is what I have thought through about him and with him and live out in my life.

With these footholds my agonizing to find God's will has decreased. Not that I'm not as concerned about doing it, but I no longer need look for the dramatic forms of guidance. Consequently, I can spend more energy on my particular ministry at this stage of life, aware I need to replenish my resources for doing theology continually and not depend on what I learned and experienced at an earlier stage in life. Change will always be with me.

CHAPTER 7

Loneliness, a human condition

Because we don't lose our humanity at the point of redemption and reconciliation, we still need from others the human experience of belonging and being understood.
—Craig W. Ellison

When I was young I never saw myself as having any problems. I never saw myself as living alone. I never saw myself as widowed, and in particular, I never saw myself as lonely. Life itself would be my ticket to happiness.

But it never worked out that way. The loneliest years of my life were the first year of marriage and the first year of widowhood. After our wedding in my home community, we headed west to where my husband had a teaching position. I had not counted on spending my days alone in a pint-sized apartment in a strange community waiting for Walter to come home. Community customs forbade me from looking for a job. I had not counted on becoming a member of a congregation where I could not understand the language of worship. I had not counted on becoming part of a culture where I was considered an oddity because I did not understand the ethnic and religious traditions. I cried more that first year than I had in my lifetime. I was lonely.

But then I cried even more fifteen years later when my husband died. I found myself in another world—the world of the widowed—with four young children, no money, no job, no education, and desperately alone and lonely. There is one kind of loneliness after the death of a spouse. But there are many other kinds that pursue us throughout life and which need to be dealt with as they appear.

A few years after Walter's death, I thought I had a handle on the problem of loneliness caused by the death of a spouse. Now, suddenly, fifteen years later, without children wandering in and out of the house, I felt besieged again. Part of my written agenda had been to be more open to people. The time to learn more about friendship had arrived.

I didn't need to be told what loneliness was—often the worst problem of people living alone. Most of us know what it feels like. It comes in waves, ups and downs, undulations of pain. It's Saturday night with a long evening before you. Television is boring. The phone doesn't ring. The mail had nothing interesting today. You've done the crossword puzzle and taken out all the trash in the house for the second time. Nothing around the house appeals. Your conscience says, "Well, then read the Bible and pray," but you aren't listening to your conscience at this moment.

So you go to the refrigerator, only to close the door after a brief look. Nothing there. The book you brought from the library looks dull. You can't think of a person to phone. Who would want to talk to you anyway?

Loneliness is a form of hurting that is triggered by a change involving the loss of something or someone you value. There's no Band-Aid big enough to cover the hurt. It's that feeling of psychic pain, dread, alienation, hopelessness, fear, and futility all rolled into one and as easily recognized and felt as a third-degree sunburn. Only this pain is felt in the pit of the stomach, in the tension in muscles, by the ache in the soul.

People respond to loneliness in various ways. Some react

with depression and isolation. One widow lived in a dressing gown for several years after the death of her husband. Others respond with mindless motion and activity—cleaning, working, drinking alcohol, and eating food. Some engage in intemperate sex, endless shopping, nonstop television watching, continual travel, which only increases the loneliness. Others cling to memories of good times, reliving them again and again. Still others may pretend that the lonely life is the whole life and subside into meek creatures, peering out at life but never being a part of it.

People are freer today to talk about loneliness, but some myths related to loneliness still exist: *Myth No. 1*: Normal people aren't lonely, so if you're lonely, you're abnormal. People who believe in this fallacy forget that there's an existential loneliness, which is a normal accompaniment to every stage of life because it is an aspect of being human. Everyone experiences some loneliness at some time because human beings are self-conscious people. A rock isn't lonely because it has no self-awareness. Most people handle such loneliness well; others refuse to admit it and stumble along.

Another kind of loneliness thrusts itself upon us at the moment of a specific loss of something or someone. Loneliness occurs when life becomes thin, when there are too few close relationships, resulting in a lack of intimacy and feeling of rejection. Daniel Perlman writes, "Loneliness exists to the extent that a person's network of social relationships is smaller or less satisfying than the person desires." Children become terrified when parents leave for an evening, wondering if they are being deserted. Adolescents agonize over not being wanted by their peers, or being rejected by a girl- or boyfriend. Dr. James J. Lynch in *A Broken Heart: The Medical Consequences of Loneliness*, writes that most people don't realize that "loneliness can be translated into physical problems." Lonely people have higher death rates from heart attacks, strokes, and high blood pressure.

During my parents' first years as immigrants in Canada, Mother was desperately lonely, she told me. She could not speak English and had no opportunity to learn it because we five children occupied her entire time. She had no way of making friends at first without language as a facilitator.

I can speak the language of those around me, yet I feel the pains of loneliness when I lose a book or a favorite scarf. I feel lonelier when I lose a friend, or when someone deserts me and leaves me stranded with the feeling that I am the last person to be chosen on the team. This Saturday evening no one chose me. For this vacation I have no one. For this family festival, I am alone. This week no one chose me. This year. This life. The man lying by the pool of Bethsaida was asked by Jesus why he didn't go into the waters when the angel stirred them. He responded, "I have no one," some of the loneliest words in Scripture.

I felt lonely recently when I flew into Wichita late one night from a speaking engagement. The night was dark, the rain was coming down in sheets, I had forgotten where I had parked the car, I was wearing new shoes, and I had no umbrella. As I slogged through the rain and standing puddles, I bathed myself in self-pity and loneliness. Why me?

I find it helpful to think of each stab of loneliness as a reminder that God has made us with a need for intimacy and people contact. Infants and children thrive in the context of human warmth and physical affection. Everyone needs some strokes. Even adults living alone need close contacts with people. I like to be hugged.

Myth No. 2: People who are having sexual relationships aren't lonely. I have sometimes succumbed to that view in my heart, yet knew in my head it wasn't true. When single persons convince themselves that all their friends enjoy deep satisfying sexual relations, while their options for marriage are becoming slimmer as the years go, the loneliness is heightened. The truth is that the marital relationship is not the only relationship in which intimacy is possible, and sexual intimacy is not the only type of intimacy. Furthermore, just spending a lot of time with someone, or even having sexual relations with that person, doesn't guarantee the end of loneliness and the existence of a strong friendship.

Widows, divorcées, and singles think they are the loneliest because they live alone, yet some married couples living together remain far apart in their emotions. Statistics show that widowers are the most lonely of all. Their pattern of life is the most disturbed by the death of their wife, and frequently they have the fewest resources for coping.

Myth No. 3: Strong Christians aren't lonely, so if I'm lonely, I'm not a strong Christian. The truth is that some of the greatest biblical leaders were lonely to the point of wanting to end their lives. Moses cried out to God, "I am not able to bear all this people alone ... kill me ... let me not see my wretchedness." The prophet Elijah prayed, "O Lord, take away my life; for I am not better than my fathers," and "I, even I only, am left."

One young woman told me, "Single women friends never allow me to say how I really feel. They always say right away that God will supply all my needs if I let him. I have not found the Lord sufficient for my needs." Another questioned what difference faith in Christ makes to a person in grief as compared to a person who has no faith. These questioners are probably closer to finding help than the one who says, "My Lord supplies all my needs," and then buries her head all day in the bedclothes.

It didn't take long for me to understand some of the reasons for my own loneliness. Part of it was my own problem. I am an independent person who enjoys my privacy and individuality. I like becoming involved in my own creative projects, but when I come up to breathe, I sometimes find I have lost touch with friends and family.

But part of the reason for loneliness is also that we live in a society that orients itself toward those considered normal and average—healthy, not disabled; married, not widowed, divorced, or single; young, not elderly; well-to-do, not poor—although some changes have taken place. Society finds it difficult to make room for people who do not fit the norms even though single parents and the elderly are two of the largest groups in many congregations.

I enjoy my regular adult Bible class, but even its members in their willingness to make room for a few of us who are not married, occasionally fall back into old patterns. At one of our regular breakfasts, I sat alone at a small table for four, for the first one had already been filled with diners. The next persons to come sat at an empty table, filled it, and then began another one, leaving me and another single woman sitting by ourselves, growing ever more uncomfortable. I sat there lonely, angry—until I was able to tell my friends I felt stranded.

I have learned I am lonely also because I hesitate to tell others I need them. I fear pity. Mother has told me that when she and Dad came from Russia, as poor immigrants, they lived in a small two-room shack with my two older sisters, both toddlers. I hesitate to call it a house. A picture shows it unpainted, weathered, hugging the ground. Dad's two young brothers lived with them and slept in the kitchen. Before Mother could make breakfast, they had to move into the other room. The second winter Dad enlarged the shack by filling in the ell. Every Sunday, from Christmas to Easter, other immigrants came to this small house to eat and talk. "We needed each other," Mother told me. "We were very happy." Her face shone as she remembered her experience in the two-room shack. They needed one another. And so they came together. Who admits such need today?

I find it difficult to say, "I need you," for fear of being considered an inadequate Christian or a whiner. I know some people are ready to help, but others will do so only reluctantly when informed about a need, which shuts a lot of needy people up. Who wants help given under constraint? I remonstrated with a friend whose husband was absent for a considerable time because she failed to let some of us living nearby know she was alone for weeks at a time. She preferred loneliness to sympathy. Another friend, whose husband is a church executive, shared that she knew she was expected to act courageously, joyfully, when he was absent. But the truth was she hated his absences and yet couldn't open up about her feelings for fear of being judged. But would I have acted any differently? My daughter asks me whom I talked to when I felt so lonely after James left. I belong to a generation which does not admit need readily. We have been too well conditioned by a church community which has not learned to deal with emotional hurt.

But there's another reason for loneliness. Our society stresses competition rather than doing things together for the enjoyment of others. "How can I top the other person?" "How can I make sure my contribution—casserole, Bible lesson—is the best so it gets good comments and is accepted?" The loneliness of being chosen last is painful whether it is a child on a ball team or the maker of a salad at a church supper. At one potluck, I brought a new recipe of cranberry jelled salad—which was my mistake. When it was time to leave for the event, it still hadn't fully jelled, although it had been in the refrigerator long enough. I took it anyway, but after standing in the warm room for an hour, it turned to a thick syrup with blobs of red something-or-other in it. No one took any. I felt lonely for it as it stood in all its brilliant red liquidity alone, untouched. I wanted to take it into my arms, and pat it a little. I also felt rejected.

We need to also consider that in a technological and informational age, emphasis is on efficiency, productivity, and making money rather than on human relationships. Thirty or forty years ago, when life was slower paced and the winter doldrums had set in, the local men in our community spent hours in my father's store, talking and laughing. Women spent many afternoons at teas and sewing bees, learning to know one another. Intimacy begins with learning to know someone. And learning to know someone takes quality time and effort. Today people with two jobs, or marriage partners both working at full-time jobs, have a difficult time developing and maintaining friendship in a marriage and outside it.

Church services don't encourage intimacy—people are lined up in rows, looking at the back of one another's collars and haircuts, making worship seem more like forced fellowship with near strangers than community. One school of thought says you must not whisper in church and tell a friend you missed her or him. This is the place to make God-contacts, not people-contacts, so you count the bricks above the pulpit between prayers.

Our social entertaining style is likewise a hindrance to intimacy. Who visits without a formal invitation? Whom do you dare drop in to see, except close friends and the elderly in retirement homes?

In coping with loneliness, I have been a slow learner. I thought I should be able to lick this new bout of the disease easily, but one winter, compounded by other problems, it hung on month after month like a low-grade infection until I sensed the loneliness had permeated my whole being. I wanted other people to help me out of it. I wasn't prepared to make much effort. The story of three men who were challenged to discover the cave of wisdom and life illustrates what I mean. The men made long preparations for the journey, and traveled many miles. Finally they found the cave. At the door, the guard asked them, "How far into the cave do you want to go." "Only so far that we can say we've been there," they replied. Loneliness can't be overcome if we come to life wanting to go only a short distance or carrying only a small dipper.

Paula Ripple in *Walking with Loneliness* writes that people can run away from loneliness or enter into it, look upon it as an evil or as a challenge, ignore or explore it, see it as a personal weakness or limitation or as a possible source of greater inner strength, treat it as a problem or cherish it as a mystery, fear it as God's way of punishing, or accept it as God's way of loving us to life. This is good advice.

The best way to begin the battle against loneliness is the same way one begins the fight against alcoholism: Recognize you are lonely. "I am lonely," I told myself one evening. "I am lonely." I had said it. All right, now what could I do about it? This pain belonged to me. Could I challenge its mystery to open to me? I couldn't expect friends, neighbors, congregation, or colleagues to pull me out of my hole. If other people didn't recognize my need, that wasn't their problem. If I saw myself only with self-pity or bitterness, I was the one who had to figure out what to do. I was free to be discouraged, to be despondent, to feel imprisoned, to feel lonely. I was also free to accept, to love, and to move on. I told myself that if the caring community isn't present, the lonely have to start building it.

I asked the question all lonely people ask: Why must I live my life alone? I don't know. But God has permitted it. That doesn't mean I am unlovely. As a child of God I am entitled to respect myself and to expect respect of others. I yield to God and pray his grace may touch me. I may be lonely today, but I can choose to make loneliness my manageable companion, to control it, rather than to let it control me. I must refuse to remain "carefully folded together, like a precious silk, never used." I must avoid for a time those who boast that "God took away all my loneliness." I rejoice with them, but I am not yet there.

Can any good come out of loneliness? Not as long as it controls one's life. We cannot look on personal adversity as God's curse, but as a gift and challenge. This is the essence of the gospel. When we face adversity with such faith, it becomes contagious and spreads to others. When all the world is crying and protesting that life isn't fair, as Christians we need to respond with the psalmist's words: "Therefore will not we fear though the earth be removed, and though the mountains be carried into the midst of the sea."

What had the speaker in India said? "Joy is peace dancing!" That word had finally caught up with me. I claimed to have peace of God. Then let it dance! I accepted that the goal of loneliness is not just to get rid of the pain, but to develop a potential for intimacy.

The next day I shared my feelings at the college cafeteria with a few colleagues. I was shocked that so many "normal" people were willing to admit to loneliness. I hadn't figured on that. The next day I came back with a plan. Why not become one another's support group by meeting regularly for a time? They agreed. The result was a small group which has been meeting fairly regularly for several years to talk, to laugh, and to share burdens and joys, sometimes in the evening, and at least once a year over a marathon breakfast that may last three hours or more. As some members leave the community, others join us. I enjoy being part of this close social group, and sometimes a group of strangers works better as a support group than close relatives.

I am convinced about one matter: The good life in a land of plenty has always been synonymous with abundance—lots of youthful vigor, lots of money, lots of clothes, lots of sex, lots of vacation spots, lots of long smooth stretches of superhighways, lots of stereo music, lots of eating places, lots of drinking—the list is endless. The good life, however, is not dependent on any or all of the above. It doesn't require excessive mobility or a trunkful of play equipment. The good life depends on the most renewable of resources—friends. As C. W. Brister says in *Take Care*, life without true friends is hardly life at all; some people don't value them because they have never experienced friendship. Friendship is highly valued in Scripture, probably more highly than today's society fosters it. David and Jonathan stuck together closer than brothers, but their relationship would probably be highly suspect today, and Ruth and her mother-in-law Naomi would become the butt of some stand-up comic's idea of a joke. Jesus was close friends with John, Mary, Martha, and Lazarus. Paul had many friends that he kept in touch with through letters.

Americans prefer to keep in touch with their cars rather than their friends. Some have owned more cars than they have had friends. They can list with faithful accuracy each model they acquired through the years, how much they paid for it, its main faults and good traits, and why they traded it in—but they couldn't list as many close friends. They grow up with several cars at a time and give them names as if they were family pets. They jump in and out of them daily. They argue with their starting and stopping systems. They curse them, praise them, polish and repair them, and sacrifice to make payments on them and to keep them running. They aren't ready to do as much for friends.

The desperate pace of modern life has made deep and long-lasting friendships almost a rarity. People haven't got time to be friendly, for friendship costs. Like a car, friends need regular checkups by letter, phone, or personal contact, and a steady investment of time and interest. If they don't have the oil checked regularly, they give out.

Yet our lack of emphasis on close friends doesn't mean our society doesn't have friendly people. We have lots of people who smile and shake hands and welcome newcomers to church and community within minutes of arrival. They move immediately to a first-name basis. But they hesitate to allow others to know the real person behind the quick smile and generous phrases. Friendship, the David-and-Jonathan type, has no value for them unless it brings customers to a business or newcomers to the congregation.

A friend affirms and supports in times of disappointment and failure as well as achievement. A friend encourages risk. A friend is balm for the pain of loneliness, someone to listen to one's need to talk, someone to pray with.

Friends restore the lost art of conversation, one of life's most interesting activities. Friendship is the cement that makes marriages stick. Husbands and wives who are friends as well as lovers have greater insurance against breakup. A sad sight is a husband and wife who have nothing to say to one another. I see them occasionally in restaurants. They enter solemnly, chew their food in drab silence, and as distantly from each other, walk out again side by side. Friendship has its treasured silences, but not this kind.

If lack of friends is a big factor in loneliness, there are others. Maintaining a victim mentality is one. I asked myself if I would want to be my own best friend if I had to overcome the walls I had built around myself? Hardly. I knew of people I hesitated to come close to. Some talk about their problems within twenty seconds of greeting me. Some can never be persuaded to decide anything or offer an opinion on any matter from what to eat for lunch or when to go home.

Loneliness has no one solution, but must be worked with constantly through the development of spiritual resources in Bible study and prayer, through the development of gifts and talents, by maintaining a home whether one is single or married, and by accepting the risks of moving ahead alone. A period of being alone is a divine gift to think, to learn to know oneself, and above all to learn to know God. One's situation and the purposes of one's life are of one piece and cannot be separated. Solitude should be welcomed.

When I made my initial list, I felt convicted that I had taken too little time to be open to people, giving lack of time as the excuse. But now I had made a new resolution. The tests of new resolves, however, come quickly. Soon thereafter I rushed past a small figure sitting alone after the church service. I stopped to say hello. Small, frail, silent, she sat alone at the end of a row of chairs in the area where untidiness soon sets in after a church service.

"How are you?"

Her voice answered automatically, "Fine," but her eyes,

dimmed with age, checked me over. When recognition arrived, the voice said, "Fine" again, this time with a smile outlining the soft voice. She was waiting for someone to pick her up and deposit her back home. "My, it's good to have someone even ask me how I am," she added. It didn't happen often anymore.

I sat down. There were many empty chairs around her. We talked briefly about her family, about mine. A few other things like that. Then they came to take her home. She thanked me for the conversation. She considered five minutes of small talk a gift. I had almost bypassed her in my hurry to get to what I considered more important.

Some people hand out time and conversation freely, like free samples at the supermarket, assuming every contact, even a few backslapping moments, constitute dialogue. Others are so "parsimonious," writes Oswald Chambers, they won't spend a thing in conversation unless it is on a line that helps them. So, with eyes straight ahead we rush ahead, hoping the person whose every question digs deep into our personal lives like a dentist's drill will accept the hint. We steer away from seats beside people who might engage us in small talk. We raise the newspaper high when someone sits beside us. At home we turn on the television or turn up the radio to silence unwelcome contacts. Our message is clear: You may be a spouse, child, acquaintance, co-worker, or stranger, but don't bother me.

In *The Meaning of Success* Michel Quoist has strong words for people who never have time to make contact with others, even briefly, but keep apologizing for being so busy. Hebrews 13 encourages hospitality as a ministry for Christians. In those days, Christians, particularly those fleeing persecution, needed a place to stay. Traveling preachers looked for the home of a believer to spend the night. But hospitality meant not only the gift of lodging and food but also of one's person. Quoist speaks of this kind of hospitality as being present to the people we meet in our daily round of activities and welcoming them into our lives. He writes that some people are so full of self, like the overfull bus that doesn't stop for the passenger waiting on the curb, "they have neither time nor space for those waiting to get on." He cautions that if people say, "I didn't dare disturb you the other day, you looked so busy," you probably are too busy.

I think many of Jesus' encounters probably started with small talk, for he was the friend of publicans and sinners. I doubt he made appointments to see them. First meetings may have been casual—questions about Mary's garden and the state of taxes for Matthew, the tax collector. These could have led to profound statements about eternal life.

So I rush to my next appointment. Someone approaches. Shall I lower my eyes and move on? Then I'll avoid the wearisome question, "How do you like your new home?" or "What will you be doing this summer?" I remember Quoist's words, "It is the Lord—these are invitations to make contact." I smile. I stop. "How are you?"

CHAPTER 8

When am I old?

*Old age is neither inherently miserable nor
inherently sublime—like every stage of life it
has problems, joys, fears, and potentials.*
                                    —Robert N. Butler

I sit here contemplating that strange powdery substance we
stir into our coffee to whiten it—cream substitute. Still stranger
is the fact that coffee drinkers accept it and other substitutes
gladly, even asking for them, strewing little envelopes and
plastic containers around them like empty hulls. Few people
expect real cream anymore.

At what stage of life will I be satisfied with substitutes? What
whiteners do I reach for?

Is there a stage in life when many of us acquiesce and accept
second-best readily?

Adolescence? Admittedly the transition from childhood
through adolescence into adulthood has a few bumps and
holes. But youth live with the dream. It haunts them.

Middle age? One businessman thought his life was moving
along smoothly. No middle-age crisis for him. Then, in the next
sentence he mentioned that after the last child left home he felt
so unsettled by the strange emptiness of the house, that he
woke at two in the morning and drove around the block for a

while to calm down. But after the calming down, did he tend to let go of life? Unlikely. In middle age, the dream continues to pursue.

Old age? When one must accept that one's life must be the way it is, is this the time to shed dreams and live with substitutes? When children leave home, when parents die, fear of old age enters. One is being forced to take a step forward toward old age. Or is it backward? Like other people looking ahead to being among the elderly, I struggle to resist the temptation to let go of my dreams. I am not retired yet, but the next decade will introduce more forcibly the idea that life in the main track is finished. Even now our society gives the retiree no real role in life, not many reasons to dream.

When is a person old?

"The digestive system may not be what it used to be. The organs less efficient. The muscles not as hardworking. His whole metabolism may be slowing down. His joints may even be a little stiff. His hearing a little hard. So, of course, his nutritional needs have changed." A description of an older person?

Not this time. It's an advertisement to persuade loving pet owners to switch to special food for the older dog, the dog beginning to feel his years. When is a dog old? The advertisement seems to have the answer.

When is a person old? When hamburgers with onions are hard to digest? When the boss says it's time to take your tools home permanently? When you ponder whether to use hair color or buy a hairpiece? Or when the dream is gone and you accept substitutes for the full life—too old to become much involved, too old to have friends, too old to expect the church to involve you and your gifts?

I asked my young grandson one day what he wanted to be when he grew up. He gave me his casual look out of the corner of his eye as he pushed the dump truck across the floor. "Oh, I suppose a fireman." A superduper fireman was the main character in the book we were just reading. Next week he would probably choose to be a cowboy.

The choice of vocation for the young is mind-boggling. They can fly a balloon or fly to the moon, paint spots on toys or paint a wall mural, design lace or design a skyscraper. No limit.

I asked a sixty-year-old friend with silvery hair and friendly eye wrinkles, "What do you want to be when you're old?"

His mouth fell open. "When I'm old?" he asked with a chuckle.

Must we expect life to have more and more of the cream skimmed off it as we age? Can one fantasize about old age like a child does about adulthood? Can one build castles in the air about life after seventy and expect to live in them? Of course not, says my friend. Old age is simply old age. Nothing more. There are no categories to choose from once you're old. Old is old. If God had intended the end years to be other than dismal, dull, and drab, he would have arranged for more variety in hair color for this time of life.

Should I believe him? Not entirely. Admittedly, at times our society overemphasizes the process of personal actualization until death knocks. Each of us is pressured by the media to refuse to accept pain, sickness, discomfort, and even the possibility of death. Yet I refuse to yield to the sinister message my friends on the way to sixty send my way that this next period of life, the sixties and beyond, is a dead end and has no redeeming features, and that its appearance, its non-activities, and its non-involvement shape the size of the tunnel. If one is unfortunate enough to get caught in it, it's best to go gently into the dark night and carry a bottle of aspirin in one hand and hair dye in the other.

Yet a dozen times a day I'm reminded that old is old. I get the message every time I pass the hall mirror. I glance at the baggy woman reflected in it, suck in my stomach, and throw back my shoulders. I can lick it. Then, as I glance back, the sun streaming through the window reassures me the color of my hair is now the same as my mother's.

Gray hair, salt-and-pepper variety. Gray hair, any variety, looks well on friends but resembles the dispirited froth of a weary ocean wave on me. I am devastated. My spirit shrinks. Old age has finally caught up with me. I'm over the hill. People will soon refer to me as the little old lady-writer in pink Nikes who is over the hill.

Then, during the day, a friend I haven't seen for several years, says, "Katie, you haven't aged a bit in ten years." I lap up the compliment like the soil during the rain after a long Kansas drought. I'm beating old age after all. I knew it all the time. I'm restored to good spirits. I sing with the old sourpuss writer of Ecclesiastes in one of his merrier moments, "There is a time to weep, and a time to laugh; a time to mourn, and a time to dance." I'm dancing. I see myself as coltishly young, kicking my heels in the meadow.

The day progresses. Another friend says, "Katie, you look younger than your pictures." I preen my soul feathers. The jowls under my cheeks disappear. The wrinkles smooth out. God is with me. The world is good. These comments from friends are true words—not flattery.

I look in the mirror again to gloat, but the person with graying hair glares back indignantly: "What's wrong with looking older today than ten years ago if you've lived ten years longer? What's wrong with looking older than your pictures? What's wrong with looking old and letting the sound aging wood shine through?"

I flinch. True words. Very true words. Is it treason to look my age? Because an image of uselessness has overshadowed the image of older people as contributing individuals, some of the elderly accept this negative stereotype as their dismal lot in life. Some believe that being old is bad, a personal and social disaster; that it is a disease nobody will admit to having; that it means giving up responsibility, beginning with enforced retirement, a shock some people never get over because they equate retirement from work with retirement from life; that the mind stops functioning during old age and regresses to bingo and soap opera with time for naps.

If I don't accept this image, why then did I waste time in the discount store yesterday looking for skin cream and hair coloring? Why do I peer at my face each morning for new wrinkles? Why should I disguise myself like a teenager in jeans and T-shirt? Looking old has its merits in more places than the shoe store when I ask for comfortable shoes. At a wedding the bride looks radiantly pretty, her mother looks charming, but her grandmother has a patina a photographer would pay money to capture on film.

Now I know I've beaten the "old is ugly" bit of nonsense and can smile beneath my halo of growing gray without feeling guilty about being a traitor to my sex. I intend to take advantage of my age. I intend to accept activist Maggie Kuhn's advice to stop speaking of myself in euphemistic terms, such as senior citizen and golden-ager. "We are the elders, the experienced ones; we are maturing, growing adults responsible for the survival of our society," she states.

But the television commercials remind me again our society thinks women depreciate more with the years than men. Men develop a dignified mien, making them more distinguished and attractive; women just get scratched, dented, and baggy.

I am strengthened by Avis D. Carlson's words in *The Fullness of Time*: "I am a child of God and am therefore entitled to respect from myself and from others," even though the congregation doesn't expect much of me at this point except to be grateful for small mercies, keep reading Psalm 23, listen to admonitions to avoid sending money to TV preachers, and keep bringing casseroles to church suppers. If I saw pastors vying for the job of ministering to congregations which have over half their membership mature, experienced, disciplined elderly, I'd know there was gold ahead instead of only silver hair.

The next day the paper upsets me even more by screaming

at me: "A New Answer to the Problem of Aging." The article
sets forth a sad picture of the elderly struggling with poverty,
loneliness, poor health, and meaninglessness in dark airless cu-
bicles in slums, high-rise apartments, and convalescent homes.

I'm back to square one. I sadly accept the article as true, for
it includes statistics and testimonials. I can see myself twenty
years from now becoming one of these statistics. I look at the
church. It doesn't recognize the elderly as the experienced
ones, the maturing growing adults, responsible for the future
growth of the church and society. It wastes them. It trivializes
them by encouraging them to pass time, to not develop images
of inner strength. I hear leaders speak of churches with many
elderly as "dying churches" and their services as being *for*
them, not *with* them.

My day is gray again. Aging is after all a problem, not a
joy—until I hear the excitement in the voice of an eighty-year-
old friend working on a new research project and catch the
gleam in an older woman's eyes as she makes a new discovery
about life.

I straighten up. I put the news story into perspective. The
article is true, but only for a small segment of the elderly. Only
about 5 percent of the elderly are invalided in homes and
unable to function. The larger percentage of people over sixty-
five are living in their own homes, blowing out enough birthday candles each year to set the house on fire. Articles about
the plight of some of the elderly make invisible all the others
who are so busy at meaningful living they haven't time to read
about themselves as a problem.

So, aging isn't a problem, any more than middle age is a
problem, or adolescence is a problem. It is simply a stage in life.
When you are old, you feel no different than when you were
young, except that you have experienced more and therefore
have more to remember, your appearance has changed, and
you probably have more physical problems. The only thing the
elderly have in common is that they've been around longer, so

they do not deserve to be treated like a box of factory-cut crackers.

The elderly have the right to mourn when they experience loss but also they have the right to ask, "Why can't I die?" Those who minister to the elderly in the interests of keeping up the image of a strong Christian faith want to cheer them up, one gerontologist said. Sunday is cheer-up day in nursing homes, even though reassurance may be the worst thing one can do, because it says to the hurting person, "I don't want you to grieve because it hurts me too much to see you in pain. Grieve when I am gone."

True Christian faith allows others to lament, for Christ said, "Blessed are those who mourn," not "Blessed are those who refrain from mourning." Faith allows people to grieve, because the Lord understands sadness and aloneness, because it was part of his life. A stiff upper lip in time of sorrow may be good stoicism, but not good Christianity.

Solaced by such ideas, I charge ahead like a car with a clean carburetor. Then as I adjust my bifocals, I spot a gem of a paragraph, tucked away in a corner of a favorite periodical, intended to inspire the middle-aged and elderly. It's the kind of sentimental goo I would have clipped and mounted on a refrigerator door twenty years go.

I read it now with brand-new insights: "Youth is not a time of life—it is a state of mind. It is not a matter of ripe cheeks, red lips, and supple knees. . . . Nobody grows old by merely living a number of years; people grow old only by deserting their ideals. . . . You are as old as your doubts, as young as your self-confidence; as old as your fears, as young as your hope."

Beautiful words. Challenging words. For a moment I wish I'd written them. Until I reread them. These choice words are actually saying that it's okay to have a tired, worn-out body as long as the attitudes in it are young. That the attitudes of the young are to be admired. That the attitudes of the elderly should be put out with the garbage. That the young have ideals; that the old have doubts. That the young have confidence; that the old have fears.

Nonsense! Youth, as I know them, aren't all self-confident eager beavers. Any incoming class of college freshmen includes a bumper crop of uncertainty, loneliness, and hidden fears. Youth are characterized more by insecurity, inhibitions, and foolhardiness than by self-esteem, self-confidence, and stability. Who would want to be perennially plagued by the doubts of the adolescent, always wondering, "Do people like me?" Not me. My age is a more comfortable fit.

To cling to the values and attitudes of youth when you're old is as ridiculous as my turning up in my classroom in a pinafore. Hope, fear, doubt, and self-confidence have never been age-coded. I rip the clipping to shreds. Now I'm sitting solidly on top of my problem. I feel the courage of an Esther about to walk into the king's chambers surging in me as I talk back to it.

I write my own space filler for magazines: "Old age is a time of life and a state of mind. Old age has its splendors—if you look for them. There's the freedom from competition to keep up with the neighbors in acquiring stuff for the house or in keeping the windows gleaming. Old age means feeling comfortable using stainless steel while the silverware tarnishes in the felt-lined box. It means wearing comfortable shoes while watching the younger set stagger around on high heels. It means being able to admit freely you don't like music that goes boom-boom-ka-boom so loudly the windows rattle. Old age may be a matter of wrinkled skin, creaking knees, and failing eyesight. It is also a matter of the temper of the will, of the quality of the imagination, and of a strong measure of faith, hope, and excitement about life lived with God and at peace with humankind."

I smile at the woman in the mirror. She smiles back. We like each other. At least for a while. I hope the period of liking gets longer each time I face the issue.

Meaning in life in old age is not achieved by what a person

does or produces but in what a person is. Yet I and my peers are hesitant to discuss our aging as openly as football scores and good restaurants, other than to rage, "It's tough getting older."

We have one generation now in deep retirement (those who live in retirement homes and get some help in some aspect of living). They are sometimes referred to as the omega generation, the last in a series, the end ones. We have those who enjoy a fair measure of good health and live in their homes. Neither group, however, says much about what it's like to grow old in the church today. Will my generation, moving quickly into the post-work years, also clam up about our feelings because we view old age as something akin to the bubonic plague that wiped out half the European population during the Middle Ages? We know that old age, like the plague, takes everyone.

Yet old age is happening all around me. The brother and sisters with whom I played in the backyard only a little bit ago are thinking of retiring. Children are beginning to sound like reasonable human beings, and grandchildren who were infants a few months ago stand nearly as tall as my shoulder. Yet I wish the topic of aging weren't either avoided or treated as a joke in this period before I get there.

How do I continue liking the person I am when I am old? What is the relationship of discipleship to aging? I'll admit I resent those frustrating moments when I walk into the bedroom to get something only to stand there, wondering what brought me there. So I go back and start again. My psyche aches a little then and also when I can't fit a name to the friend I've known for years. Getting out of my son's low-slung car makes me feel like a newborn camel struggling to its feet. What happened to the agility I had ten years ago? How can I admire that awkward person struggling in and out of vehicles?

If I try to pin down elusive feelings about aging, I focus on the fact I don't know exactly when I will be old and what I will be expected to be like. A little girl knows she is a child. A young adult knows he is a young adult. But the person at the other end of life is never quite sure. Am I old or am I not? People told me life began at forty, became delightful at fifty. But now at sixty? What does it mean? When am I old?

"The only answer to the age of anguish is a sense of significant being," writes Rabbi Abraham J. Heschel. "The sense of significant being is a thing of the spirit. Stunts, buffers, games, hobbies, slogans are all evasions. What is necessary is an approach, a getting close to the sources of the spirit. Not the suppression of the sense of futility, but its solution; not reading material to while away one's time but learning to exalt one's faculties; not entertainment, but celebration are approaches."

To grow old with integrity is to know how to live. As I grow older, I need to be reminded that God is where I am now—not ahead and not behind—but in the possibly smaller living space, the smaller circle of friends, the narrower range of activities that will come with decreasing physical strength. As I sit in a church service I watch the intent faces of the many elderly. I remind myself that spiritual maturity is seldom reached at a young age, even though spiritually precocious youngsters are frequently shoved into positions of influence and authority far beyond them. The great saints of the faith only seemed to perfect themselves after they were fifty and older. As someone has said, a young minister may be brilliant, but an older man is more often wise. The young show great zeal and spirit, often rushing tempestuously forward in support of great causes. We need such enthusiasm, but we also need the one who sees the world steady and whole and who can match zeal with wisdom and inner stability.

Each age has its own temptations, and those of the elderly are difficult for a younger mobile person to understand. How can one put oneself into the worn shoes of an eighty-year-old who feels forsaken because of fewer visits and letters and who has limited physical and economic strength with which to cope? The denial of a car license because of poor eyesight becomes a major catastrophe; the decision to move into a retirement center, the equivalent of signing a surrender treaty. Always there is the feeling of being managed, of being shunted to the siding like an uncoupled railway car unless these moves are chosen.

Persons in each stage of life get their attitudes toward the next stage in the aging process from those who model that stage. As youngsters we watched and listened to adults, modeling our behavior after theirs. We pieced together enough information to get us going. How to live as an omega gets picked up in the same way. It comes to the next-in-line from coffee chatter, advertising that insists one must look young to feel alive, and from contact with the elderly in their own homes or in strolls down corridors of homes for the elderly and visits to them.

I take my models from two older friends. Unfortunately, on two occasions I returned home from a trip to the information one of them had died. I felt I had lost a part of me. I never called the first woman Hannah, the way all her friends referred to her, but Mrs. Willems. I remember clearly the first time I met her walking up the aisle after a service, confidently, with a warm smile, reaching out to me. She wanted to meet me, she said. After that, little by little, we, as a family, moved into the lives of her and her husband in their pleasant frame house across the track from us.

The evening before the funeral, I visited the mortuary. I'm not quite sure why I went. I am not much given to viewing "remains." Perhaps I wanted to assure myself someone hadn't made up a story about her death. But there she lay in a favorite navy blue dress with white polka-dot collar. Her hands were calmly folded, unlike the way I had learned to know her. They were usually busy making meals for others, writing letters, or helping in some way.

As I stood at her coffin I wondered who would take her place in praying for our family, for she believed in prayer. Who would take her place in making meals for lonely people? We often sat at her table, sipping tea, eating ice cream, just talking. Who would take her place in leadership in women's work in the church and community? Who would take her place in encouraging me? She knew I experienced life differently than she had during the same period and that my contribution to the church might take a different path from hers. She forged ahead in her area; she allowed me to do the same.

After she was gone I felt bereft for a long time. Then somehow I began short after-supper visits with Esther Ebel, who picked up in loving, encouraging, and praying where Mrs. Willems had left off. She made it a rule never to speak unkindly of another person. Or to be upset by something she couldn't change. She maintained an active visitation ministry to residents of the home where she lived. She wrote letters and sewed beautiful items for gifts, for mission groups, and to meet individual needs. And she shared with me the story of her life.

One day I gave her a box of mixed tailor's samples to do with as she pleased. Later that summer one afternoon her car rolled into my driveway, an unusual event, and she stepped out carrying a large box which she presented to me. She had pieced the samples into a quilt for me instead of laprobes for the elderly.

Inside was a note: "I have pieced covers of wool, cotton, and synthetic fabrics and always had uniform pieces. Here was a new challenge: a mixture of textiles and four sizes of patches. Surely, these pieces can be arranged in some design to make harmony in a cover without bulges and wrinkles. One day I discovered myself in the patchwork of the varied textiles. I look at the quilt cover and see myself as a patch that fits into the fabric of this retirement home. Yes, we are of different shapes and sizes, yet there is harmony through acceptance and willingness to be trimmed to fit into the spot we are to fit."

So I move ahead with the years. My models challenge me to learn to live fully. In so doing, I will learn to bless as I grow older.

CHAPTER 9

The absence of a present God

There is an enormous difference between an absence after a visit and an absence which is the result of not coming at all. Without a coming there can be no leaving, and without a presence absence is only emptiness and not the way to a greater intimacy with God through the Spirit.

—Henry Nouwen

Life for depression people was waiting. Waiting for a return of better times. Of greater opportunity. Of relief from suffering. For God to show his face.

We who lived then have its stamp on us as surely as a branded steer, assert survivors of that era. We brought with us into the next decades attitudes toward life that are reflected particularly in our buying. Because we lived in a "next-year" world, year after year, waiting for conditions to improve, we depression people dislike the installment plan. For us, it's pay for all or wait. Depression survivors are cautious buyers.

I was a child during the thirties, but I recall clearly how the hoboes, waiting for the dream to catch up with them, attached themselves to the roofs of rumbling freight cars like barnacles to a ship. Some of them dropped off temporarily in our community to comb it for a handout. Occasionally one sat at our table, invited in by my mother, and ate swiftly, while silently surveying the amount of food on the table.

Men with professional degrees dug ditches. Artists followed much-mended machinery around fruitless farms. Christians who wanted to serve the Lord as missionaries stayed home. All waited for times to change.

In school we studied Milton's "On His Blindess," which asks the question, "Doth God exact day-labour, light denied?" Even as children we understood the answer: "God doth not need either man's work, or his own gifts: who best bear his mild yoke, they serve him best. . . . They also serve who only stand and wait."

Yes, life for depression people was waiting.

It continues to be that for many people, even in a more affluent economy. They wait for God to show his face.

One morning in the seventies I began a journal entry with "This is the summer of my deep content." For once circumstances seemed favorable to easier living: no daily 50-mile trip to the university for summer school, no eight-to-five job for a few months, no major changes for any family member. I felt at peace.

In the morning each dew-bejeweled rose on the trellis waved an individual greeting to me, and I waved back. I knew the sun had risen specially to make my day brighter. I indulged in grand thoughts of catching up on sweeping out the dust and cobwebs, of enjoying friends, of reading and writing.

However, within a few days one of my daughters, who had been struggling with ill health for some time, became acutely sick and spent the rest of the summer in and out of the hospital. Roses, sunshine, friends—anyone and anything that had wholeness and beauty—became the enemy. I began the summer of my discontent. And of waiting.

I regretted less the opportunity for housecleaning and writing than that once again I had to face the question of suffering.

Everywhere I turned that summer, I met it in some form: in the patient in the hospital room next door struggling for breath, in the older person living alone, in the casual acquaintance whose son had chosen a lifestyle to his self-hurt and the parents' heartache, and in the young woman who felt rejected by her family.

I found myself asking, demanding, why God, if he is both powerful and loving, permitted so much needless suffering. Why was he absent from me? Why was he silent? Why had he forsaken us? In an age of push-button or at least prepackaged convenience solutions for every type of distress, when help does not come in quickly delivered forms, impatience followed by bitterness is the most frequent consequence. I struggled not to become bitter.

I wanted to shove the experience of dealing with suffering from me. Like Tolstoy's Ivan Ilych, I didn't want to crawl into the narrow black bag without an opening. I was struggling for air as much as the one on the bed. The solid ground was gone, and I couldn't find my footing. Faith, prayer, darkness, hope, despair, and courage all floated alongside me, disconnected from me and from one another, like pieces of a shipwreck.

I learned again the need to keep working at the problem of pain. It burdens us at the death or sickness of a loved one, when relationships break, when we face problems of any kind. The pain I was experiencing during these middle years was of a different sort, but still a recognizable pain. Life was not fitting into neat, compact packages I could deal with easily.

It has been my habit for a number of years to spend a winter, or longer, thinking, studying, writing, about a specific topic. One year it was servanthood, another year creativity. This year I returned to the topic of suffering about the same time as Kushner's *When Bad Things Happen to Good People* became a best-seller.

No life stage is without pain, although we wish it were. Oswald Chambers writes, "I am sorry for the Christian who has

not something in his circumstances he wishes was not there."
Do some persons actually have all circumstances in perfect
order? Many Bible characters didn't. Hannah felt cursed because she was childless. The priest Eli suffered because he had
children who didn't obey him or God. Caleb, one of the ten
spies, probably felt squeezed between a rock and a hard place
when he returned with a favorable report and the Israelites accepted the unfavorable majority report that they couldn't
possibly take Canaan.

How the ancient patriarch Abraham must have suffered
when God asked him to sacrifice his only son. Did he have a
counselor to help him decide? Or did he struggle alone? What
convinced him that the angel in the thicket with the ram wasn't
the devil's illusion? What if Abraham had told himself God was
being inconsistent? What if Abraham had disregarded the
angel's offer of a ram?

One summer I spent many days with the ancient patriarch
Job. We introduced ourselves cautiously. I had heard he wasn't
easy to get to know. The apostle James speaks of him as
patient, and that's his most common image. But I found that
description didn't hold. He became quite depressed, even a little feisty with his friends occasionally.

After a while I got to like the old man more and more. But
that only came after we had spent a lot of time together.
Friendship is like that. At first I had only pity for his boils, his
loss of family and wealth, and his wife's rejection of him. Even
worse seemed his friends' accusations that he was sick because
he was a no-good guy.

One day it dawned on me that Job's real problem wasn't
why he was suffering but why God wasn't acting predictably,
dependably. If there is anything we like, it's a predictable God,
like a computer. Job and his friends hesitated to let go of their
traditional image of God. They saw him as a divine change machine—a dollar in, a dollar out. Which was a low view of God.
But that's what they had been taught. Job had put a whole

lifetime of good living into the slot and was getting nothing out, creating his dilemma.

To let go of a view of God picked up through preaching and teaching, literature, movies, television, and radio, which seemed right at the time we latched onto it, but which later doesn't match either biblical teaching or experience, is tough. More painful than boils. We don't like to change our minds. That's akin to cutting the rope before throwing the anchor overboard.

Job had grown up believing that a just God in partnership with his people rewarded good and punished evil in this life. People got what they deserved. Today, it would be like saying the poor or anyone face down in the mud could be singing and throwing money around in the park if they would straighten up their act. Live right and life will be rewarded with prosperity.

Job thought of himself as a decent person, yet he was getting what the wicked deserved—no home, no family, no servants, and an undiagnosable illness all over his body. Naturally he got uppish with God. His friends insisted he must have sinned. He insisted he hadn't. But if he hadn't sinned, why the sudden end to his cash flow, his family, and creature comforts? Something was out of sync. Such things happened only to bad people.

People get caught in Job's dilemma when their experience goes counter to what they have been taught about God. People who embrace the view that God is their private genie or celestial errand boy, waiting for the signal to bring them more creature comforts, are heading for Job's experience when God doesn't hop to their bidding. "Far and wide, contemporary Christianity is the suffering-free religion for a world perceived as without suffering," writes Dorothy Soelle. "It is the religion of the rich, the white, the industrial nations."

Job had to shift his low view of God to a higher one. To make this transition is not unlike hanging over a ledge, unsure whether the rope you're clinging to is the same strong cord you brought with you for the climb. It looks and feels the same, yet you're not sure it isn't a gossamer thread provided by the enemy.

Job learned God is not exactly like anything or anybody. He wanted to pin down God to his own image of him, but God is bigger than any image we may have of him, one reason the early Israelites were not to make graven images of him. His sovereignty means he doesn't need to answer to human complaints about his character. What he wants of us is "steady confidence with no ulterior motives, the faith that trusts not for comfort, not to get an answer to prayer, or even to escape damnation," writes Jacques Ellul in *Living Faith*. As soon as we set ourselves the task of believing in order to solve our problems, to save humanity, to get the strength to carry on, to ensure the world's survival, as soon as faith is not simply itself for God's sake, but an instrument to reach some other goal, it's just one more illusion. God is not the Great Repairman or the machine that dispenses solutions. He doesn't answer people who have designs on him, he states.

Dorothy Soelle in *Suffering* writes that the essential thing is whether "we carry out the act of suffering or are acted upon, indifferent as stones.... All who learn in suffering, who use their experiences to overcome old insights, who experience their own strength and come to know the pain of the living in the realm of the dead, they are beginning the exodus."

In late July one summer I flew to Saskatchewan to visit my sister-in-law, who was dying of cancer. What do I say to a dying person, I asked myself. Pious phrases, neatly chosen words, are trite in the face of suffering and death. A dying person shreds such words quickly and casts them aside.

Joyce made it easy for me, for she talked freely about life and death, faith and doubt, hope and despair, a present and absent God. Only we who think we are more alive separate them. Like Milton and Job we waited together. She was tired, she told me, of the "how-to-be-successful-in-the-faith" books—stories of people who had had a serious problem and then achieved a big victory, such as healing, a new lease on life, a new calling, and over-abundant joy. Friends were inundating her with such literature.

Our short week together moved by quickly. We talked about many things as I sat beside her as she lay on the living-room couch with the morning sun streaming in. "I'm not afraid to die," she said one day. "It's the long suffering I dread and knowing what the family will have to work through." I agreed.

"Why don't I feel God's presence closer?" she asked. Again the matter of the absence of God's presence. She felt an emptiness, a drabness, a darkness, to this dying from cancer. A loss of all emotion. Sort of like the child, who when a parent doesn't respond to a plea to intercede in a sibling fight, thinks the parent doesn't care. "Help me, Lord, I am being overcome. Why are you absent?" was Christ's cry on the cross. God's absence seems terrible because if he is gone, there seems to be nothing left to love.

I, sitting beside her, who was supposed to be alive, also longed for more feeling in the faith—a stronger experience of divine hands holding, lifting, stroking me. To simply know God is with me even if I can't feel him and that his presence doesn't depend on my feelings is not enough. When I think of him as absent, where is he?

"Why doesn't God heal in answer to prayer?" she questioned one day. She had prayed. She wanted to stay with her husband and family of young adult children. How could some religious leaders promise healing? We talked about the fragmented Christian church, some of whose leaders promise healing in exchange for "bold faith." Was she a failure because she hadn't had enough faith for healing? To be sick and then to be accused of lack of faith is cruel, I argued. Can anyone promise what God himself does not promise for everyone?

"What is supposed to give meaning to life when you're waiting to die? What am I supposed to talk about when friends come? They don't want to discuss dying. I don't know enough about living," she asked one day.

Again I agreed. We who are well don't want to know about dying. Unlike Job's friends, we avoid the topic of suffering. We talk about our work, our family, our good times together, our memories, our plans. What we can say about death and dying wouldn't take sixty seconds.

In time our conversation became freer. "What if faith in Christ is a hoax and there is nothing on the other side?" I saw both faith and fear in her smiling eyes. Together we came to an answer. You are no loser if you trust God. If there is no life after death, yet Christ has sustained us here, we gain on this side. If there is life after death, we're a double winner.

Joyce died several weeks later at home in the house built into the high bank overlooking the slow-flowing Saskatchewan River. The wildflower garden she had planted outside her window was already touched with frost. She chose the foolishness of the cross of Christ to the rationality of a faith-less death.

What does it mean to wait for an absent God when we have been promised that nothing, "neither death nor life, neither angels nor demons, neither the present nor the future, nor any powers, neither height nor depth, nor anything else in all creation," can separate us from his love? Why did Christ cry out that God had forsaken him on the cross if God was with him?

Waiting on God is an indication of hope. When the psalmists cried, "Why do you reject me and hide your face from me" (88:14), or "How long, O Lord? Will you forget me forever?" (13:1), their plea was an act of faith in a present God, not an absent one. In time of difficult waiting we are tempted to fake our belief and speak empty words of faith and joy when questioned ("How are things going with you?"), though inside there's a churning of disbelief and despair. Some believers continue the motions of being a Christian—attendance at services, giving a token offering, saying prayers—but the joy and power has gone. The psalmist freely admitted he felt God had turned aside, but he came to him nevertheless.

I repeat. Waiting on an absent God is an indication of hope. The psalmists, even when they lamented God had forsaken them, were convinced God was. Their cries to a silent God were cries of faith. They turned to the only one who could help them, for only if a soul does not stop loving in the darkness, can the object of the love be rightly considered God. "Though he slay me, yet will I trust him," wrote the psalmist. As Soelle writes, "The only salvation for a person in this despair is to go on loving 'in the void,' a love for God that is no longer reactive, in answer to experienced happiness . . . but instead an act that goes beyond all that has been experienced." Then one day, God appears again.

Though God may seem inconsistent when he does not appear to be devoting every moment to us, he is always consistent with himself—remaining in a covenant relationship of long-suffering love with his people. As in marriage where there is a distancing and coming together of the partners, so in the Christian life. God is with us; God is absent. This is a consistent pattern. The absence however is always an indication of his presence. The psalmists who cried to the God who had left them didn't think the relationship was broken, even though the "absence" created strain and pain. As believers we are faced with the paradox of God's promise to be with us always and the actuality of his apparent absence at times.

To explain this paradox, Henry Nouwen in *Living Reminder* points out that there is an enormous difference between an absence after a visit and an absence which is the result of not coming at all. "Without a coming there can be no leaving, and without a presence absence is only emptiness and not the way to a greater intimacy with God through the Spirit." The elements of communion—the bread and wine— are signs that speak first of God's absence—he has not yet returned—but also of his presence—he has promised to be with us. Hope of God's coming extends life's horizons into the future and acknowledges that though what one has been waiting for has not yet

come, the promise of his being with us gives the future a
reality.

The waiting in suffering can mutilate the spirit, chewing at
its edges until strength is depleted. It can become a selfish
thing—like the Dead Sea—shutting out life, love, and light,
and refusing help. I sense my temptation to withdraw, not to
talk to people, to nurse my hurt privately when I suffer. Suffering can also produce beauty as believers work in their suffering.
Yet because we witness many sufferers waiting patiently in
hope, we accept that God wills evil and suffering because of the
excellent way they handle oppression and affliction. To attribute to God the evil of pain and suffering brings God in at
the wrong point. God needs to be credited for the grace in the
person's life.

Admittedly, waiting for the years to bring an end to the
depression was difficult. Any waiting in pain and sorrow is difficult, especially if we don't know what we are waiting for. We
ask impatient questions: When will this interruption be
finished so life can continue? We cast about confusedly for a
handle to manage this waiting for the unknown. Nouwen
advises that in the waiting we "find the connection between
our small sufferings and the great story of God's suffering in
Jesus Christ." God also suffered when Christ died on the cross.
He also suggests that all the "randomly organized incidents
and accidents" are a constant opportunity to explore God's
work in our lives with memory one of the best tools to do this
exploring.

For example, though we wait for someone to come to us, rich
memories of times spent together with that person can bring us
closer to one another than physical presence. Though we may
wait for God to manifest himself, memories of times when he
was with us can be a stronger support than his actual presence.
God absents himself to "convert the pain of the Lord's absence
into a deeper understanding of his presence," says Nouwen.
He has not yet returned. He will return.

At the Lord's table, we gather to remind each other of his promise of return. The minister may be much concerned with making people glad and creating an atmosphere of "I'm OK, you're OK," and with affirming God's presence. Yet to only affirm leaves no empty space for acknowledgment of our basic lack of fulfillment without him. "If we deny the pain of his absence, we will not be able to taste his sustaining presence either. We will be unable to affirm 'The Lord is my shepherd, I shall not want,' " concludes Nouwen.

How then does one wait for God's presence in the midst of pain? Waiting is easier if you have someone waiting with you. I remind myself of the story of the man in the Old Testament, waiting alone in the middle of the desert on a starless night. Fear is in his heart. Even shame. Some apprehension. In the morning he will have to face his brother whom he deceived.

What does he think of in the inky darkness? The speech he will make to his brother to placate him? Tactics for fighting him? The hope that God will come along, gently put his arm around him, and comfort him as a mother does a child, assuring him everything will turn out all right?

As he sits, two strong arms reach out of the darkness and forcefully swing him around and pin him to the ground. He has been attacked—but by whom? Aroused, he struggles against this unknown enemy. Hour after hour the two wrestle. Until daybreak.

We know now that Jacob wrestled with an angel because we know the rest of the story. But Jacob didn't as he felt the hot breath of the other one close against his skin in the cool night air and knew the pain of muscles straining for freedom. When those strong hands grasped his shoulders, he didn't know whether he was wrestling with an angel or a night demon. As he was pushed down, I doubt that he assured himself, "This is God in human form come to teach me a lesson," as we are sometimes urged to do when we suffer.

We know from Genesis 32 that the two men struggled all

night. In the dawn, when both were weary, Jacob's opponent asked to be released. Jacob replied, "I will not let you go until you bless me." By then he knew whom he was fighting.

Some commentators argue that Jacob should not have wrestled with God, for his mistake resulted in being lamed for life. They maintain a believer should wrestle only before God about things, never with him in prayer. To wrestle with God is unscriptural, for God is never opposed to us or anything we ask that is his will. He gives freely, not reluctantly, they say.

Agreed. But what if, like Jacob, we don't know who or what has smashed us down? Then we can only do what he did—and that is struggle until we also meet God. That evening Jacob faced the opportunity of a new beginning. He was going back home to the land of his parents. But before he could cross the river, he had to face Esau, the brother who had complicated his life years ago when both were young hotheaded men.

We all have our own Esau to face. Sometimes he is a family member, a friend, an acquaintance. Sometimes Esau is within us. Sometimes the situation across the river may be the loss of trust, failure, a death, disappointment in one's calling, bitterness. It may be caused by our shortsightedness, stubbornness, lack of love, misjudgments, and hasty tongue. Sometimes it is suffering.

We wait with Jacob in the desert, wondering how we can escape facing Esau. As we squat in the darkness, feeling bereft of God's presence, we pray for comfort, for joy, for hope. We ask God to reach down deep and pull out the hurt. We pray to be rescued from deciding issues that lie ahead. We do not want to go through the pain, the suffering.

One of the weaknesses of this generation is its unwillingness to accept any kind of suffering or emotional pain, including the pain of making decisions. People try to escape from themselves through drugs, alcohol, sex, television, and work. As I write this a wave of teenage suicides is sweeping the nation. One writer comments teenagers turn to suicide because they lack too few models of older people facing their pain. When people refuse the pain, they also reject the opportunity of an encounter with God in the darkness of the night.

"Don't waste the pain life brings with it," a Catholic religious told my daughter during an illness.

Waste pain? We waste time, energy, money, people. But pain?

Yes, don't waste the pain. Learn from it. Let the suffering teach you the lessons of life. Let it bring forth from you what needs to come out. As you wait, let it make you aware that God suffers with you. He hangs on the cross in the person of his Son Jesus Christ.

The Genesis story has an ending. When Jacob looked up, there was Esau. "Esau ran to meet Jacob and embraced him; he threw his arms around his neck and kissed him. And they wept." Jacob now had a memory of God to pass on to his children and to strengthen him in future times of doubt.

During my daughter's illness I strengthened myself with memories of how God had been with us during my husband's illness and death in the love of friends and family, in giving courage and hope to continue, in the intimate communion with him in time of sorrow. Later on, other kinds of memories strengthened my faith.

Memory is a strong provider of hope. Memory can bless. One summer I visited my childhood home in Saskatchewan for the first time in years to revive old memories. Like most people my first reaction was how time had shrunk our former family home. Did all seven of us actually fit into that tiny space without feeling crowded?

Garage, playhouse, sandbox, swings, sauna— all were gone. Weeds overran the yard. The ivory and green frame house stood empty, rejected, and vulnerable to time and weather on a street in which all the other houses were noticeably loved and occupied. I felt affronted. But then these others didn't know about the "memories that bless and burn." My brother who was with me and I could have matched memories all day.

His: Thoughts about the gray-blue porcelain jug, always overfilled with custard sauce for Saturday waffles.

Mine: Lying in the backyard on a patchwork quilt made of tailor's samples, watching the northern lights twist and tumble across the star-studded sky.

His: Drowning prairie gophers in their holes, then twisting off their tails by swinging them around his head. Tails meant pocket money in depression times.

Mine: Listening for the smooth hum of the tire of the 1929 McLaughlin-Buick when we hit the pavement twelve miles from the city after bouncing over fifty miles of dirty and gravel. Angel's wings couldn't have sounded smoother. "Ah!" I exclaimed then. And "Ah!" I say now.

Literature speaks of epiphanies or breakthroughs of insight. "Before I was blind and now I see," said the blind man to Jesus. The Greek word *kairos* refers to the pregnant moment before dawn breaks, before the fragile butterfly bursts from its cocoon, before the rosebud releases its fragrant beauty.

These "Aha!" experiences are as real as waffles and smooth roads if we watch for them. You've read something ten, maybe twenty times, then suddenly the murkiness clears and you see clearly. Words that were just strings of words become meaningful truth.

I knew all about forgiveness, about caring for the weaker person, about the need to affirm others, but that knowledge was public knowledge. Then, strangely, in India at a meeting of Christian national communicators, I could say, "Aha! I have learned something new. This truth-territory now belongs to me. I claim it for myself. Something new has begun in me. God is with me."

These "Aha!" experiences can originate from memories of the triumph of hope over frustration and failure. Remember when you got to the end of the piano piece at the same time as the metronome and it felt so good? Remember when you fixed a leaky faucet by yourself, or made a computer obey your commands, or walked the first time after a long illness, or spoke stumbling words of unfamiliar faith? "Amen," you said then. "Amen," you say now as you remember, for you can put the words into past tense. Love overcame, love suffered long, love was kind and was not provoked. Faith endures in the absence of God knowing he will return.

The humble cobbler, Jean Lenoir, living in Paris, wrote in his diary for July 14, 1789, "Nothing of importance happened today." But we, looking back, know that a world-shaking event took place that day. The mob stormed the Bastille, beginning the French Revolution. Like this cobbler, we see "through a glass darkly." We see God as absent. But the memory of his presence keeps hope alive. And then he comes. As he promised. Anyone with this view need no longer be a depression child waiting anxiously for a new day but possessing perfect quietness of the soul.

CHAPTER 10

We shape faith through choices

From the cradle onward life is choice, and all choice is a shedding, an abandonment of a possible reality, a step from the multiple to the single.

—Selected

A few years after my trip to India my middle-age crisis, if that was what my earlier feelings of discomfort were, was subsiding. I could now admit to there being a middle-age crisis that varies from person to person. For some people life moves along without interruption from the last heart-breaking adolescent crush to the rocking chair stage. For others, middle age may be a heaving ocean of emotion related to job change, health deterioration, concerns about vocational and personal success or failure, and even something as expected and planned for as children leaving home. I had to admit, for example, that the house seemed twenty feet longer with no child to answer the doorbell, and the grocery store and post office in another country when I had to do all errands myself.

It sounds trite to say we live in a world of change. Yet change is the twentieth century. It is inevitable and apparent all over—in clothing and hair styles, music, art, language, architecture, education, methods of going to war, book publishing, family structures, eating habits, and worship styles. By this time I could admit that adult living would mean much change.

Change is normal, people assure themselves. They're ready to admit that our institutions need change and also that tradition may be hindering church and personal growth. But because change means a period of uneasiness and insecurity until one has become accustomed to the new, these same people will argue that specific modifications that will affect them do not necessarily mean progress. Stability looks more appealing for the moment even if it means stagnation in the end. Change is for other people, not for them.

Many people fight change related to time, appealing to cosmetic surgery, hair dyes, and youthful clothing, mannerisms, and slang to keep them static. They are convinced that to look younger is preferable. Resistance to change shows up in other ways: Young mothers wish their children were grown up and out from under their feet. Middle-aged parents wish they still had children coming in and out of the house. Older people long for something purposeful to occupy their time. These are all normal feelings, and not to be belittled unless they cripple development.

A friend asked me what have been the most difficult changes I have had to make living alone in the past few decades. I didn't need much time to think about a response. Not adjusting to loneliness, I told him, although that is what many people place first, but to work out my value system in relation to the many social, technological, and political changes around me and then to adjust my lifestyle accordingly. And to do so alone. Whether to travel by plane or to use slower transportation has never been an issue. Whether to use new labor-saving devices or adopt a higher standard of health and sanitation is easily decided. I finally adjusted to even the children's leaving home.

I struggle most with pluralism within and outside Christianity, and with the way people mix and match theology to suit their lifestyle. Most difficult has been sorting through the changing attitudes toward issues such as human sexuality and its related topics: the modern family, abortion, homosexuality, the singles movement, divorce and remarriage, working women, and how the Scriptures speak to such issues. For example, in an earlier era, men gave women their identity and social status through their relationship to them, so failure for a woman was not being selected by a man for marriage. Husbands were heads of families, sires, not always partners in marriage and fathers. A wife asked her husband to baby-sit for her. A husband had the right to say, "I've got a meeting tonight, so I can't baby-sit for you." I had grown up accepting such an arrangement as right and normal and that a mother employed outside the home was out of her natural sphere. Yet as a working mother, friends commended me for supporting my family singlehandedly. I was confused.

Some people fear change, particularly related to Christian thinking, because it means making decisions and accepting more responsibility, choosing not so much between good and evil as between better and best and without specific biblical proof texts to support their decision. We don't like to be self-responsible Christians. We middle-American Christians are what we are because we were taught zealously and in great detail to do what we do. Part of this teaching was that God always does the leading for us, which is true, and therefore also the choosing, which is easily misinterpreted. We have confused leading and choosing, neglecting to remind ourselves that as God leads, we must make commitments to him.

As I've already mentioned, during my young adult years a tremendous amount of Christian literature was published on finding and knowing the the will of God. Although probably not intentional, much of it emphasized "letting God choose for us," and becoming only a vessel or a passive channel of his love and grace to a needy world. So we waited for signs, for omens, for wet fleeces, for letters, and sometimes also for a shove from God, ignoring the many passages in both the Old and New

Testaments that clearly teach the Christian life is a series of choices and commitments directed by God's compelling love. Joshua called the Israelites to commitment: "Choose you this day whom you will serve." Jesus commended Mary for "having chosen the better part." She acted, not just reacted. We have to take the first step in the decision, whatever it may be, as if there were no God—but when we do, we find he was there all the time.

Devotional writer Oswald Chambers writes that the "remarkable thing about spiritual initiative is that life comes after we do the bucking up. God does not give us an overcoming life; he gives us life as we overcome. When the inspiration of God comes, and he says, 'Arise from the dead,' we have to get up; God does not lift us up." Chambers adds that our Lord said to the man with the withered hand, "Stretch forth your hand," and as soon as the man did so, his hand was healed. But he had to take the initiative and raise his powerless hand.

Making definite decisions—becoming a co-actor in the drama of life with God—was a new thought to me. It forced me to write my name on the bottom line to some faith commitments. Did the man with the withered hand feel fearful when he stretched forth his hand? I know I did the first time I received an invitation to speak in public or enrolled in a university class. I also recall waking up one night in a cold sweat, overcome with fear that my classmates considered me too old for a seminar I was planning to attend. In my dream 'I felt the sharp ridicule of my younger classmates. Yet growth takes place during times of decision. Decisions consolidate our position, whatever it may be, and gives God or sin an opportunity to enter our life.

Many people resist change for fear of being judged by others, of becoming conspicuous. We also fear failing, losing our respectability, if it means moving out of familiar patterns. Some people never change their hairstyle because then they wouldn't recognize themselves in the mirror. They want to see the same familiar face greet them each morning.

Yet how can one reconcile choosing and making independent decisions—not waiting for God to shove from behind—with being submissive to God's will? His goal for us is holiness. The details are ours to work out. For this he makes his infinite resources available to us—Scripture, prayer, the guidance of the Spirit, the counsel of friends. At the college where I teach, each year I am given a contract, which if I sign commits me to being responsible for a certain number of courses and other types of responsibilities. No one supervises my every class period. I am given wide latitude in making certain decisions both within the classroom and without it as long as I fulfill the goals of the college. Anything less would be an abuse of academic freedom.

Psychologist Paul Tournier writes that in every person is the idea of God's plan. Some do not call it God's plan, but the concept is the same. The plan for an apple tree is to grow apples, not pears. The plan for a human being is glorification of God. God expects something of us. We all come to life with our unique gifts, heredity, experiences, and inner leadings that grip the mind. Each person feels he or she is on a unique pathway that leads to some destination. Finally the moment comes when we are forced to make a choice of some kind, and take charge under the inner direction of the Spirit and God's call.

Submission and decision-making are not mutually exclusive. God gives us freedom to follow him in discipleship, not in a knee-jerk relationship, but through the paradox of both Spirit-led and humanly determined decisions to bring us further on the pathway of holy living.

Part of making decisions regarding change (I dislike using the word "coping" because of its negative connotations) always has to do with how we regard our own past. Sometimes the past, instead of serving us, hinders us. When we allow all kinds of hairy beasts to lurk back there, year after year, we move into life with a victim mentality, convinced at each turn that life is not fair. The unpleasant things back there that we would like to forget frequently involved personal relationships, yet they keep popping up in our minds. They stand in the way of change.

I grew up in comparative poverty during the depression and never had the opportunity to continue my education until several years after high school. Most of it was done after age forty. Even after I acquired a university education and had written a few books, I was still bothered by the fear that people would see me as the limited, underdeveloped, unsophisticated daughter of immigrants in a conservative denomination. I had an image of myself as someone who spoke mumbling, bumbling words—the kind of person we made fun of as children. At one point I had to deal with my history, and cleanse my spirit of all that the past controlled or I would never be free to tell others of God's freedom in Christ Jesus. I embraced my past and found treasures there I never knew existed. When I claimed the past as belonging to me, I could change my attitude toward it.

Maxie Dunham writes in *Dancing at My Funeral*: "For the first time I saw that my past had power to undo me because I myself was energizing it. My past was back there and couldn't hurt me unless I let it hurt me. I stopped in my tracks and faced the hounds of hell." Whatever the past contains cannot destroy us unless we let it. We need to face the hounds of hell and say, "It's happened. I wish it hadn't, but it is over now. Pain will be there from time to time but I will learn from it and go on." Though it is amazing what the human organism can handle in terms of pain, suffering, and stress, when people are pressured to give in against their will, they may be tempted to pull the trigger and hurt someone they don't really want to hurt. They lunge at others in criticism and anger. Life has little joy if you are running around like a wound-up toy pleasing everyone and no one. Self-pity and loss of self-esteem, followed by joylessness and often bitterness, are frequently the result. So dealing with the past cannot be evaded.

I find that making decisions is easier if I have not only dealt with the past but also have a vision of what can be, if I see with the eyes of the sanctified imagination (Ephesians 1:18) the possibilities God has in store for me, for family, for friends, for the church of Jesus Christ. Most of us have visions of our next purchase—a car, dress, sofa, microwave oven, VCR, or compact disc player. We wait for the next paycheck and scrimp on this or that so that we can turn our dream into reality. We can see the goal accomplished—new paint, flounced curtains, new bedspread, and maybe some new lamps and a new chair for the guest room. To accomplish our goal, we make changes in lifestyle. Few real changes occur in the Christian life without seeing life through Christ's eyes.

Decision-making may mean we will have to weigh the possibilities for the future dream against the realities of present. What is it in this change I am resisting, I asked myself when I first considered selling my house and possibly changing church membership. Will it enhance the opportunity for friendship and service? Will it provide opportunities for creativity? Will I be able to risk failure without being squashed or caught in power struggles or gossip circles, equally as harmful?

A friend told me she was contemplating changing her Bible study class because it was not meeting her need, although she had been a member of it for years.

"Change to another," I advised her. "Join a group that will encourage your spiritual growth."

"But what will the people say?" she replied. So she stayed where she was.

One Sunday morning as I was teaching my regular adult Bible class, a most enjoyable group of people, I suddenly realized as we went over the material that I knew almost to the word what the response of each person would be—and I also knew my own. We were going over a different lesson each week but not allowing it to stretch us to the point of changing our lifestyle. I knew then I had to make some changes.

Organizations can hinder maturity, so it is important at times to let go of those gatherings that keep us shriveled. To decide for growth means making choices and changes, sometimes uncomfortable ones. Yet it is important to ask leading questions: What do I value? I opted to be free to be myself, to be creative, to use my gifts, to explain my life, to share, to love, to live deeply, to endure, to fail if need be.

Not making firm decisions can result in frustration. A decision, even if a wrong one, at least means movement in some direction. Earlier I had asked myself what I was doing with life at my age. Life was swirling past me. At my age, could I still get on board?

I had begun my decade of learning feeling the pressure to change. Here I was over fifty and not sure what direction life was taking me. I felt somewhat satisfied several years later that even my small decision earlier to list goals for my course in adult education had resulted in some change. Old dogs could learn new tricks.

Since then I've met many "old dogs" in their fifties, sixties, seventies and even beyond who are learning new concepts, new attitudes, and new skills with each passing birthday. Old dogs can learn to build, to draw, to paint, to write, to teach, to lead, to speak, even to use computers and to change their minds about long-held ideas. These "early-borns," as an older friend calls his peers, may have arthritis in their bones, but they don't have to have it in their attitudes, unless they want to. I didn't know if I could put myself in this category.

I was surprised a few years later that I could list a few changes. I could admit freely that I no longer believed evil resided only in individuals. Even as goodness and truth resides in social systems and structures developed by humans, such as the family, church institutions, and so forth, so evil also may control them. When Christ spoke against the Pharisees, he was speaking against the evil in the religious structures and systems of his day. When he spoke to the woman at the well, he was addressing her as an individual. He worked both fronts. I had to also. This was a far-reaching decision for me.

As the result of consciousness-raising, I could now identify myself as a Christian feminist. I dislike the term "women's liberationist." I could accept the necessity for inclusive language, especially when talking about people, and had begun to consistently work at changing my own usage. My language awareness was slow but gradual, starting with a minister who preached a sermon that began with the reading of a Scripture passage beginning with "brothers," and then throughout used only masculine nouns and pronouns. All illustrations dealt with males of various ages and occupations and their emotions and responses to life. Clearly, the speaker did not consider any women or girls as having had interesting, challenging, or enlightening experiences worth repeating in public. His application was to "go preach the Word," an activity traditionally reserved for a small minority within the congregation, of which often more than half are women. Women were not included in that invitation "to preach." I felt left out. I decided to become more inclusive in my language myself.

Each decision to change has also required a commitment to the goal or to a new model to make the commitment hold and a letting go of old patterns. A child learns to walk by giving up handholds or the security of creeping. An adult learns to walk by surrendering temporary securities—familiar but sometimes limiting patterns, safe but possibly unrewarding work, values we mouthed but didn't live by. The result will not be assured success. We are told daily by the mass media there is no substitute for success. Winning isn't everything, it is the only thing. But there is noble failure—and sometimes it comes through the willingness to risk with God. Failure is not fatal, only what we do with failure. The fleas sometimes come with the dog, but that doesn't mean we throw out the dog.

Nor does all of life afford the same opportunities for growth. Fiction writer Flannery O'Connor frequently writes about the moment of grace in her characters' lives. For a brief few seconds the revelation of God penetrates them and they can decide for or against Jesus Christ before life moves on in the same patterns. These few special moments count for more than all the rest because in them the characters must take a stand, make a commitment or decisive choice.

In *The Seasons of Life* Paul Tournier writes that "these turning points in life are generally few in number. They may have been slow, almost unconscious . . . or they may have been like the flash of lightning, a sudden burst into consciousness of a process worked through in the subconscious." He explains that they are always an encounter with an idea or a person before which we cannot remain neutral. The encounter may be with a few words, a glimpse of a life through a book or a film. We have to take sides, take responsibility. At this moment of decision we get a special knowing, the Aha! experience, a knowing that can take place at any time in life.

I have found that these special moments frequently occur when we are out of our regular routine at a conference, in a new setting, on a trip. On my European tour the sign at the bottom of the hill near the city of Zurich, Switzerland, said "Anabaptist Cave—15 minutes." The destination of our tour group was one of the secret caves where Christians of the radical wing of the Reformation had gathered for fellowship about four hundred years ago. The cave is now along a regular hiking trail and open to anyone. Fifteen minutes up the hill. I fell in line behind the others.

As I trudged up that steep hill that bright shining day, beside me in imagination walked the believers of a previous century. A husband and his wife, taking turns carrying a small child. An older man with an ax hoisted over his shoulder. A middle-aged woman chasing a cow. All walking with deliberate steps toward the hidden meeting place. All knew that if they were apprehended by government officials, the price might be death. So they trudged up the hill, camouflaging their destination by chasing a farm animal or carrying a bundle of vegetables to give to a friend.

Curiosity drew me up the hill to the cave. With what anxieties and hopes had these people picked their way up this path, now slippery from a recent rain? How long had they sometimes waited in the darkness of the cave for others to show up? Records say five hours of waiting did not daunt them.

The waterfall rushing over the cave entrance muffles human sounds. In the semidarkness, these Swiss believers had sung hymns and shared the week's experiences in the faith, possibly concluding with the Lord's Supper. They were always aware their lives were in danger, but they were apparently more concerned about the strength they would receive from this meeting with other Christians than the fear of death.

Our tour group, sitting on logs in the dampish cave, joined in communion and attempted to reconstruct what faith in Christ might have meant for these early followers. Something had shaped their faith and made it a reality that directed their life to the point of their being willing to yield it up if need be. Some of that shaping had happened in this very cave.

What has shaped my faith, I asked myself, as I visualized the kinds of people who might have squatted on the dirt floor at an earlier time. Not what started my Christian life, but what had given it identity, strength, roots? At what point in life had I said, "This truth challenges me to the extent I want my life to be identified by it and am willing to change?"

I checked back in time. Reading and study—yes, obviously. These have shaped my faith. These have brought about change. The hymns sung repeatedly in our small congregation when I was a child. Sermons, but not as many as I would have thought. Family, too. Most assuredly. The witness of friends at crucial times in their lives and mine. Very important.

All that—but especially fellowship at special times around the Lord's table with other believers. At various times when other life options looked attractive, I recalled saying "Yes" to

Christ and his truth at a communion service.

Before I was married, an older highly respected minister and Bible teacher spoke from Ezekiel 47 at one such service about believers entering the waters of faith. At first the water comes to the ankles, then the knees, then the waist. Fear of drowning intrudes, overwhelms. The believer is tempted to turn back to shallower water. But faith buoys the person in the deep water. James Baldwin in his short story, "Sonny's Blues," makes particularly clear that deep water and drowning are not the same thing when the protagonist, after an absence of several years from his Harlem home, returns to jazz piano playing freed of his earlier fears. To risk by moving out to water beyond our depth can be a life-giving and life-changing moment because we have to have faith to trust the water to hold us up. The footholds are gone.

Life with change needs these checkpoints of commitment, like runners in a marathon, at which times we self-consciously identify our faith position to ourselves and to others and tell ourselves that being a Christ-follower is not just a good decision—but the best one. And that it will require making more changes and commitments on the pilgrimage toward holiness.

Without such checks, our lives soon take on the identity of those who have no commitment to discipleship except for maintaining a few religious phrases and customs and whose moral decision-making is limited to deciding whether to stay up to watch a late talk show or get some sleep. Such living may be with less pain, but also less joy.

To live is to change. The journey had only begun. Now I was beginning to look forward to the adventure of faith that might lie ahead in the rest of the middle years.

CHAPTER 11

Moving the inner baggage

*Everyone thinks of changing the world, but no
one thinks of changing himself.*

—Leo Tolstoi

Within four years of my initial consideration of what I
needed to do to meet the years ahead with more grace, I had
changed church membership, written several books, tested
various personal spiritual disciplines, and sold the house, the
only home in which I and the children had lived without my
husband. Purchasing the house fifteen years earlier had been a
big step of faith, selling it now was another.

You learn a lot about yourself when you move—even if it's
only five blocks down the street. Moving has biblical
precedent— Abraham moved long distances as did Moses and
a few other Old Testament characters, like Jacob. Some
American families make it a regular practice every two or three
years. The journey is a popular motif in literature, for it represents not only a geographic shift but also an inner shift. For me,
this house move was the first one in over fifteen years.

Now that my children had left home and I had accepted
their leaving, I moved into a home with less floor space (less
cleaning and lower utility bills), a smaller yard (less complain-

ing from me about mowing lawns), a shorter distance to the town's business section (more walking and less driving), and closer proximity to neighbors (more opportunity for backyard frendships). Loading my boxes of belongings onto the truck was easy compared to getting the inner baggage to come along.

"You'll enjoy your new home," friends told me. I knew I would—in time. "Do it, Mother," said the kids. I appreciated their willingness to let me leave behind the house that housed many of their growing-up memories and not demand a large place so that they and their families could all visit at one time. I have seen too many parents build the big house after their children left home to regret it a decade later. I wasn't against the move, but on moving day the thought of leaving the only place where I and the children had battled life together, hit like a sledgehammer.

I had a love-hate attachment to our long hall—all thirty feet of it—a remnant of the army barracks the building had once been. On cleaning day I saw it as wasted space, but a godsend when the doorbell rang. While rushing down its length, I could pull a comb through my hair or even change my skirt or blouse. In winter when it was too cold to exercise outside, it was useful for doing laps, and when anyone was tense, it was most useful for pacing out frustrations.

Then there was the queen-sized bathroom, remodeled from a regular-sized bedroom. Daughter Christine immortalized it in a poem in which she claimed it would sorrow "with more pathos than any mourner" after our leaving. She vowed she could "hear the shower gush a wet outburst on patient porcelain—and toilet tank sighing the end of its cycle of rushing and flushing, and silver faucets dripping their quiet tears—remembering a million morning splashes." And remembering also the many discussions that took place in it because it was large enough for four or five people to move about in freely at one time. Our bathroom was a main room, not a bypass.

Many things had to remain: the oak tree planted by Susan

and her husband early in their marriage; the holly I found growing in the trash pile, having sprouted from some discarded Christmas decorations; the roses and pussy willows in the back.

In moving I discovered I had more worldly goods tucked away in odd corners and drawers than I cared to know about. The yellow towel with the crocheted basket to hold a washcloth had waited more than twenty-five years for the right guest. Some dishes and linens had never been used, and were now useful for only show and tell as were some shelves of books, padded with extra volumes like the bustle of a woman's dress for ostentatious display. A church library or friends could use them better than I.

I found I owned a lot of period pieces. Some items belonged to the camping period, the candle-making period, the model airplane period, the electronic period, the woodworking period. Each was part of our family history.

But the history that was hardest to leave behind were the visible tokens of the love of friends. Often when our sky was falling down, friends had responded. The insulation, the siding, the paint job, the partition in the family room, the hotwater heater—these were not just mechanical objects but visible signs of mutual burden bearing. The old house represented a lot of living for a family that had had a lot of lessons to learn quickly following my husband's death.

The new home was a chance to start anew. Immediately, Joanna and her husband planted two maple trees. I could begin again amassing memories, dreams, and skills.

The years immediately before and after the move, as reflected in my journal, I was thinking a lot about many things. With no children around, I could think of other concerns. I tried to overcome my fear of inanimate objects by enrolling in a woodworking course at the local high school. Though I may never again guide a radial saw through a board, I conquered my fear of power tools by learning to use them under guided instruction. The proof of my skills stands in my office in the form of a too-solid walnut-stained bookshelf on which hammerhead marks and drips of glue mysteriously appeared after it was completed. But it is a recognizable bookshelf. It, too, is a step in the journey.

Health and nutrition came in for close scrutiny during this period. Whether overeating was a big sin or a little weakness, a person should be able to quit cold turkey, I'd told myself often. All I had to do was acknowledge my need, pray, and shove off in a new direction. My theory worked well until I applied it to my own eating habits.

I wasn't grossly overweight. I wasn't battling breath at each step. But I sensed a slow leakage of energy, occasional sleeplessness, and shrinking clothes. I took on the battle, for like many Americans I had fallen into a pattern of eating what was ready-cooked, near, and not dear. Often I watched slim and trim joggers in appropriate gear float past my window. Older couples, although not quite jogging, clipped past at a determined pace, barely pausing to greet me.

One winter, advertisements for aerobics and charm courses appeared, sometimes with the added incentive of "Christian music." The final clincher was my son's gift of a pair of hot-pink Nikes. For me, the age of the well-cared-for-body had also arrived, although I admit each of us has to sort through our involvement in it.

I had grown up believing cleanliness was next to godliness. I liked the image my faith tradition had of its members being an orderly, clean people without serious vices. Alcohol, tobacco, and drugs are on our taboo list; but coffee, tea, rich desserts, and high caloric animal protein foods remain on our protected list. Good eating meant good fellowship in our home. I can still hear my mother urging, "Children, eat, eat." It was her way of showing love. She had known what it was not to have enough to set on the table for the family during the post-Revolution days in southern Russia.

Now, to my dismay, I found that I, who could discipline

myself to write a book, couldn't discipline myself not to eat a piece of rhubarb pie.

At first Fat was the enemy. I soon realized that that view gave thinness more divine worth. Because I didn't know the factors complicating overweight people's lives, judging them was not my concern. I changed my goal from primarily losing weight to achieving better nutrition, and hopefully better health. I wasn't interested in crash diets. I hoped I wasn't buying into the powerful messages that entangle themselves with the concern for fitness: shapeliness is godliness; firm muscles mean a firm faith; graceful movements mean graceful character; a color-coordinated wardrobe and makeup means coordinated fruits of the spirit; that an alive faith requires lithe muscles; and that without beauty of body, you're always a second-class citizen of the kingdom of God. I just wanted to be more responsible for my body the same way I saw myself responsible for my soul.

I admitted to myself also that this present attention to wellness could take place only in an age of affluence. The poor are concerned only with getting enough to eat, not which foods provide the best nutrition. To exercise or not isn't an option for them either. If they don't work, they don't eat.

I dislike sociological and psychological jargon, but I decided on "behavior modification" in eating. I wanted to change my eating habits—kind and amount of food. I laid out a fairly simple plan: less meat, more beans, whole grains, cheese, and eggs; less refined food, more bulk through fresh fruits and vegetables and bran; fewer empty calories, fewer desserts and snacks, less coffee and tea (deciding on that hurt!), and less salt.

The first hurdle was the grocery store. I was still stacking up sale items as if I kept a daycare center for teenagers.

Rule No. 1: Buy only food suitable for my needs. Skip down supermarket aisles loaded with canned goods, snacks, jams and jellies, prepared cereals, and similar items.

Rule No. 2: Consider the pantry full without large supplies

of cookies, cakes, and pastries, even though my family background kept softly insisting these are essential for good eating and good living.

Rule No. 3: Eat three meals a day, and no more. I saw too many overly busy people who omitted meals and ended up feeling shaky, headachy, and unable to function effectively. Three regular meals keeps energy levels constant.

When a family member went on a low-salt diet, I joined her as an experiment. I learned that more natural foods, spices, and herbs added to food eliminates the need for as much salt.

Rule No. 4: Forget the saltshaker.

Rule No. 5: Drink more water. Our city council came to the rescue on this one by providing drinkable water from the kitchen faucet for the first time in our city's history. Now I wouldn't have to buy bottled water anymore.

Rule No. 6: When you eat alone, make meals enjoyable. I put my food on a small plate to make smaller helpings look bigger and read the newspaper, a book, or watch the news so I will eat more slowly.

Change in diet wasn't enough, however. I needed more exercise. But how could I stretch arms and legs when they jarred a chair or table with every movement? "Walk," my better self told me. "Impossible," I replied. "No time for walking. Anyway what will people think if I wear low-heeled shoes, my hair gets wind-blown, or my skin glistens in the summer sun? I carry heavy books daily. The extremes of Kansas weather rule out walking." "All pride," responded my better self.

I walked, under great inner protest at first. I bought a warmer coat, boots, raingear, and a cap, well aware some folks think the well-dressed look should dispense with headgear. I found groceries and books can be carried easily in bags or bicycled home. I told myself, unless there's a tornado blowing, walk; and carry combs in every pocket.

After about a year on my new regimen, not a rigid one intended to make life miserable for myself or friends, I surveyed what I had gained. More energy, the need for less sleep (or possibly the recognition that I needed less sleep), and more comfortably fitting clothes. My biggest shock—and disappointment—to this day is the discovery of how little food a middle-aged adult in a sedentary occupation needs daily to maintain weight.

I have not conquered all my vices or answered all my questions. I still have an affair going with ice cream and yogurt. I keep looking for a good replacement for a hot morning drink. Decaffeinated coffee has only slight charms. Buying cheaper and therefore less tasty brands of coffee or using herb teas hasn't been the entire solution. When my children were home, my first goal was nutritious food, but a close second was providing lots of cheap fillers to keep food costs down. I found wholegrain breads, fresh fruits, and vegetables were more expensive than a hot dog in a pasty white bun. Now I was learning to enjoy whole grains, beans, and cheese.

But I was concerned about another area of my life, that seemed unrelated, yet was an integral part—the inner spiritual disciplines. Something had to change regarding my way of Bible reading and prayer. I didn't know what to do.

One day I quit one of these disciplines altogether. The decision wasn't a hasty one, nor do I advise others to do it my way. But one day I stopped reading the Bible—to fast from it like one fasts from food to cleanse the body of excess wastes. The reason was that as I studied my King James Version I found myself reading into certain passages interpretations I knew didn't stand up to more recent scholarship. I couldn't help myself. These interpretations were as much a part of me as my fondness for chocolate milk shakes. I hated to give them up. But to achieve greater inner strength, I had to discard those interpretations that didn't agree with the truth of Scripture and to reach zealously for new understandings.

I was also slowly grasping that in some passages the King James Version incorporates the bias of its translators and that much theology claiming to be based on "the biblical perspective" actually is built on the perspective of the Bible as read from a white, male, Western, bourgeois, intellectual perspective rather than from the perspective of the biblical writers themselves. I felt misled when I learned, for example, that Romans 12:1 challenges Christians to offer their bodies as living sacrifices, because it is their "reasonable worship" (NIV). How could that be? The word in that phrase should be "service," the way I grew up reading it—something one does.

Another example. Psalm 68:11 reads, "Great was the company of those that publish the word of the Lord," yet the Hebrew version is explicitly feminine: "Great was the company of those women who publish the word of the Lord." Why was the word "women" omitted?

At the time I let go of my King James Bible, my concern wasn't primarily with passages like the preceding, but with proof texts in general. I found I could no longer duck them with grace, dignity, and humility when someone hurled them at me. Furthermore, I was starting to hurl them back with good aim as well as mean curve.

Like proof text fans, I found myself making doctrines out of texts I liked and avoiding those that didn't fit into my system of beliefs. If someone shot Proverbs 3:9,10 at me, or something similar, I'd reply with Luke 1:46-53. There are no strict rules in this game. It doesn't even matter if the verses don't exactly cancel each other out. It is important to have individual pieces of ammunition and to use them.

Sitting back for a time and listening to proof texts being hit back and forth taught me one thing: We use them primarily to gain control or to manipulate other people, not as gestures of love. A proof text usually contains some phrase or clause that refers to something a person should or should not do.

I came back from my temporary fast, the better for it. I still enjoy the rich, dignified, and simple language of the King James Version. I chose the New International Version for my personal Bible study. I appreciate the attempts of newer translations to come closer to the meaning of the original text in language I can grasp more easily. If sometime, newer scholarship brings the meaning even closer to the original, I hope I have the grace to shift more readily.

The next step was to become more systematic in Bible study. As a new Christian at about age nineteen, I read the Bible ravenously—like a teenager who has discovered double cheeseburgers for the first time. I needed what I read. It fed me. It tasted good. It told me what this new life in Christ was all about.

Then I enrolled in Bible college. A new factor entered in. As students we studied the Bible each day, so personal Bible study seemed less necessary. Yet my roommate and I read the Bible and prayed for ten to fifteen minutes each morning and evening. That one or the other might fall asleep on her knees to be poked by the other into renewed mumbling didn't bother us. We squeezed Bible reading in at both ends of the day, even if the ends nearly met. A friend mentioned that one evening as he and his wife were praying, she was called away by one of the children. Left alone by himself at the bedside, he didn't know what to do. Should he keep on praying? Was his audience his wife or God?

After college I married, and the pattern of personal devotions changed again. The reason was partly that I confused an important principle. When I yielded to my brand-new husband the spiritual leadership of the home, I gave up also my right to serious Bible study. Sitting at a desk with an open Bible seemed to fit his role as husband and minister better than mine as wife and homemaker. Then when the babies came, their morning cry always sounded louder and clearer than God's call to Bible study. I felt guilty about what I vaguely knew was escaping me, but I didn't know what to do.

A little was better than nothing, I reasoned at the time, so I resorted to the Promise Box method of spiritual nurture. I picked a verse for the day, meditated upon it briefly, sometimes memorized it. Recently as I sorted some old treasures, I found my set of small cards, edges worn, tied with a frayed shoestring. Perhaps the shoestring symbolized what the cards had been to me—a faltering faith in God's promises rather than a strong one in the Giver of the promises.

As life became busier and more complicated, I longed for a deeper knowledge of the Word of God, so I used a popular method of Bible study, best termed the existential method. It is used often individually and in groups. A passage is read and the reader is urged to explain what the words "now say." This method brings with it no great concern for what the words were intended to say to their original audience or in their original context. It is important to feel God speaking now, directly, to be blessed.

If I needed guidance, I prayed God to direct me to a verse that spoke to the issue, like the woman, who, after a long hard day, wondered what to do with the three hens she had penned under a tub earlier in the day. She opened her Bible at random, counted down seven verses to read, "Rise, Peter, kill and eat." Subconsciously, I wanted God to show me the same way. I wanted to know his will outlined in neon lights. I did not want the pain and responsibility of making a decision.

I experimented with other methods such as reading a chapter a day and using books of devotional readings. While all these methods provided some strength, they did not give me the solid base I needed to survive in a world not very kind to little old ladies in pink Nikes or young ones in sandals. I needed more, much more. Enthusiasm for Bible reading was not enough. Either I had to accept Christ and his Word as a living reality or forget it.

My Scofield Reference Bible was worn out, the binding broken and many pages loose and torn. I retired it from faithful service. Dispensationalism was becoming less popular anyway. I found some of the paraphrases popular in the Bible market too cutely familiar and the King James Version too distant. But how to begin Bible study again?

Though our society demands convenience foods, God's truth cannot be quick-served at the golden arches at discount prices. I would have to dig for spiritual food. As I have already mentioned, I was working through various problems such as self-acceptance, the purpose of suffering, and my new role as a single professional woman in a very much coupled society. Could the Bible actually lead me through the morass to sure footing though I was not a formal theologian? I believed it could. I had the advantage of living alone and of setting up an office in my home. The calls of little children no longer disturbed the early morning hours.

Now I work with several translations, a concordance, Bible dictionaries, handbooks, commentaries—and much patience. I keep notes. I sort, reject, synthesize. Quicky answers to sticky questions are not my goal. Studying the Bible this way has changed my life. I believe fewer things, but I believe them more intensely.

The biggest hurdle at first was the realization I might have to let go of favorite interpretations taught me by wise and respected Bible teachers whose own lives were impeccable and therefore seemed to support such views as unchangeable. For example, I had learned Christians should deprecate themselves for "he must increase and I must decrease." One older friend who had been infected with this teaching told me that as a young man he refused to sing solos because of his fear of taking glory to himself until he had interaction with another theological perspective that showed him singing solos was not sinful. My Bible study taught me that I had to love and respect myself before I could love my neighbor. The best prod to keep at regular Bible study has been to teach a Bible class, for as I study for it, I am studying for my own life.

I changed my attitude toward the Bible, but I also decided to change my language. Sooner or later, nearly everyone has to come to terms with the fact that language is alive but transitional, and when people are uncertain about their language—its origins, grammatical functions, and nuances of meaning—as they are today in a visual age, it changes even faster.

A few decades ago some Christians felt affronted at being nudged to shift their "thou" and "thee" prayer language to "you" and "your." Some remonstrated such language was too bold, too intimate to be used before the almighty God. Without the more comfortable archaic language, they felt naked before their Creator, unaware that "thou" language was actually the more informal address for God at an earlier period and "you" the formal usage.

I worked at changing archaic pronouns for God, which at first resulted in an awkward fumbling when praying in public as I exchanged thee and thou for you and your. I worked even harder at using more inclusive language for people. Today I seldom hear people saying, "Man for man," "to a man," "salesman" and similar terms. The challenge to "men of God" to rise and be done with lesser things has lost its punch in the aftermath of this language revolution. Masculine pronouns for generic terms are still sorting themselves out and will continue to do so for some time, but language change is here.

Bible translators are more open to correcting earlier versions that reflect an unnecessarily strong male bias. A critical passage is Romans 16:11, which reads in the Revised Standard Version, "I commend to you our sister Phoebe, a deaconess of the church ... a helper of many." Scholars now state the terms "deaconess" and "helper" should be translated "minister" or "servant" and "ruler." The office of deaconess was not instituted until the third century, so the term is inappropriate here. The translators didn't know what to do with a woman minister and so changed the word to suit their views.

Romans 16:7 is also under scrutiny. Paul writes, "Greet Andronicus and Junias, my kinsmen and my fellow prisoners; they are men of note among the apostles." Translators made the feminine Junia of the early manuscripts into the masculine Junias to avoid giving a woman the status of apostle. The word "men" is a translator's insertion. In other passages the Greek indefinite "anyone" has been translated to read "any man" tipping the meaning to lean toward men.

I presently reject the option of changing masculine terminology in Scripture referring to God to something more neutral. I recognize that we tend to image God primarily as masculine, although the Scriptures use many images to refer to him, including feminine ones. How one addresses or refers to God is a function of one's theology and another issue. However, if in hymns and prayers, we freely speak of God as a "rock, fount, shepherd, and lamb, would an occasional feminine metaphor be out of place—especially when the Bible speaks of the believer being "born of God"? I want to be free to change when I have thought through my theology regarding this issue.

Prayer remains a difficult assignment for me, and I believe also for many computer-age Christians. Although I sense a groundswell movement toward a more reflective life, it isn't a mass migration as yet. I have problems in other areas, but I want to keep reaching.

A friend asked me recently, "When did you get your life in order?" I chuckled. Yes, when? Does one ever? Adults tend to think they are the only one experiencing ambiguity and unexplainable feelings in adult life, so they shut up. They believe they are the only ones who haven't got it all put together in one neat package, so they hesitate to speak about the pilgrimage of the later years. Yet I am discovering that life at any point is a journey, a pilgrimage, lived with God, in which we continue to discover new aspects of his grace, love, and goodness.

CHAPTER 12

Jumping new hurdles in the journey

You come alive as a middle-aged adult when you are convinced that as an adult you are capable of more—and that the range of possibilities is not fixed.

—Found in my files

It's a reflex action. I shudder whenever I see someone grab a whopping handful of paper napkins to wipe up a spill. If a cloth were used, I reason, it could be rinsed and used again. Paper napkins make a dead-end landing in the garbage can.

I also agonize to see large amounts of food wasted, as at banquets, on airplanes, and even in restaurants. I recall walking out of a large city restaurant where a high school tour group had just eaten. Half-finished glasses of milk, large clumps of string beans, partly chewed pieces of fried chicken, and barely tasted desserts cluttered the deserted tables. I stood dismayed by this callous waste of food.

It's all part of the depression complex. As a depression child, I grew up conscious of the need to save and recycle. Water in which we had washed our hair was used later the same day to wash the floor. Wax-paper bread wrappers were folded and stored for future use. Envelopes were slit open for scratch paper. The mail-order catalog was taken to the outhouse for another look and a new use.

I brought certain habits out of the depression: buying with cash, using water sparingly and electricity frugally, and finishing the food on my plate. I also brought out memories of dust and grasshoppers, dirt roads, poverty, five-cent ice-cream cones, the value of a copper, and playing Run, My Good Sheep, Run in the empty lot.

From the depression years I carried with me into adulthood few artifacts—a round wooden cheese box, a doll, and a gabardine skating jacket—but many hopes of new things, like shoes and dresses, the joy of reading, a delight in little things, the fear of fires, a need for closeness, and a grasp of how strongly the human spirit struggles against all odds.

We who began grade school never dreamed of owning, let alone using, a typewriter. A computer was the equivalent of a trip to the moon. We, who belonged to the stubby pencil brigade, were not permitted pens until about grade three or four. Inkwells that spilled, pen nibs that broke or accidentally poked a neighbor's arm, were the obstacles to joining the next level of written communication.

A few grades later on, we were allowed fountain pens—the kind with little rubber tubes inside for ink. We felt we had arrived. And then, in adult life, we acquired typewriters and ballpoint pens—even the kind that could write underwater—although I don't know why. We were set for life, we thought. Then I was supposed to learn to use a computer.

"Mother," said my persuasive salesman son. "You can't let yourself get much older without learning to use a computer. It'll only get harder to learn."

"But my parents and their parents before them lived to a ripe old age without learning. Why do I have to?" I had all the arguments against change down pat.

"If you want a head start into old age, you've got to use a computer. Old age and computers are a compatible team. Can't you see yourself in your apartment several decades down the road—you're old, you're making doorstops out of catalogs—but with a computer you could have fun playing games—Mystery Sermon, Adventures in Medications, Board Strategy, and so forth."

"I can also see myself with a scrambled brain trying to learn all these new commands. When I was learning to write, the teacher only talked about curves, straight lines, and whether to write above or below the line. Now with a computer I'd have to learn about word wrap and soft hyphens and booting the system. I'm too old."

"Old, nothing. Why I've heard of people of ninety-five sitting in front of a keyboard and mastering it in a few hours. Nothing to it . . . ."

"If there's nothing to it, how come some of my computer friends are growing extra fingers in their desperation to reach all the keys? They try to hide their hands in their laps, and never shake hands any more. I've seen them . . . ."

"You're exaggerating, Mom. Using a computer has never yet harmed anyone's health. You'll soon find the keyboard exercises excellent for arthritis—nothing like it. What is more, you'll be an excellent model to your grandchildren. They'll admire you sitting at your personal computer, writing them letters, balancing your checkbook, logging into daily financial reports from New York to find out how well your investments are doing."

"But, son, I'm already drowning in information, and what if I haven't got any investments?"

"Well, think of other advantages. You could have your name put on a waiting list for admittance into a retirement center. Every day you could check the list to see if your name was getting near the top."

"But the thought of a computer in the house scares me. Furnaces scare me, car engines scare me. You know that. Even the insides of a bicycle spilled over the street sends me rushing for air to the other side. I could never deal with a computer talking back to me. I'm sure I'd break down and cry. I couldn't sleep nights, wondering if the computer was plotting against me for having told it to Change Logged Disk Drive when it wanted to Abandon File Without Saving."

"Listen, you could take a computer to bed with you and it wouldn't hurt a bit. They're tame as a kitten, like a pet, in fact. Before long, you'll find yourself saying good night to the computer every evening. It'll become your friend, your adviser—"

"But I can't afford one."

"Nonsense, never let money stand in your way. You don't want to enter old age without a computer at your side. If you haven't got one before you hit sixty, Mother, I can see you becoming a bag lady on the streets of Hillsboro."

Me, a bag lady?

No way. I bought. I learned. Now I wouldn't give it up.

My generation is being asked to learn one new skill after another. For example, women have to learn to speak in public and function as responsible committee members. The first time I spoke in public, a local women's gathering, I rattled through my short presentation, then sat down to tremble visibly for thirty minutes thereafter. The second time I worried beforehand and wore a longer skirt. The first time I got up before a mixed group at the request of the pastor, the shaking was both inward and outward. Was I possibly flouting not only human nature but God's laws this time? But after each time, even after some miserable flops, I was ready to try again despite the hazards of the road. Few men ever share what it means to travel alone so I assume they never make the *faux pas* I have suffered through.

For example, after receiving a request to speak, first I have to subdue thoroughly my typical female response to rush out to buy a new dress. Next, I face the first problem: Will the person sent to pick me up walk off with some other woman who fits the image of a woman speaker better? So how should I dress? Casual-like in sneakers and jogging pants or formally in a subdued tailored suit? I've learned since to dress in something that will be suitable for whatever occasion I face, for my baggage may not arrive with me, and time limits may make a change of clothes impossible.

I don't know how men get recognized, but I breathe great sighs of relief when I see someone waving a sign with my name on it or wandering around matching the news clipping in his hand to the faces of women in the waiting area.

It is a real joy, when, after wandering all over a six-acre airport, a woman leans over the down escalator as I am going up to ask, "Are you Katie Funk Wiebe?" But this delightful moment of recognition is more than offset by the picker-upper who, after having been assured that I am the person she was looking for, says, disappointedly, "I didn't expect you to look like this."

I've found that an unexpected hazard of the journey is that on arrival I may find plans have changed. Once, in a sudden surge of expectation regarding the size of the audience, the local committee changed the site of the gathering and forgot to notify me. So I sat in an empty church building wondering why everyone had left before I got there, and the committee sat in front of a full auditorium wondering why I had never arrived.

Another serious peril I've had to consider is platform behavior. Men bury their heads in their hands in solemn acts of devotion, or swing one ankle over the other knee and then lean back nonchalantly to pick out the sleepers and beepers. But a woman? Should I cross my legs at the ankles like the other women, making the row look like one side in a big game of X's and O's—or at the knees? Or not all so I look like the woman in American Gothic, straight, stiff, and steadfast?

What do I do with a purse? Hide it behind my chair? If I leave it in some back room, what if I suddenly need a handkerchief? Without pockets, do I carry a lace-trimmed hanky with my notes like a bride a bouquet? Or do I stuff my Bible with tissues?

Then there's the peril of the podium. These come in all sizes, mostly high, heavy, and massive, intended for six-foot, six-inch men, yet excellent for leaning frail female flesh against. But there are the other kinds. Eventually I've learned a method of attack for all kinds—those with only a small ledge, sending notes, books, and papers to the floor, forcing me to clutch all my belongings with both hands at all times; those with two ridges, which eases the situation; those that look like angel's wings in full flight, sliding everything into the center ridge; those that are so high I have to wear my bifocals upside down to see; and those that are so spindly, one good lean sends me and it to the floor.

Some have clocks glaring at me, rushing me through my material in half the allotted time. Others have microphones that pick up the slightest extra noise like metal sleeve buttons, forcing me to keep both arms slightly elevated at all times like a praying mantis.

Men never have to decide where to stand. Women missionaries used to stand slightly to the side, so as not to appear to be behind the sacred desk. If I want to see my audience, I find it's the better part of wisdom to stand in front of big podiums. If I don't want them to see the run in my hose, I stay well behind it.

Yet there are other decisions. Do I pound the pulpit and roar like thunder or do I aim for the rippling brook effect? Do I tell a story to give myself time to think? One soon recognizes ploys men use in public speaking, but also what gives them finesse.

I hesitate to write about the program perils, for their number exceeds legion. Do men also suffer in this regard? I have come planning to give a thirty-minute talk, so have brought only a few notes, to find I am expected to be responsible for each of three or four two-hour sessions during a weekend retreat.

Spending the night in strange places also has its risks. I wait with anxiety wondering what the night will bring in terms of mattresses—firm, soft, hollowed out; roommates—none, one or two; and bed or roommates—cats, dogs, gerbils, or human beings? And coverings. I froze through one night because I didn't realize the blanket was electric. I remind myself to feel the blanket well to find out if it has bumps and cords. I assure myself my hostess didn't deliberately plan for me to shiver through the night; she only forgot to mention where the hidden switch was located. I froze through other nights because I was accustomed to central heat and these bedrooms had none.

I've told myself to think through ahead of time to the morning when I will need bathroom privileges. Lack of information as to its whereabouts can constitute a major peril if I retire uninformed of this facility's location and awake the next morning with six similar doors facing me, none marked, yet knowing that the house is full of house guests, mostly male.

I've laughed at some responses to presentations. One woman came to me after what I thought was a fairly reasonable presentation—no Billy Graham speech, but possibly a lesser glow— looked at me with admiring eyes, giving rise in me to the expectation of profound words of affirmation. Then she said, "I sure liked your dress. Did you make it or buy it? Where can I buy the pattern?" Another time the fan said admiringly, "You have beautiful hands."

I try to forget the time when after having given the presentation my all, convinced I had moved mountains and molehills that day, I removed my corsage which someone had thoughtfully given me, changed clothes, and sat down at the table to enjoy a meal with fellow retreaters. The woman across from me smiled and said, "Tell us who you are, where you're from, and why you came." Ouch!

I found it disconcerting at the time to turn into a hog caller because the mike wasn't working or a choir was practicing the "Hallelujah Chorus" behind me. I've tried to adjust to shifts in time zones, to being stung by a bee twice, to helpful people who insist on carrying my brief case, to inviters who never write or phone after the first contact and haven't left an address or phone number.

I haven't been too upset when my hosts have told me they're sure I've probably been eating all day because all airlines overfeed passengers and so skip making a meal. I've even gotten over having to revive fainting committee members when I've presented my travel expenses and not fainting myself on being told openly they hoped I had a slush fund to bail me out, for their treasury didn't plan for all the costs.

On one occasion, the financial confusion turned to my advantage. I had been upset by the very low honorarium I received, but decided to forget it, and chalk it up to experience both on my part and that of the committee that had asked me to speak. I had hoped for at least $100, in fact, needed it. At the ticket counter I was asked to volunteer my seat due to overbooking and travel another route. In exchange I received $136.

Yet the rewards of moving about are well worth the trials.

I've learned a lot about church women. We are as varied as we are the same. We're moving ahead in kingdom work. Allowing women to travel means cross-fertilization of ideas, more female bonding, and development of greater confidence in ourselves as God's servants. I've met leaders, of course, inexperienced as I once was, who are tense before a session begins. "Are you nervous?" they ask to assure themselves their own nervousness is not unusual. Until women get more experience in leadership, there will be times of insecurity and uncertainty, but that is to be expected. I have noticed that women find it hard to close meetings strongly, possibly because we lack the inner authority to bless others.

Women will always be more concerned about appearance and comfort at meetings than men. Decorations and flowers are important to us. We like to eat on time and to stick to schedules. And that is to be commended. But some women can be quite upset when the coffee isn't ready on time.

In my limited experience on the road, I've learned why speakers demand to stay in motels other than for privacy. People ask the same questions again and again. Some seldom move into the area of ideas but stay with topics related better to the game of Trivial Pursuit. But I think it has more to do with a matter difficult to discuss openly. On one occasion as I was telling a story about my own past, the audience suddenly grew very silent. Here and there I saw someone wiping an eye. Why? I asked myself. It's only Katie speaking.

To know the power of words to affect people's lives leaves one vulnerable to the temptation to overstep one's integrity to manipulate and to say what is expected of one, to keep speaking after the well has gone dry, to become an impostor. Piety can become a sin when words are said for effect, when one speaks for God but does not identify with him, when one complacently mouths beautiful religious platitudes. I think some preachers quit because hanging onto their own integrity in the face of the pressures to speak what people want to hear becomes too difficult.

I gradually became aware that as I moved about I carried with me the intense fear of being considered a fraud, of moving away from reality to words that were not true for me. Then one day I read in the newspaper that this feeling is common to women moving into new arenas of work and thought in this age. It's called the impostor syndrome. Women can't quite accept they have the authority to do what they are doing because they have never been officially blessed for the task. They can't bless themselves because they see themselves as trespassers in uncharted territory. It helped to know I was not alone in this feeling and that it was another form of false guilt women carry unnecessarily.

Although I prefer writing to speaking, even though it requires more precision, speaking offers the opportunity of more immediate feedback. I admit I enjoy it, and often think if I had my life to live over, I would have been open to vocations other than teaching and writing. Yet unlike my attitude toward wiping up spilled milk with paper napkins, no skill is a reflex action. It requires hard work. Another generation of women whose roots are in the radical sixties rather than the depression years as mine were may accept public service for themselves as a given but struggle with another area—the right to stay home and look after the family.

CHAPTER 13

Password: Discipleship, not widowhood

*Modern American society has been phasing
out the status role of "widow," with its all-
pervasive identity and its main function of
maintaining the distinctions between a woman
so labeled, and wife, a single girl, and
divorcée...."*

—Helena Z. Lopata

I told a friend I had decided I was no longer a widow. I had never liked the term. Its connotations were all negative. It came to me suddenly that I didn't have to be one anymore if I didn't want to. Legally the term would always apply, but psychologically—that was another matter. I did not want my main identity for the rest of my life to be "widow."

"But you are a widow," she responded. "Your husband is dead."

"But I don't feel like a widow," I insisted.

She figured "widow" was better than single. A little more prestige. And in our society, take all the prestige you can get.

I disagreed.

In Zindel's novel, *Pardon Me, You're Stepping on My Eyeball*, the father of the young boy, the main character, has died. His mother is an alcoholic. The boy cannot accept the death of his father, so he keeps the urn with his father's ashes hidden under his bed. He writes himself long letters of advice, always ending with "Don't let anyone step on your eyeball."

What did Zindel mean by that? What happens if someone steps on your eyeball? Obviously, you can't see. As I associated more and more with all kinds of single persons (widowhood frequently changes the entire pattern of friendships), I sensed some of them were letting other people step on their eyeballs, making them literally blind to the wonderful things of life. Death or divorce had robbed them of a spouse; they were robbing themselves of the opportunity to return to life by clinging to a victim mentality with society as the villain. I knew. I had been there.

I returned home after one widows' seminar haunted by what I had seen. Among the numerous alert, alive women were some who looked repressed, depressed, unexpressed. I kept thinking I had seen flat cardboard standup figures fashioned by an amateur instead of persons made in the image of God and declared by him to be good. These women's entire stance said that life had become uninteresting and meaningless. They had not found the courage to recreate their lives. Their primary identity was widow. Yet is a person the sum of only one aspect of being?

In Bible times the identity of a widow was a poor person, frequently victimized, dependent on others for support, and generally considered a useless creature. Widowhood was the woman's main identity, although it was only one aspect of her life. Their dark widows' clothing identified them openly and set them apart. "Widow" became part of their name, an identity that included shame, reproach, and deep affliction. Instead of encouraging widows to stand upright, free, facing the world with joy and vigor, society had pushed them to the bottom of the social ladder and kept them there.

Many aspects of widowhood have changed since then. I recall my sister bringing me a black dress and hat to wear to my husband's funeral to satisfy social conventions. While today's widows are not expected to live out their unwelcome role wearing dark colors and subdued styles, or even to carry on under their deceased husband's name, other aspects of widowhood have changed less.

I think through conversations and correspondence I have had with widows from many parts of the country. Little notes. Long letters. Phone calls. Coffee talks. What has not changed is how few people understand how the death of a spouse affects the survivor unless they experience it. It doesn't take many weeks of widowhood to learn that widows or other people who do not fit into the coupled society are not a valid group but a problem, especially if they do not allow themselves to be painted into the backdrop.

A middle-aged woman, only two years into the struggle, shared her confusion and hurt at finding that the church hour was still one of the loneliest events of her week. Why did former friends and even relatives, who came in pairs, continue their round of social activities unmindful of her desire to remain part of that circle? While there is greater sensitivity to labeling Bible classes as "couples classes" or to holding "sweetheart" banquets, many widows and widowers admit that finding their way back into congregational life is almost a greater hurdle than working through their grief.

I am convinced that aging and widowhood will always be women's agenda. Older widows populate homes for the elderly and make up a large proportion of some church membership roles. While most congregations do not have official roles or lists of widows who get assistance, as Paul advocated to Timothy, some of these older women point to a welcome change: The financial situation is easier for more widows today than it was even a generation ago.

Women widowed years ago tell stories of incredible hardship to support families: scrubbing clothes on a washboard, doing housework, janitor work, or truck gardening—anything to keep a few dollars coming into the family treasury. Social security, better education, and more work opportunities ease the financial load. Widows today are not necessarily at the bottom of the economic ladder, listed with strangers, servants, and slaves.

What has not changed since Bible times is that widowhood represents one of life's biggest opportunities for spiritual growth—or for defeat. The new state, in which some people feel like a tree with roots severed and branches lopped off, challenges the person to work toward a new and clearer sense of self-worth in God's sight. Worthwhileness in his eyes is not determined by the marital state. Jesus Christ determines a person's identity—not one's marital state. It is only wrong to waste the years waiting for marriage or to set aside discipleship for widowhood.

The call to discipleship is for all believers. Some will work it out in partnership with a spouse; others will remain single. But no one is excused from discipleship. The password to a new life when one returns to the single state is discipleship. Sometimes a crisis is needed to bring this identity into sharper focus.

Psychologists tell us we get our self-identity from various sources outside ourselves. To a large extent others determine who we are or what we think of ourselves. If I ask, "Who are you?" what would you say? Probably your name, work or occupation, and position because you think that is what I expect. We tend to respond with the answer society expects of us.

Some friends were doing custom combining in the north. Their young children went along. Before long the young daughter of the outfit owner learned what response people wanted when they asked her, "Who are you?" She immediately said, "I am John Kaufman's kid." "Where are you from?" "Kansas." She didn't give her own name or the city she was from. When you're in another state and only a child, you tell people who you belong to and where you come from rather than your own name. That's what they want to hear.

Identity also comes from relationships. I grew up at a time

when women were identified by their husband's name. Some people have a hard time yielding an identity to a woman without a husband or without knowing her husband's name. Wiebe is a common name in my area. Frequently in the early years of my work at the college where I teach, I was asked, "Which of the several Wiebes who teach or work at Tabor College do you belong to?" People wanted some point of reference to identify me. Some women cherish this kind of identity determined by a husband, especially older widows. My mother, who was widowed at age 91, found it hard to open a letter addressed to Mrs. Anna Funk. It didn't seem right to her if for sixty-six years she had been identified as Mrs. J. Funk.

When we get our total identity from something impermanent or unstable, we are in for a rough tumble when circumstances change. Being a retired businessman has a hollow ring to it. Being an unemployed teacher is even more unsavory. To have to answer "I am an invalid" is even more objectionable. To suffer such drastic change in status in society affects one's self-respect.

People with power determine the identity or self-image of those under them by their affirmation or criticism. Minority racial groups are given their place in society by the dominant groups. Blacks were once defined by whites as less than human beings, only ⅝ of a person in the eyes of the law. In William Faulkner's *Absalom, Absalom*, the son of Colonel Sutpen, the main character, is discovered to have 1/16th black blood in him, inherited from his mother, and is therefore rejected and forced to live with the social limitations of a black person rather than as a white person, the way he was brought up as a child. That post-Civil War society said to the blacks, "You may be free, but you are still inferior." The blacks believed these words until their consciousness with regard to themselves was raised.

As a culture educates its children, there is much it tries to train out of them, including a primitive sense of equality. They must be taught the cultural walls or they act free. Black parents taught their children to keep their place in society in relationship to whites to stay alive. One young black man asked his father why he worked at precarious self-employment when he could have steady employment with a white employer. His response: "My son, a black man cannot be a man and also work for white people." He wanted to hang onto his own identity with pride rather than lose his integrity.

This determination of self-identity by what other people think of us occurs in various settings. Teachers establish the identity of students as stupid and inept, or bright and able, by reinforcing their view of the student by their attitudes, words, and actions. Adolescents with a certain social ease or even a false bravado may make life miserable for their peers by labeling a classmate as ugly, clumsy, a nerd, or other denigrating term.

The process of determining identity has infiltrated our society. The elderly are over the hill. Singles are failures at the marriage game. Divorced people are persons with a big X on their backs. Widows are less than whole people. Consequently, some people accept that their lovableness is determined by what they haven't got—youth, social ease, presence or absence of a spouse.

I found that in my quest for a new identity, many myths about the single state abounded, looking for takers and getting them. One of the most prominent was that all normal people are married. Abnormal people stay single. Singleness is a fallback position in life, never a permanent, steady, enjoyable one. A friend conversing with a new single acquaintance asked her about her family. When she replied that she was single, his shocked comment was, "How come you're so normal?"

I've found that singleness always requires an explanation at any age. It starts with "How come a nice girl like you never married?" Then, "How come you never married again?" The idea is that singles are abnormal in personality, treading water until the right person comes along. And as a result some do. A single friend, on leaving our community after nearly two decades here, told me with a wry smile, "Katie, do you know that I've lived here seventeen years temporarily?" She had never let down her roots and made herself a home. She was living out society's image of a single person.

Some people are firm in their belief that without sexual experience you become sexless. Singles can never be happy whole people until they find the right person to have sex with. One evening of watching television reinforces this erroneous idea dozens of times. Since sexuality is an aspect of entire being, it is not limited to sexual intercourse.

A third aspect I found myself now rejecting was that the single person is not quite as wise, as mature, as capable, as the married person. Because the gifts of the Spirit are given only to mature people, to have a gift for service you have to be married. It didn't take long to recognize that young married men were frequently given positions of responsibility in the church while both young and old single men and women, possibly wiser, more stable, better equipped and more capable, were left idle. One young single man told me that he had spent most of the last ten years of his life fellowshiping only with a singles group, not with a church body, because he felt he didn't belong. I sorrowed with him at the loss of his gifts and service to the church.

Where can widowed persons find that elusive identity that enhances their life rather than identifies them for life as a spouseless person and nothing more? Earlier I mentioned wanting to regain the zestful spirit I had enjoyed as a younger person. Did I really want to be like that starry-eyed girl in the feathered cap again? Sometimes as I taught, traveled, and talked, I caught a glimpse of her—free, self-confident, open, not easily cowed by others, with dreams. That was the remarkable thing—that younger person had dreamed dreams. That person back there had wanted to be and do. She had become class president, worked on the school paper, but for some strange reason had allowed her ambitions to be weeded out too thinly when she left home, married, and moved closer to the church. And especially when she was widowed. What had happened?

I examined many old wedding pictures in albums and books to see if I could make a connection somewhere with something I couldn't identify between this husband and wife before they were parted by death. I didn't know what I was looking for. What had brides of a century ago thought about on their wedding day as they faced the unknown? What had I thought about? How much did they know about life lived intimately with a man? More than I had? Some men in these fading pictures looked confident, almost arrogant, and the women inscrutable. But maybe that was because posing for a photograph took a long time.

Some of these women had been brought up carefully protected from contamination by a sinful and worldly society. Reading material was limited. Some of them married without knowledge of intercourse or the process of birth. Some were not prepared for the quick succession of births and the resultant drain on health, emotions, and finances. One older woman admitted that she had married at fifteen, borne seven children in ten years, had wanted to leave her husband but couldn't because she had no means of support. So she stayed and endured.

I heard of couples who after a number of births in quick succession never slept together again. I chuckled with Letty, the widow on the television series "Flickers," who when she mentioned her frequently absent husband, spoke of having had the privilege of being married but without the "inconvenience." An older friend told me how another woman gave her a long hooked wooden stick to use when she was in the tub to induce an abortion. She couldn't do it. Recipes for suppositories were secretly passed around during pioneer times. Why hadn't these women felt free to speak of their deepest needs and concerns about marriage? If openness about life hadn't been present then, it certainly wouldn't occur in widowhood.

I had to admit that at twenty I didn't know about homosexuality, bisexuality, or hermaphrodites. We children knew about crazies and dummies because they were part of our immediate environment. We watched carefully the young woman who occasionally came home from the "lunatic asylum" and we discussed her with one another for days thereafter—what she had said, what she had looked like, what she had done. Neighborhood children teased the young deaf mute boy at the corner into frenzied frustration, but we never questioned that he could be other than of low mentality. In our ignorance, because of societal conditioning, we identified these people in a way we could deal with them.

As Evelyn Underhill writes, "We have arranged to see what we want to see." We create our realities from the multitude of cultural traditions handed down to us, generation after generation, without reexamining them. So to move from perennial widowhood, we have to be willing to clean up false perceptions of it, spend less time waiting for life to happen to us, and less time being the victim.

I had allowed life to flatten me too easily. Now it was important that I return some texture to it.

For some time, on an impulse, I had tacked a sign above my desk, "What do I want to do before I die?" not in a morbid sense, but with the awareness that life was moving along swiftly. We die the way we have lived. If we have chosen a pattern of diminishing life choices, life ends with a whimper. If we choose a pattern of positive life choices, the end can be as good if not better than the beginning.

One day when I was speaking to a women's group, I experienced another Aha! experience—the awareness that love of life is one of the greatest gifts we can give another. If we have lived under the tyranny of ought's and should's, life becomes a burden. If we change the words "I have to do the dishes" to "I do the dishes because I choose," we change the experience. If I kept saying, "I have to live the way society says a widow should live," I became the bent woman in Luke 13, bowed over for eighteen years, never seeing the glory of dawn or sunset because her eyes were fixed to the ground. If I said, "I choose to live as a disciple of Jesus Christ with joy," I could stand erect and praise the Lord.

The redefinition of myself became an important task in the years following my first listing of goals. Obviously, my job, my marital status, my family, and my professional ties tell people partly who I am. But I had to see myself as God saw me. It's okay to be a widow, he said. It's okay to be single. But it's not okay to accept society's definitions of a widow, a single, as one not blessed by God. I was blessed by God. I could bless others. With that new awareness I moved from the dead edge of life where nothing happens to the growing edge.

Life is tough, and it's all right to say it's tough. I lament the loss of male companionship, the sensual experiences of marriage, the working together toward common goals, and the many other kinds of intimacies, but that doesn't mean life isn't good. What a wonderful day when I grasped that God loved me. And if he loved me, I was a worthwhile being.

When we make peace with our imperfections, we can accept ourselves as stewards of our personality, our gifts, our opportunities. When Christ redeems us he doesn't give us back a shell of muscles and bones with the Holy Spirit rattling around inside, but the right to let the Spirit direct our personality.

That event, as definite as any conversion, turned me into a freer spirit—someone not as easily threatened by what others did, for I was not responsible to them but to God for who I was. My concern was discipleship—obedience to Christ.

So, once again, I see widowhood as a psychological state. I am no longer grieving. I have made a new life. My children have grown up and moved away from home.

I am unmarried.

I live alone.

I eat alone. Meals are five-minute affairs or fifty-minute celebrations. Dishes can be shoved to an every-other-day schedule
or can be done every meal.

I've got time to kill and time to create. I have time to waste
and time to invest.

I don't need to share the television or the bathroom. My
toothbrush stands alone in the holder.

I don't think of what it was like to be married often. Sometimes when friends go out for dinner together, I wish I were
among them. Very much. Sometimes when I have some special
news I want to share with someone, the pain inside reminds me
I am alone. Then I hurt.

I'm no longer the poor widow with four small children
whom everyone pitied. I'm a college teacher. I'm a writer. I'm
a grandmother with four children each making homes for
themselves and their children. I'm a friend. I'm a Christ-believ-
er. I'm a person uniquely made in God's image. I'm a dis-
coverer.

Yes, I think I'm no longer a widow. I am Katie.

Grief is a process, a work that must be done. To grieve is
natural, but to grieve for years and years is not healthful. The
time must come to finish grieving and move on. Ahead lies the
challenge to learn new skills, sometimes in a vocation, more
often in decision-making or new types of services, always to
choose between good and better.

Those widows, who though hurting deeply and subdued by
experience, are more than survivors if they can say freely about
those who disregard or slight them, "Father, forgive them, for
they know not what they do." They fathom, if with dim vision,
that widowhood is not an unending state, but for a time. Part of
the healing process is to turn one's eyes once again to others
and to offer one's gift to the Lord. Like Elijah, when our brook
dries up, we have to move on. That's what I meant when I said
I was no longer a widow. I was choosing discipleship over
widowhood. I was moving on.

CHAPTER 14

Passing on the faith

*My capacity for care is rooted in my awareness
of personal power. It is this power that I use, I
spend, I "give away" as I care for others.*
                              —Evelyn Eaton Whitehead
                              and James D. Whitehead

It is impossible to examine the process of aging without en-
countering an important task of this period—mentoring. A
traditional task for men assuredly, but also a task for women.
Therefore a task for me.

My interest in mentors for women grew from an awareness
of my own young adult needs, those of my daughters as they
left home, and those of other young women. But also from a
study of Scriptures. I kept reading Titus 2:4 about older women
teaching the younger women and wondering what that had to
do with modern Christianity. It took a while to find out.

From even a limited study of social history, it soon becomes
apparent that women of one generation have always felt a
concern for the needs of the next one. Female students at
colleges and universities had "dorm mothers" and deans of
women to whom they could turn for advice and comfort when
they faced situations beyond their experience. Parents felt
comfortable sending their daughters to a college knowing that
at least one woman in that distant institution would keep a

watchful, loving eye on their child. Many missionary endeavors at home and overseas were initiated and supported by women out of concern for women and children of another country. These included orphans, the poor, and women behind the veil. Organizations, such as the now secular YWCA, and church groups were begun by women concerned about the spiritual nurture and development of young women in the church.

"Matron" and "housemother" have almost become antiquated words, if not concepts, yet the task of guiding the next generation and modeling an integrated lifestyle of faith and deeds is not outdated. Even though young women move to the cities, rent apartments, and become responsible for themselves, mentors are still needed.

But my interest in mentoring had another origin in addition to the above. Each time I sent my daughters into the city alone, I had a vague feeling of unrest I couldn't identify. They were leaving home and home community. "Let go," said one voice. I wanted to. At the same time I wished for some old-fashioned houseparents in the city to which they were going. Granted, girls today are more sophisticated, and know better how to manage, but their need for emotional support from an older person remains the same. I asked myself why church women haven't taken up this concern to a greater visible degree.

My interests in mentors also developed out of my own needs in life as my roles shifted from single person to wife, to widow, to working person, to writer. As a young woman, I wanted to write, but I knew no one who could advise me how to get started. Neither I nor my parents knew any writers, and I didn't even know it could be a calling. My parents encouraged my sisters and me to turn to teaching, nursing, or secretarial work because that was all they were familiar with. Only years later did I realize that what I had needed during those developing years was a role model and mentor, someone to guide, support, and encourage. Psychologist Daniel Levinson states that a mentor acts as sponsor and facilitates early efforts to realize the younger person's dreams. The mentor champions the young adult and models an effective style of adult living and working.

I see a mentor as a combination of heroine, role model, friend, and supporter in a relationship that extends over a short or long period of time. It is a form of adult friendship without sexual or parental overtones. Mentoring is simply one woman (or man) who's been over the path, smooth or rough, reaching back and helping the younger one stay on it. Her expertise isn't in recipes for scalloped potatoes and zucchini bread (those can be gleaned from magazines), but in how to face life head on with joy, courage, and faith in the Lord—and above all to risk, not because risking assures personal growth, but because growth is impossible without it.

The apostle Paul instructed the older women in the church at Crete in his letter to Titus to mentor the young women. He pleads, no, lovingly urges, the older women "to teach the younger women" (2:3). The word here for teaching is stronger than a formal teaching situation. He intended that the older women, mature in the faith, were to be the link that would bind the younger women to God. They were to be a steadying influence, a source of encouragement and strength. If they failed in this task, the Word of God would be open to reproach.

The course of instruction was the home, which may seem strange, yet the concept of the Christian family in which love, forgiveness, and self-giving were to be dominant, was new to women coming out of paganism. It was not love that bound husband and wife together, but political alignments, family wealth, and physical survival. Paul's concern was that the Word of God not be discredited by the new Christian families. If God's truth and power didn't work at this basic level of society, the home, how could it work at other levels?

I see mentoring as a type of servant ministry of older women to younger women—discipling but not in an authoritarian way. It is in effect saying, "I've been over this path before you. Use me as your model." Earlier I couldn't understand the apostle

Paul's bold words in 2 Thessalonians 3:9 encouraging his followers to use him as their model, but with the concept of mentoring in mind, the passage becomes clear.

"Isn't mentoring an academic term?" asks a friend. She was thinking of the ancient Greek man named Mentor charged with the care of the son and household of Odysseus when he went abroad. The word "mentor" admittedly evokes images of heavy-robed students with serious mien gathered around an aging pedagogue. Men, more often than women, have had mentors, or a close association with an older person because they are expected to move into new areas of thought and activity for which they need guidance. In the professions, particularly in corporate business, young men are groomed by experienced men from the ground floor up for higher positions.

In our early married life, I had often envied my husband his mentor in the pastorate. An older retired minister spent many hours with him, yet allowed Walter freedom in the public area. The older man found much fulfillment in seeing his young friend develop under his guidance. My husband mentioned he felt more secure knowing he had someone behind him to lean on when congregational problems got rough.

Women have had mentors, particularly in the extended family, but because the mentoring was in a different area—the private sector, they were not considered as such. Young wives and mothers attest they were guided, or encouraged, by an older woman through the crises of early housekeeping and married life. Marriages held up better after hearing an older woman tell of her loneliness, fears, doubt during pregnancy and childbirth, or her way of solving conflict with her husband.

Though dorm mothers are gone, young female students need someone to counsel them on college campuses in areas other than academic work. They need women as role models at all levels of college life, particularly in administration. As women have become a larger group on seminary campuses, some need an older person assuring them, "It's okay for you to be here in an M.Div. or Th.D. program."

Mentors are needed for women moving into the uncharted territory of church life and service. Women missionaries overseas have more often had a previous generation of missionaries to use as role models. As women move into more committee and board work, both here and abroad, they need both men and women to recognize and affirm their spiritual gifts for these new roles. They need someone to nominate them for positions, to make living space for them on boards and in conversation during breaks, and particularly to defend them against criticism and ridicule. A mentor acts as a buffer to committee members who feel threatened by the woman's presence.

A mentor is one who blesses the younger women as Jacob blessed his sons. Several years ago I accepted a speaking engagement in a city about three hours away. I left the house in the darkness before dawn, asking myself if I was crazy. What indeed did I think I was doing, traveling to this church? One word of blessing from leaders, male or female, would have changed my attitude and allowed me to go with joy and courage.

Women in the home, who have chosen to be career homemakers, need older women to affirm their freedom to make this choice and not feel downgraded because they aren't working outside the home. Women who don't stay home need affirmation in their choices as working women.

Young wives and mothers, especially those separated from their own families because of geographic distance, need the wisdom and steadiness of older women to assure them God's grace is sufficient for the most trying problems in family living. Closely graded Bible classes and other types of adult groups make it almost impossible for different generations to become close friends, yet it is a goal worth striving for.

"I limited myself too soon," a former assembly-line worker told me. "I went to a small rural high school and so never thought I could make it to college. What I needed was someone to encourage me to hitch my wagon to a star, not the first paying job. A woman who had returned to college in her forties got me started back."

Another woman said, "An older friend showed me I could change original decisions that I thought were life-lasting. I thought I couldn't make any changes after I started teaching, although I hated teaching. My friend had switched from secretarial work to nursing."

Jesus was a mentor to his disciple Mary. He defended her against the criticism of her sister Martha, who wanted Mary back in the kitchen when she chose to sit at Jesus' feet like any male disciple. He said she had chosen the better part. Her choice to sit calmly at his feet was a better one than Martha's choice to fret in the kitchen. At another supper, Jesus defended and affirmed Mary when she broke the vial of perfume over his feet. He told her critics her act would be remembered as a memorial of him.

Mentors are particularly needed for women in leadership. Each time I hear of the breakup of the marriage of some woman in the public sphere, my heart aches a little for her and for all womanhood. When men travel for church and business purposes, they return to wives who help recharge their emotional and spiritual resources. Unless husbands of women leaders are supportive in the same way, some such marriages may flounder.

Mentors are also needed for women moving into the professions and the arts. If a new mother or a new board member needs someone cutting away the underbrush to make passage easier, in the same way the developing novelist, poet, or artist needs an affirmer until she is established.

When I was quite young I knew I wanted to write. I wanted to discover the meaning of life through writing and let others know what I thought. But I never let my dream guide me until I was well over thirty, for I had no one to show me how to make it real. I knew no women—or men—who were writers, and books on writing and publishing were practically nonexistent.

Later, as a young married woman, far from my family, I struggled to be content at home in a community that frowned on women working outside the home. After enjoying the heady intellectual life and wide circle of contacts at college and in the working world, I found that wedded bliss in a stamp-sized apartment was eluding me. No one I knew was ready to discuss my questions. I was expected to know answers naturally.

Fifteen years and four children later, my husband died. How do I act and function now, I asked myself, as I ventured back into a society indifferent to single women. What do I do differently as a manless woman? Where are the single parents? I found a few, but they were floundering as I was. We asked questions together, but no one was giving out answers, and we had no yellow pages to turn to.

In recent years I have faced other new situations. After the first few times speaking in public, I sensed a strange discomfort, brought about in part through inexperience, but also because I didn't know what I was supposed to sound like. I had heard few women speak publicly, other than to give gentle devotions and restrained missionary reports. My mind drew a blank for an image to guide me. Should I pound and shout like Billy Sunday or attempt a more modified and gentle approach like the local pastor? Should I slip in popular male phrases like "I submit to you" and conclude with an authoritative benediction, arms outstretched, or forget the ending? I didn't know.

Now I consciously encourage younger friends in their writing goals, and when possible steer assignments their way. One free-lance writer sent me a copy of an article she had sold on my suggestion. A poet who was terrified to conduct a poetry workshop wrote to say it went well. She had wanted to back out. I wrote her that "they wouldn't have asked you if they didn't think you could do it." She knew she was good; she just needed encouragement once again. I like to affirm older women who have returned to school. Another young writer, after a series of contacts one summer, overwhelmed me with the largest bouquet of flowers I have ever received and a note thanking me for being her "friend, mother in the faith, and mentor."

I feel good about offering this kind of help because I know how much I wanted and needed it at various points in life. For a time I received it from an unexpected source when I was struggling as a would-be writer and a recent widow. My mentor showed up in a most unlikely person. She was neither a career person, nor a widow, nor a writer. She had never completed high school. Her own children were grown. She had a staunch faith in Christ and a keen interest in the church. And she was a neighbor.

For about fifteen years until she suddenly died, Mrs. Willems supported me in every endeavor from children's discipline to trying to get published. She told me about her early experiences as a farm woman moving into the city and her embarrassment at her clothing and country mannerisms. She was an avid reader. As she became more involved in women's church work, she took a Dale Carnegie course in public speaking. She respected my choices and supported my interests when I felt discouraged. "I'm praying for you, Katie. It'll work out." I felt she enjoyed watching me grow into greater confidence.

Like my older friend, a mentor helps the inexperienced person withstand group and societal pressures to conform to its values. The homemaker who says dejectedly, "I'm just a housewife," needs affirmation in flesh-and-blood form, not just in beautiful four-color illustrations in a magazine. Women who choose new roles need it as they check the fit of the new position.

Mentors model an integrated attitude toward work, recreation, career, and personal relationships. A Christian mentor also models the integration of faith into all aspects of life. The best kind of mentor is one who shows that struggle in life is unavoidable, and that one can meet obstacles and injustice without all gears promptly slipping into reverse.

Mentoring by men in midlife has long been accepted as a replenishing force for them. As women learn to accept this task, especially those who face the empty nest, they, too, will find new meaning. Losing the power to procreate forces women to redirect their energies. The empty nest can be a signal to continue nurturing beyond one's own family.

The challenge to the Christian mentor is to trust God's guiding presence within the community of faith, and to remember that the Spirit of Christ is with us from generation to generation. Mentoring is a way of gradually turning over to the next generation responsibility for our society and its institutions, including church and home. It is done deliberately and voluntarily. And if done in this spirit it is enriching and freeing. Giving up power and responsibilities gets easier. In the process of making room for others, self-indulgent attitudes and attempts to hang on to positions and to control are unnecessary. Mentoring does not bring with it the spirit of authoritarianism.

I find some older women hesitate becoming involved in the lives of young women whose lifestyles look so foreign to their own. Obstacles to "teaching the young women" come primarily from within ourselves. Women have been taught to compete with one another more than to accept each other as sisters. Women have been encouraged to compete for boyfriends, for grades, and for jobs. Some of them say they prefer men for friends; to develop friendships from among their own sex is a waste of time. To develop a friendship with an older woman is even more of a waste when the whole world is waiting to be conquered. What can Jenny's grandma do for them?

Some successful women fear that if more women are helped into the circle of leaders, writers, and speakers, they may be surpassed and eased out before they are ready to leave. "I made it the hard way; no one helped me, so why should I help anyone else?" said one successful office manager. She had made it on her own. Others could follow her example.

I hear other reasons why Paul's word to the older women at Crete wouldn't work today, but my main concern is that in this age of swift social, technological, and economic change, that demands independence of us, not mutual caring, we need another spirit to live by—the Spirit of Christ. Servanthood as exemplified by an older person serving a young person is this spirit. Psychologist Erik Erikson calls it generative caring. I call it passing on the faith.

CHAPTER 15

A voice from the past

Christianity is a rebellion of everything that crawls on the ground against that which has height.

—Dorothy Soelle

It came as a shock to me that I had inherited some theology from the religious tradition I belonged to that I had never made my own. I knew I was expected to support it, even possibly live up to it. But deep down I knew it belonged to the church, perhaps to my parents, but not to me.

One day as I sorted a box of old papers after my move, I nearly threw out a thick letter written on pale blue paper. Instead I opened it. The date was 1947, after the war, and the signature read "Mike." Mike? Who was Mike?

Dear Katie: Remember the bargain we made in—I forget when—that after so long—I forget how long—we would get in touch with each other some St. Patrick's Day and see how far— and how far apart—grade 12 of old had gone.

Had we, that small cocky grade 12 bunch, made such a promise? I had forgotten, but Mike, a classmate, had remembered, and apparently I had thought his letter worth keeping.

I suppose most of those in our grade 12 class now tread the highroads and byroads of fame. Mike had always been a bit flowery. *I took the road back. As you know, I was attending Normal School, seeking those laurels of learning to impart to others—but not that for me, said Fate.*

I made myself comfortable on the trunk as I looked for the next page.

The call came—first to kill and then to help in doing so. I took a stand and our ways divided. I suppose that was the greatest division point of our paths. Here I think I turned back. I spent four months at hard labor in Moosomin Common Jail.

Now I remembered. Mike had been a "conchie," as they were then called. A Doukhobor conscientious objector, during World War II. Doukhobors and Mennonites, both opposed to war, were always mentioned together in government orders and news reports.

My mind flitted back to September 10, 1939. I had been in grade 10 about a week when our teacher announced that Canada had joined the Allies in war against Germany. My classmates and I listened quietly from our straight rows of bolted-down desks as he talked. The boys scuffed their new winter school shoes on the oiled wooden floors or played with their pencils. Our country was at war. I didn't know what that meant. Maybe they had an inkling.

The heavy black newspaper headlines the next day thundered the news "CANADA AT WAR." I searched inside me for some bit of information or experience out of the past to settle my fears. I sifted through bits and pieces of wartalk shared by my parents, who had grown up in the Ukraine in southern Russia and had lived through a horrible war and a worse revolution. Families had been separated, fathers killed or imprisoned, brothers had disappeared. Plundering bandits, sickness, and famine had added to the hardships. I comforted myself that the war zone would never reach across the ocean to the tiny village of Blaine Lake in northern Saskatchewan, where we lived.

Conscription didn't begin at once, but young men were encouraged to join the army. Canada needed soldiers to fight in the front lines in Europe with the Allies. Within days of the war announcement, some of the older high school boys left for the city and came back almost immediately dressed in heavy khaki uniforms, putteed boots, and the little flat caps they tucked into a tab on their shoulders. They burst into the classroom even though the teacher was talking, eyes bright, step jaunty, to say good-bye and to show off their uniforms to the girls. Often they hung around until recess, joking with the students about army life and the adventure ahead, yet reluctant to leave their youth behind.

I knew that I had been born into a Mennonite family and that Mennonites traditionally didn't go to war, but I had never discussed this matter openly with anyone. Why should I? Girls didn't need to make decisions about the army. Fighting was a man's job. Deciding not to fight, therefore, was also a man's decision.

On September 23, 1940, shortly after my sixteenth birthday, I registered at our local post office according to National Registration Regulations of the National Resources Mobilization Act passed in late spring of that year. The act required people to place themselves, their services, and property at the disposal of the King. I carried my card in my wallet faithfully throughout the war.

My parents, not two decades in this country, were concerned that our family obey the laws of the land that had offered them and about 20,000 other Russian Mennonites refuge during the 1920s when the Bolsheviks were pressuring them in the Ukraine to give up their traditional beliefs. Other countries had turned down their request for a new home. The Mennonites were grateful to the Canadian government. Mother and Dad were convinced that national registration for my sisters and me would mean only being placed in some essential industry. War in a good country with a just government was somehow different from war in an unjust and godless land.

Most of the boys in our two-room high school stuck to their studies until graduation, but male teachers resigned one after another to become officers in the military. I recall one teacher, rejected because he was overweight, grimly stalking the dirt road around the quarter section evening after evening in his personal war with his bulk. One day, he, too, was gone and re-placed by a woman teacher.

Young men who could afford a university education received a military deferment. Those without money were gobbled up by the military unless they were needed on the farm or were conscientious objectors to war. I didn't sense a great deal of unity as to what a conscientious objector was. Some of them enlisted in the army as noncombatant medical personnel. Others worked in forestry camps, essential industries, or on the farm.

I enrolled in a short business course, though I wanted to at-tend university, but the country was still pulling itself out of the depression, and government loans were not available for liberal arts programs.

My friend Mike was a member of a Slavic religious group, many of which lived in our area. Doukhobor means "spirit wrestler," and was the derisive nickname given to this sect by the Greek Orthodox in Russia for resisting or wrestling against the work of the Holy Spirit in their lives. In response they adopted the name with a new interpretation: They would not fight with weapons, only with the spirit of truth. They refused to kill humans or animals, and therefore were vegetarians. We used to joke they were so opposed to killing, they trapped houseflies and then released them outdoors rather than swat them.

I liked individual Doukhobors like Mike, but I found the quaint colorful costumes of the women and the strange cus-toms of a radical branch of the Doukhobors called the Sons of Freedom discomfiting when my denomination was categorized with them. Doukhobors didn't generally accept alternative civilian service as an expression of their pacifist position, so some, like Mike, landed in jail.

I read several more lines from Mike's long-forgotten letter:

You have no conception what an experience Moosomin Common Jail was mentally, physically, and especially emotionally. In these four months I must have aged many years. And then freedom. The sight of the sunset, the green of the grass, the breath of free air, the cool of the lake, the whisper of the wind in the trees—all this for a whole day! And then the usual attention, incomprehension, apprehension, dishonorable mention, and back to serve another nine months of hard detention. Again the bars—and I don't mean chocolate. Again the feeling of one's very soul being wrung in the hands of the state.

Of course, it had its redeeming traits, too. A man must learn to live with himself there—the first real lesson in life. There are also a host of amazingly interesting characters, for "while the mediocre tread the highways, the saints and scoundrels meet in jails." I saw a hardened thief's heart break into the sputtering sobs of a baby due to lack of consideration from a mother he loved; and I wrote love letters for an illiterate friend. But such is life, and the essence of life.

So, while Mike, the nice guy with whom I had spent hours working trig problems, was swinging a pickax in prison, I was typing legal deeds and doing the bookkeeping for a law office. During the early war years, I swung back and forth emotionally like the pendulum of our large wall clock. I was caught between the hard reality of schoolmates being shot down overseas by enemy fire (Joe with the slicked black hair and friendly manner never returned) and the romantic notions about war that bloomed and faded with the instability of the times and with the war novels I read in which young women made passionate promises to overseas sweethearts to be true forever. Life was pretty humdrum pounding a typewriter in a law office, and yet there seemed very little during those years we could grab hold of and find solid.

In the meantime, as the war accelerated, we coped with shortages and with rationing of sugar, meat, fats, gas; and with standing in endless lines to buy everything from hose to Kleenex. Older women knitted socks and caps for the Red Cross to distribute. Everyone bought war stamps. Young women were beginning to enlist for desk and technical jobs and as nurses.

On August 10, 1945, while I was vacationing near one of Saskatchewan's serene but cold northern lakes, the word filtered through that world peace was imminent. All evening my friends and I jammed the front seat of the only car with a radio to catch the news. Finally we heard it. The words of Japan's surrender could be distinguished midst the crackling noises of the receiver. The war was over. We cheered and hollered and talked late into the night, contemplating what changes this might mean for our lives.

I never learned to know well any strong opponent of corporate violence for religious reasons until about a year after the war. They were all busy in alternative service or noncombatant service assignments. I was engaged to be married to one about the time Mike's letter arrived in 1947. Walter, my future husband, had spent 4½ years in various forestry camps at 50 cents a day. He passed the test for simple living *cum laude*.

After the war young men like Walter and Mike, and those who had been in the military, picked up the current of life where it had been diverted earlier. And those of us who had been working at regular jobs continued as before. It took many years—several decades—before I sensed that somewhere, back there during the war years, my thinking had taken a sharp detour around an important issue.

Not until after Walter's death did I go back to that detour to find out what had happened. Somewhere in the New Testament Christ had taught an ethic of repaying hatred, harsh words, or violent action with love. He had taught it to all his followers, young and old, male and female. Gradually this teaching was diminished as some Christians identified with the state in countries like Switzerland and Germany. Governments, even if closely related to the church, found they couldn't keep peace with their enemies without using a club or a gun.

Then, later, some people like the Anabaptists rediscovered this truth of nonviolence as a powerful weapon to witness for Christ's love. But as they stood up for this truth and others, they were persecuted and had to flee for their lives. Gradually they became weary of fleeing and made a truce with themselves and with their enemies. Though in many places their descendants lived isolated from the rest of the people of the land, when their country was at war, they were expected to help defend it. But they couldn't do so for reasons of conscience. Out of loyalty to a higher authority than the government, they bargained for the right not to bear arms. And countries who wanted them as settlers agreed to this request.

Gradually the teaching that Christ had intended for everyone became a teaching for only some people—the young men who had to decide about becoming part of the military forces. It was reduced to one issue—taking up arms. And it became a tradition rather than a way of life accepted by each new generation for themselves. Fathers with many sons growing into military age, and sensing the threat of war in the near future, sometimes packed up and emigrated to another country. A father with a family of girls wasn't as concerned.

I was strangely surprised when, as I studied my own parents' stories of their conversion, I discovered that my father had become a Christian *after* he had spent several years as a non-arms-bearing medical orderly in the Russian army. His role in the military was obviously based not as much on personal convictions as on traditional folk views. To have been born a Mennonite granted one such immunity.

That was part of the sorting out I now had to do as an adult woman. Mixed in with the religious objection to war was another complex issue. Some people accept that it is okay for men to fight in battle and risk being killed, but it isn't okay for women to get involved in actual warring because they are too innocent, too gentle, too nice, to be involved in something as diabolical as hand-to-hand combat or bombing enemy territory. Because men are considered coarser, rougher, less moral than women, they are assumed to be better able to handle the horrors and rigors of struggling with mortars in deep mud, with life in trenches, and with destroying civilians by napalm or bombs. Women should be protected from the grosser sins. For this reason men are the prime target for the military and asked to recognize at age eighteen that the consequences of their decision to become a member of the armed forces might end in permanent disability or even death. Women are not asked to make such decisions.

One day the enlightenment came—not as a flash of understanding, but as a gradual awakening. The thinking that women are too good for war identifies women with the inner life, with the home, and with absolute good; and identifies men with the public domain, the outer life, and with evil. It loads sin and evil on men and excuses women not only from taking part in the evil of war, but also from openly accepting the task Christ gave them to be peacemakers. It allows them a safe retreat to protected territory, while men fight their battles for them on all fronts, spiritual and in the military.

I didn't like what I had thought through because it released me from hard thinking and more careful and caring living.

I started reading memoirs and biographies of Anabaptist men and women. I learned that during wartime, women often suffered as much, if not more, than men in the front lines. They endured unspeakable physical, mental, and emotional horrors and hardships though they never came near to handling a gun.

Further, my own heart told me that girls and women had as much evil in them as boys and men. They could be as hateful and violent, even if they didn't get into as many fistfights as children. The belief that they shouldn't have to face real evil and sin because they were too innocent didn't hold true.

We are always heirs to the climate of opinion in which we grow up. Unless we spot weaknesses and face them head on, they become part of us. I had accepted the idea that peacemaking was only for men. My church had excused me from rigorous thinking about nonresistance during war—but also during peace. I had not had the models of Abigail, wife of Nabal, who made peace with David's soldiers, or models of more contemporary peacemakers held before me, because the matter was not considered pertinent to young women.

Then I faced the toughie. If I accepted this kind of thinking that excused me from facing evil, I also accepted release from the responsibility of living and working for peace. I never knew why Mike was a conscientious objector. He had never told me directly, and I had never bothered to find out what Doukhobors believed on this issue—or for that matter, what I believed—because I didn't have to.

I scanned the rest of Mike's long letter. He had more court hearings to settle his status. Eventually he was released from prison to work elsewhere. I dropped to his last paragraph.

I suppose we have drifted. I expect we have. I would appreciate it if you would scribble me a note telling me who and what you are now, so that should we ever meet, we would not pass each other as strangers.

Who am I now, Mike? Not the girl you knew in grade 12 chemistry and physics. Not the girl you wrote to when you got out of jail. I hope I am someone wiser. I hope I am someone who has begun to understand that peacemaking is for all Christ's followers.

I know I am someone who recognizes that this generation of young women—your daughters if you have any, and mine—will have to decide how peacemaking fits into their lives. Mike, do you, too, tremble because you know they may not be ready for such a decision because of our present indecisiveness about such matters?

CHAPTER 16

I have tended my own garden too long

No one can truly know Christ, except he follows him in life.

—Hans Denck

"What do you think of all this?" the man waiting by the church door asked me. The question surprised me. The man was a stranger. What difference did it make to him what I thought of the peacemaking conference we were both attending?

I told him I had come to learn. That I was a member of a historic peace church in which some members weren't fully convinced of this position. That I was working my way through the nuclear arms issue and other related matters. That I recognized that prejudice is often rooted in theology. He admitted to a similar pilgrimage. He was also working his way through "all this."

I wasn't at the conference to learn how to demonstrate. I wasn't there to study the biblical basis of nonresistant love. I had gone to find out if, like the people in Nazi Germany, I was blind to something so huge I couldn't see it for looking at it.

One speaker said, "One must see evil to respond to it. We have to see the crisis to be open to it." He mentioned that a relative of one of the more than nine hundred persons who drank the fatal cyanide in the Jonestown massacre several years ago had asked, "Why didn't someone tip over the tub of cyanide-laced Kool-Aid?" That simple act might have saved hundreds of lives.

Why didn't someone reach out and dump the tub?

Possibly, and probably, because that someone had never even tipped over a thimble before.

Like many of us?

Yes, I think so. We tell ourselves that when the big crisis comes, when people's lives are seriously threatened by sin and evil, we will rush heroically into the fray. With great spiritual strength, we will push over tub after tub, freeing people from sin's domination. But we're wrong.

We think evil will invade our lives and nation like a mighty army. But Satan doesn't work that way. Evil moves into our lives slowly, gently, easily, until we are so used to it, we feel comfortable with all aspects of it, big and small. When the tub of poison is finally sitting in front of us, and everyone is urged to drink, we don't recognize it for what it is and we're gripped by a paralysis of will. Instead of action, we are ready with alibis:

•What will people think if I should speak out loudly against what I consider a serious wrong in our society? To speak out might harm the business prospects of this community or the church's budget.

•It's the politician's job to set things straight and to make rules for people to live by.

•Pastors should lead out against sin and evil and show the rest of us the way.

•It's the job of men, not women and young people, to settle serious issues. They should start tipping the tub.

•Nonresistant love isn't part of my theology just now. I believe Christ calls us to evangelism and missions, not to fight evil in systems and structures. These nonresisters don't speak my language.

•I simply don't do peace (or tip tubs or wash windows).

For me to shift from a frame of reference that accepted that the only and best way to change the world was to win people to Christ, one by one, to a theology that included that systems and structures sometimes have to be changed also was as difficult as trying to get a car with a broken gear to move ahead.

I had long accepted that the gospel meant individual faith in a personal God for redemption. That there might be evil in systems didn't make much sense until I acknowledged that good functioned in systems also. Evangelism has been organized into a system with professional evangelists, missionaries, mission boards, publications, and other media, all combining to give the gospel greater power. I approved of this system and of those which organized good works into systems of relief and development to aid third-world countries.

Surely sin could invade those systems that were originally neutral, such as government and politics. Social action and justice were snarl words in my early thought. Leaders said sin resided only in individuals and must be fought one on one. To take a stand against poor housing, underpaid employees, indiscriminate practices in employment, especially against minorities, or nuclear armament escalation was taboo. One bumper sticker was all right, but not a march of ten people. Never of a hundred.

I sensed that to start tipping the tub meant countering sin in structures that affected me most personally and most immediately, and in particular, rethinking my meaning of violence.

Violence is a strong word, connoting harm, pain, suffering, and aggression, possibly bloodied heads and broken bones. Although numbers of people experience physical aggression each day, I have never had my face smashed into pulp, my head clobbered at a board meeting, or my body knocked into the chalkboard at school. Like others, I have tended, therefore, to associate violence with street muggings, rapes, murders, and robberies, with wife and child abuse in other people's homes, with riots and wars in other countries far removed from my quiet corner. Yet to be serious about making peace a way of life, I needed to change my definition of violence to include more than the mugger's blow to the jaw and a gunman's bullet to the head.

Where did I see violence in daily life? Where did I use it?

The classic definition of violence distinguishes between force and violence. When force is good, it is called benevolence. The dentist's use of force to pull a tooth, or a lifeguard's use of force to save a drowning person, is deemed acceptable. Unacceptable violence is force used to limit the rights, well-being, and dignity of a person, destroying God's image in that individual.

Violence says to the other person by word, action, or attitude: "You are less than a person. I am up here. You belong down there." It prevents the victim from functioning as a free moral agent by fostering fear and doubt that the person can control his or her own life, or is not as worthwhile as other persons. Violence destroys people and their relationships. Love draws together and restores to life.

According to Jacques Ellul, all violence is the same whether it is physical or psychological, overt or quiet, personal or institutional. Jesus taught his disciples that the thought is equivalent to the deed (Matt. 5:22, 28). We tend to sift out certain kinds of violence and relabel them more acceptably as "personality conflicts" or "opinion differences"—justified behaviors to attain a good cause. Yet each such event sows seeds for greater and more violence. These relabeled, and sometimes unlabeled, acts of violence abound in daily life. I listed some I had noted recently:

An administrator seemed determined to destroy an employee's career. The young woman's voice rang with terror as she faced hard-nosed authoritarianism for the first time. "I'm probably too independent to suit him—not one of those clingy types who kowtow to his every ego-need," she said. "But how can he do this to me?" She felt powerless.

A pastor was informed by letter that the vote of confidence by his congregation had not gone in his favor. He would be expected to leave in three months. He felt destroyed, broken, and unhinged by the sudden and swift move to oust him without personal contact.

"She treats me like a child. She makes daily lists of things for me to do as if I were a five-year-old. Then she looks over my shoulder constantly as I work. She doesn't trust me," said a middle-aged experienced office worker, feeling robbed of her self-worth.

"We want one of our own people for such an important position," an American black overheard someone say in the church lobby of the nearly all-white congregation he attended. Clearly this congregation was no different from any others. Blacks would never make it to positions of responsibility. Not good enough for that. He should not have let his name stand for election.

"My husband won't even let me get a library card," she whispered to me. "Waste of time as far as he's concerned. He's afraid I may get into the women's lib stuff. I'm supposed to serve him and the children—nothing else." She moved on quickly so she wouldn't be noticed talking to me.

"We have no openings for you—sorry," said the church moderator to the woman seminary graduate applying for the position of assistant pastor. She had many years of teaching experience before seminary. A few weeks later she heard they'd hired a young inexperienced man without degree or experience.

"You can't publish that story about the board," ordered a church administrator. "The constituency can't handle that much unfavorable news at one time. You'll hurt giving at a time when it's much needed." The editor knows church boards have more political clout than he does, and gives in.

I could have extended my list to include the cutting remark, the refusal to speak to spouse, neighbor, or friend because of some imagined slight. Around this daily kind of violence in intimate relationships is another circle of violence, such as rape, muggings, burglary, and murder. Around that one, another circle that includes exploitation of workers by a factory owner, raising rents of the poor to get rid of them, withholding information from a constituency or laundering it before releasing it, "releasing" persons who disagree with people in control. The circles grow larger to take in more people and more territory through riots, political oppression, economic imperialism of multi-national corporations, colonial exploitation, and war.

To make peace a way of life meant I had to stop my uncritical acceptance of one kind of violence—psychological violence in daily life—while decrying another kind—physical and political—far removed from my private life.

I soon found out that violence in routine situations is difficult to deal with because it sometimes wears the language and dress of Christian virtue. Because success often seems to be the reward of such violence, psychological violence looks like the right approach to problem-solving in personal and institutional life. Because it cannot always be spoken of in mass terms and be related to specific events, it is dismissed as trivial and inconsequential. However, the feeling of being raped by the harsh, biased decision of an administrator, or being slashed by the unjust criticism of an underling, is no less painful because it happens to people one at a time and out of sight.

Because every situation where two or more people live and work together has potential for violence, to make peace a way of life means bringing Christ's love into every relationship, especially those mentioned by Paul in his ringing statement of unity in Galatians 2:28: male/female, social hierarchies, and racial diversity.

Every time we face a violent situation, we respond according to patterns we have seen modeled before. The neighbor's dog has dug up my tulip bed for the third time. It is too late to re-plant this fall. What do I do?

I can repay violence with violence. I can buy a gun and shoot the dog. If someone harms me or my property, my human reaction is to protect and vindicate myself: "My cause is just. I must prove I am right and get revenge, not just an eye for an eye and a tooth for a tooth, but two eyes for an eye and a jaw for a tooth." Someone has to pay.

Today women as well as men are encouraged to buy handguns and take assertiveness training to deal with the ag-gressor who threatens life and possessions. Women are en-couraged to take karate lessons, carry Mace, and learn to knee an attacker. So if the neighbor's dog damages my flower beds, in an aggressive mode I could present the neighbor with a bill and alert the other neighbors to the objectionable menace run-ning loose in our midst. I think people fall into violent patterns because they are most natural and normal. Might makes right. The end justifies the means.

We accept this pattern of solving differences because specta-tor violence is one of life's most enjoyable experiences, often head-of-the-family approved. Television blood and thunder by bullet, word, and action belittles life and human relationships. A character kills deliberately, then without any show of emo-tion steps over the body, to crawl into bed with the victim's wife. We switch off newscasts about war, famine, and earth-quakes when we weary of them. We train ourselves to be bored, shocked, amused, or to watch the screen passively.

Violence has become such an integral part of the fabric of daily life, to excise it would mean a radical change in lifestyle and to become traitor to one of life's greatest pleasures—watch-ing someone get clobbered psychologically or physically. So the issue of violence is deliberately cut from personal and institu-tional agenda, or dealt with by means of sweet talk, proof texts, or silent support of an unjust and violent status quo to keep a lifestyle intact.

The strong need to be a winner is an integral part of this pattern of violence. Children learn military games from the toys and games parents supply as soon as they can point a forefinger and say "Bang!" At football or hockey games, parents and children join in shouting, "Kill! Kill!" as the players slash at each other with sticks and fists. "But we don't mean what we say," they respond when someone remonstrates. "It's just words." Yet language scholars argue that even as thought affects language, so language affects thought. We can't escape the effects of our own language on us.

The pattern of violence is passed on through culturally ingrained prejudices against the poor as lazy people who enjoy their dependence on the government, of minorities as inferior and unprogressive, of women as deserving less pay than men for equal work. Emma LaRoque in the *Defeathering of the Indian*, describes her encounter with prejudice, which is simply the subtle use of violence to maintain one's place in the pecking order. One year the school board, without warning and without consultation with the Indian children's parents, closed the small, mostly Metis, school and forced the children to attend a large predominantly white school. Because of poor vision, Emma had been sitting in the front row in the Metis school. It took only one class session in the new school to drive her back to the "Indian row."

From such attitudes, we subconsciously pick up an image of humanity as dispensable and a style of life in which the way up is to push others down. We also develop a language that not only reflects our thoughts but influences our actions. Whether it's the neighbor kid taunting another child with "Bully" because he's been offended, a church pillar denouncing another woman for aspiring to the pastorate, or a board suppressing discussion of issues because they don't like conflict, the result is always the same: feelings of degradation and a loss of unity in the family, neighborhood, or congregation.

A second approach I could use in my problem with the

neighbor's dog is to talk conflict resolution loudly, with great enthusiasm, particularly with regard to nuclear armaments and war taxes, but never consider how Christ's love might apply to my situation. Such an attitude means we see the death principle operating at only one level—institutional overt aggression—not at the personal level. For example, one church leader noted how parents were much concerned about peace issues, but weren't as concerned about caring for their children whom they dumped on the baby-sitting service at the peace conference and sometimes forgot were there. An area junior ball team received the good sportsmanship award at league playoffs. The official making the award made it quite clear, however, that the award was going to the young men and not to their parents, who at times had become overly involved in game decisions. A few parents couldn't see why they had been singled out for admonition publicly.

This much-talk/little-action approach has another subtle aspect that occurs when dominant groups manipulate subordinate groups through incorrect teaching to keep peace. The poor, for example, are taught to submit to God in their suffering because God wills it and that they will be better Christians as a result. During slavery, blacks were taught that God had cursed the black race, making them inferior to whites. In a society in which there aren't enough men for all women to marry, women are still being told that their only fulfillment should come from being a wife and mother. For some women to speak of having heard God's call to ministry in America is ruled out of order. Teachings that are structured so that they can be accepted only in the terms offered are a form of violence because there's always a catch-22. If the person wants to remain acceptable in the Christian community, he or she has to assent to all or bow out.

This approach to peace, or more accurately, to the absence of conflict, is particularly harmful if the person admonishing, ruling, or teaching is in some position of special authority, like a minister, teacher, elder, husband or wife, parent, wealthy businessperson, or political leader. Black history scholars write that once established, a system of oppression such as slavery, colonial oppression, or American ghetto life, requires relatively little overt violence to maintain. The oppressed have internalized the rationale for their own suffering. Some Southerners used to boast that their slaves were happy and didn't want any other kind of life. Raised in the system and sheltered from the violence of lynchings, whites believed in slavery sincerely.

Such people allow themselves freedom to control other people without their power being questioned because that's the way it's always been done. In Shirley Jackson's short story, "The Lottery," every year in June the citizens gather to hold a lottery. Some aspects of this annual ritual have changed, the meaning behind it has long been forgotten, but the citizenry responds faithfully to the forceful need to continue the tradition of the lottery in which the winner is stoned to death. No one questions the system—the lottery itself—only departures from traditional procedures of holding it. Likewise, we seldom question our own bigotry and intolerance, unless it involves lynching or tarring and feathering. But the intolerance is there, nevertheless, and sometimes only very subtly manifested.

Jesus taught and modeled a love that was not a tactic, gimmick, or technique, but a deep-rooted willed attitude (not emotion) that has the welfare of the other person as its greatest concern. In Matthew 5:38-42, he presented his disciples with an alternative method of dealing with situations with potential for exploding into violence.

1. "*If someone strikes you on the right cheek, turn to him the other also*" *(Matthew 5:39)*. The talon principle in Old Testament law kept the spiral of violence in check by allowing the offended or victimized person to exact an eye for an eye and a tooth for a tooth. Jesus reviewed the principle, making a radical change. A slap on the face, particularly with the back of

the hand, was a grievous insult rather than an attempt to injure physically. The fist was used for that purpose. A modern counterpart might be spitting in someone's face. Such gestures to demean easily erupt into bigger conflict. Yet Jesus, who here said, "Turn the other cheek," when he was slapped by the high priest, used a different response. Did he therefore mean we should let the oppressor slap us around like a punching bag? Hardly.

Violence is possible only when we objectify or trivialize someone. A slap is a form of dehumanization. Satchell Paige, one of the world's greatest ballplayers, never received full recognition for his unique ability until the late 1940s because, as a black, he was denied entrance to major leagues. Prejudice in any form is a denial of full personhood. It says, "You are not equal to me."

The trend to slap people spreads to other areas when we brand those on the other side of an ideological fence with a derogatory "radical, liberal, fundamentalist, or conservative" label, or when we speak about the Big Brass, head honchos, VIPS, peasants, and plebes. When we've put people into specially labeled boxes, we can then criticize them, gossip about them, or ignore them more easily.

In any kind of hierarchy, whether between races, sexes, or social classes, in which one person downgrades another, there is potential for violence. The message of Christ's life was always love: "Don't demean another person." To the one being slapped, he says, "Don't place the person demeaning you in the category of enemy. Don't look for revenge. Don't respond by insulting him or her in return. Don't call that person by any label you wouldn't want to be called. Respond instead with an action that will shock that person into an awareness of your love." Sometimes turning the cheek may bring about such response. At other times, another response may do it, but never violence.

2. "*If someone wants to sue you and take your tunic, let him*

have your cloak as well" (5:40). In this example, Jesus turned to
the field of legal relationships. At issue here is the matter of
rights, another potential conflict situation, particularly in our
day when taxpayers, students, children, patients, prisoners, and
others demand their constitutional rights. The final word is always, "I want what is coming to me," despite the effect of this
demand on others.

In this example Christ taught his disciples to acknowledge
the existence of another order opposed to the world order—
servanthood and mutual submission in the interests of unity
and secure relationships. Relationships are always worth more
than possessions. If some object destroys a relationship, give up
the object, says Jesus. The other person may not need the coat,
but let him or her have it anyway. Yield possessions to keep the
path open for love to flow freely.

This attitude, like the previous one, says to the other person,
"You are not my enemy. I have nothing to defend. See, I am
defenseless." Though the other person may want the cloak for
selfish reasons, that should not deter yielding it up.

3. *"If someone forces you to go one mile, go with him two
miles"* (5:41). Under Roman law, a soldier could press any
citizen into service and force him to carry his baggage a
prescribed distance. Jesus recommended meeting the requirements of the law, and then going an extra mile. The legalist
says, "I have finished my obligation under the law," and
returns home. Persons with the mind of Christ go beyond the
call of duty, taking on extra burdens, because they recognize
the image of God in everyone who opposes them. In ancient
times, the model of manhood was the self-possessed, assertive
individual who imposed his will on others and yielded to
another only under compulsion. Humility, gentleness, and
meekness was expected only of slaves and servants. Young men
have patterned their lives after such heroes ever since. To
consider others better than oneself seems impossible and
ridiculous, for it flies in the face of facts if you are obviously

smarter, wealthier, better looking, and more personable. Yet others' needs always precede ours because we love Christ.

4. *"Give to the one who asks you, and do not turn away from the one who wants to borrow from you"* (5:42). In this admonition, Jesus turns to the area of social relationships and speaks again about keeping relationships intact. At issue here is not whether the person needs the money, deserves the money, or will waste the money but maintaining relationships. What will a refusal to lend money, a lawn mower, or a cup of sugar do to a relationship?

There can be no thought of revenge, of physical violence, or of psychological manipulation with the intent to harm or belittle the other person. Love begins with a forgiving spirit to heal the hostility, alienation, and wounds. Love always affirms the other person as someone God loves and cares for. Love is the goal; unity is the end. Such love allows the person who has caused the hurt the right to remain free and responsible to God rather than to the offended person.

Yet, I have to admit, that even an attempt at affirmation of the other is not true affirmation unless I include a critique of the violence I have been using to condemn that person or persons. The wealthy in criticizing the poor as a lazy lot must critique their own methods of controlling the poor. Dominant racial groups must criticize their methods of subduing other races before criticizing belligerence of dissatisfied minorities. Men and women debating sexual politics must examine their own attitudes toward the other sex and judge them in the light of Christ's words.

To confirm and affirm another person means seeking that person's good, not evil. It means never lowering someone to second-class citizenship unless the demeaner is willing to join the person there. It means never preaching submission and servanthood unless the preacher is willing to yield to the yoke advocated for the other person. It means not denying the oppressed the right to speak up unless there is a willingness to take up their battle and speak for them, even as Christ took on human form and became a servant to become our advocate with God.

Furthermore, nonviolent love is action-oriented, not silent passivity. It doesn't ignore the other's pain or the political realities of a situation and remain uncritical of violence in society by saying, "It's not my business what the neighbors do." To be nonviolent means to choose becoming part of the battle and looking for concrete ways of showing love. It means moving into battle against the evil powers at the root of the problem. It means not tending only one's own garden.

Dialogue on such concerns is often stopped with the question, "What would you do if the soldiers were at your front door?" or "What would you do if a lunatic attacked your wife and mother?" One young man said, "I plead for humility in dealing with this issue. When I'm rational I want to be a peace-loving person, but I don't know what I would do in some situations. We are called to follow Christ's model, but I have difficulty understanding it when it comes to fighting evil and deciding situation ethics. Christ said at one point to buy a sword. Another time he said, 'It is enough.' We obviously don't understand all passages."

I also plead humility in stating my case. I'm not ready to boast what I would do with the tub of poisoned drink. Or even with the dog in my tulips. My biggest temptation is to do nothing, to become the wet noodle stuck to the bottom of the pan. When the law that all Jews in the land should be annihilated was passed in ancient Persia, Queen Esther at first considered withdrawing from the struggle, for she treasured her life and feared death if she entered the king's private quarters without his permission. Like her, we must resist that urge to seek our own comfort and step forward to do something that will make the oppressors aware of their sin.

If I see vandals disturbing my neighbor's trash cans, should I let them continue? If I see burglars breaking into her house, should I sound the alarm? If a high-pressured siding salesman manipulates her into signing a contract, should I stop him? Can I say I love Christ if I stand by and do nothing? Hebrews 12:14 encourages us to "make every effort to live in peace with all men." Ephesians 6 lists the nonoffensive weapons to be used in the spiritual battle, but indicates clearly we face a battle. Prayer is one weapon, but nonviolent specific efforts to curb violence are also necessary.

It is difficult to accept that nonresistant love may initiate conflict. Christ told his disciples he did not come to "bring peace, but a sword." He came to turn "a man against his father, a daughter against her mother, a daughter-in-law against her mother-in-law—a man's enemies will be the members of his own household" (Matthew 10:34-36). These words imply that the gospel brings conflict and disagreement. Do we become silent accomplices to murder when we do nothing?

In one of the essays in *Peacemakers in a Broken World*, Stan Bohn explains how he moved from the position of nonresistance as passivity (turning the other cheek, avoiding conflict) to nonresistance as positive action to bring about reconciliation, knowing it would create conflict and suffering. One has to choose sides, he writes, in situations where there is a clear case of oppression. Persons who say, "Turn the other cheek" to the oppressed, yet stay neutral themselves are without moral power.

On one occasion Bohn sold their house through a black realtor to a black family, aware that white friends felt selling a house to blacks in a white community was acceptable, but that a Christian should not do it because it might hurt the neighbors. By sharing the hatred directed to the blacks who bought their house, he could speak with blacks and go through the painful process of reconciliation with white neighbors and realtors. In six months the neighborhood had weathered the storm and found the black family made satisfactory neighbors.

I would like to be able to say that nonviolent love leads to success, but I can't. It may not always bring about peace between wife and husband, parent and child, neighbor and neighbor, and employer and employee. Some Christians reject pacifism because it does not assure that the world's conflict and brokenness will be eliminated. We have inherited the American success theology that God rewards obedient children with health, wealth, and happiness. Some cars display bumper stickers: "Christians prosper!" proclaiming God answers sincere prayer with a gold-lined envelope.

Ellul and other scholars write that it is naive and simplistic to believe that nonviolence will always result in loving behavior. In the Matthew 5 passage, Jesus recommended a mode of behavior, but promised nothing in material returns or other results. His own life met with hatred and violence. He died at the hands of the Jews because of the way he lived. We hope our efforts for peace will bring peace and personal and social change, yet we cannot predict the response to our actions. In Esther's case, when the Jews were threatened with annihilation by the Persians, Esther went into the king without his permission, not knowing her fate. "If I perish, I perish," she told her cousin Mordecai. Fortunately for her, the king was kindly disposed to her, and the Jews were saved by a new edict allowing them to arm themselves against the attack.

When then be a reconciler? If results aren't sure, why become involved? Commitment to peacemaking must be based on the conviction that the way of peace and love, as Christ taught it, is right. It cannot be based only on affirmation of our efforts through changed actions and attitudes. One commentator on the 1960s peace movement, which evaporated when results were minimal, says, "One can't demonstrate that pacifism can exist pragmatically. One can't experiment with pacifism without being committed to it, because the ultimate commitment requires the giving of one's life."

So what about the neighbor's dog and my tulip bed? I find the best illustration of how to respond to personal injury in

Alan Paton's classic, *Cry, the Beloved Country.* Pastor Kumalo, the rural Zulu minister, makes the fearful journey to Johannesburg in South Africa to locate his son. He learns the boy has made violence a way of life as his defense against the rampant injustice in a depressed economy. The boy has taken part in a robbery and killing and will be tried in the courts.

At first Kumalo responds with anger and hatred to defend himself as a father and a minister. He lashes out against others—his son, his friends—wanting to hurt them as he has been hurt. Through another minister he recognizes his own humanity and sin, and forgives those who have hurt him. Though he prays much, his son is hanged.

The pastor returns to his village with a sorrowing heart, yet at peace because Christ's forgiveness controls his life. He starts to build anew, with fresh courage, the community of Christ in the dried-out valley where he has his parish. He accepts responsibility for his son's wife and unborn child. He acknowledges his own sin before the congregation, which receives him again as spiritual leader. He finds ways to build bridges to the whites through the murdered man's young son who sometimes visits him. Though there are no drastic immediate changes, within him is peace, for unity seems to be the direction whites and blacks in that small village are headed.

The dog who destroyed my tulips doesn't need my forgiveness, but its owner does. That and courage to confront. And the goal of maintaining good relationships. Then I will have tipped over at least a thimbleful.

CHAPTER 17

Spading up words

*In a very real sense, the writer writes in order
to teach himself, to understand himself, to
satisfy himself; the publishing of his ideas,
though it brings gratification, is a curious anti-
climax.*

—Alfred Kazin

The years following my move to a different house and
changing other aspects of my life also brought with them a
strengthening of my commitment to writing as a Christian calling. But before that happened, I nearly quit. To understand
why I nearly quit, I have to go back a ways to the time I was
just out of high school. To the time I was a bologna god.

At the end of high school, family finances decreed that I find
a way to earn a living quickly. I took a short business course
and accepted the first job available to take me off my father's
list of dependents. I worked as an order clerk at a meat-packing
plant in the city.

The blood, guts, and grime part of the process was done in a
city about two hundred miles away. The finished product was
shipped to the plant where I worked. My job was to take the
phone orders and record them for the workers in the re-
frigerated areas to fill. But that was during the war. Meat
products were in short supply, so I frequently didn't have
enough bologna on hand to fill all the orders.

Butchers, their voices broken with emotion, begged me to give them one more roll of bologna. Just one more piece. How could they keep a business going with so little bologna to sell? So, according to the power vested in me and according to my fancy, I added a piece here and deducted one there.

Sometimes the bologna arrived covered with an ugly gray slime. The men washed it off with salt or vinegar water, but I decided who would get portions of this still much-cherished cooked and spiced flesh. Then, one day, a few months after I had begun at the plant, I quit. I no longer wanted to be a bologna god. I left to become a legal secretary.

I learned something. One must make decisions—about slimy bologna. But somehow I couldn't apply that to big issues like what I wanted to do with the major aspects of my life. These were somehow different from dividing meat. I don't know when I first thought about becoming a writer. The decision to commit myself to writing came after I had done my share of dispensing dates and kisses to various young men during the war years.

Several years ago while going through an old steamer trunk, one that has accompanied me since I left my parental home at age seventeen, I found an old forgotten notebook. In it was a loose sheet of paper with these words on it:

> I'm afraid to be a writer—I'm afraid to put things down on paper, things I might regret later on, as if these things really applied to me. But then they do. These things that I want to write are my thoughts, the things that keep me going, the things that slow me up and make me wish I was anywhere but where I am. I shouldn't be afraid. I know I shouldn't. No one will ever see these things I write. No one will ever know they belonged to a girl who once had hopes and dreams but never saw them realized.

Were those my words? Had this pressure to write been with me when I was still absorbed in boyfriends and suntans? I thought it had been a product of my middle years. But there it was, "I want to write...." I must have written that after the breakup of a particularly significant youthful romance. Such breakups always drove me to write.

The urge to write may have originated during the awakening years, but I had a hard time giving that urge room to grow. I remember reading voluminously, especially about girls who aspired to be writers and sacrificed romantic love to devote themselves to their muse. Jo, the second sister in *Little Women*, appealed to me.

Yet the idea of writing was not a reality I could understand or cope with personally. No one encouraged me to write or to be creative, although no one discouraged me either. I had a vague idea that somewhere the mystique of writing held a satisfaction I wanted, but I had no one to show me how to line up words, sentences, and paragraphs to make a story or an article. What we did in school seemed far removed from "writing."

Like the man at the pool of Bethsaida, I had no one to help me into the healing pool of creativity when the angel stirred the water. Writing was for people in books: in the church it was possibly for preachers, rarely for women, certainly not for me. I had no vision of the possibility of things being otherwise, especially during the war years in Canada as I finished high school and left home to support myself as a secretary.

Now, several decades later, I am writing.

Where and how had the dream really begun? Most of my ancestors were farmers for centuries, poking the ground, making green things grow. I never knew my grandfather, the one who was a miller in South Russia. But my father? Did he ever want to describe with words how it felt to clomp around on wooden *Schlorren* in his father's mill in the village of Rosenthal? Or to spend Christmas in a train boxcar as a homesick medic in the Russian army? Or to begin life anew in Canada with a red-haired wife, two toddlers, and twenty-five cents in his Russian-style trousers? Why do I know these stories as if I have seen pictures of them?

My German-speaking parents, who could also speak the language of their adopted country, Russia, left with hundreds of others for Canada in 1923 after the Russian Revolution. So I was born in Canada. I was a New Canadian, my parents told me. But why, if I had received all my education in this new land of promise, did writing remain a silent wish, an undreamt dream, an unarticulated hope—something I could not personally envision happening to me?

Only in the past decades have my agrarian forebears moved in large numbers into business and the professions. On the traditional farm, work was divided between husband and wife out of necessity. Men worked outside on the land. They were leaders in church and community. Women worked inside the home baking the traditional *Zwieback* and *Roggebrot* in the wall oven fired with straw. Three words best describe these women: silence, modesty, and obedience.

I can still see my father walking to church, about three steps ahead of Mother, and Mother calling to him to wait. She wanted the American way, but he had no patience with it. Men moved ahead, made the decisions, took the risks, and women followed. Men walked into church in one door and women in the other. They sat in separate pews. This was the way it had always been done, and it seemed right and normal.

Women's place was not with the men. Not with thinking. Not with dreaming, declaring, determining sin, discipling, deciding to stay or leave Russia. Woman's place was at home kneading the soft dough with strong hands, stripping milk from soft, warm udders, serving *Prips* and *Schinkefleisch* to tired men when they came home from the fields, cradling children into quietness, loving deeply without open words, praying silently with head covered. The poetry of living had no real attachment to the poetry of words.

But I knew very little of this when I left high school. I had inherited a strange mixture of values—the freedom entrusted to one of the top students in a school where sex was never considered a deterrent to any vocational goal. Yet, at the same time, I had unconsciously absorbed the values of my immigrant home in other areas. Mother, while she ladled sour cream gravy and handed out Russian pancakes, drew the family together through her open acceptance of her role as keeper of the home. Father, who knew the hardships of earning a living without an education, encouraged economic survival for me and my sisters. But his limited understanding of what lay ahead in the New World for his daughters could not push me over the hurdles into writing. Poverty does not lend itself to big dreams. Yet inside me was a voice saying there had to be something else for me, something related to the world of the mind and ideas.

I decided again I wanted to write. I agonized. I prayed. Where was the will of God? During those days I occasionally wrote little notes to myself, and I find them now in odd files. One written about 1956 advised me to try writing again: "Is writing worth considering seriously or shall I just forget the matter altogether? The whole problem seems to resolve itself around the matter of having something to write about. If I have nothing to say, there's no use putting that bit of nothing down on paper."

But that winter I did begin. I set up a small table with my college typewriter on it under the chimney corner of our parsonage home. This became Mom's desk. I wrote a few news releases about our congregation for a newspaper and received a few words of praise from the editor. I was launched. I had found room to grow.

At first I helped my husband in his work editing a small youth periodical for the church. When he suggested to the editorial board that I be appointed editor, their reaction was negative. Not a woman. I was crushed. I thought my experience was unique, but I have learned of other women with similar experiences.

For a time I fought a battle against two enemies, both of whom should have been my best friends—God and myself. I felt guilty questioning what seemed right and pure: that a woman should find complete fulfillment in her role as wife and mother and never expect God to require anything more of her. She had her sphere of service. Was I trying to wiggle out from under the authority of God's Word by considering a sideline venture? My conscience told me I should find sufficient meaning in life as a wife without making any specific contribution of my own. Other women had done so. My mother had never had any other aspirations. Or had she? The thought dumbfounded me. Had she buried her longings for creative expression deep inside her as she baked pan after pan of rolls and *Platz*?

If I fought what seemed to be the voice of God, I fought myself also. The craving to write was part of me, yet I couldn't acknowledge it as mine. Men in black suits holding open Bibles said it shouldn't be in me, and I did want to please them.

My perplexity is true for many women, ethnic and non-ethnic. It stems from the subtle leeching of the woman's belief in her own power to think, to create, to choose, and to contribute as a person in her own right, especially in the arts, for this is part of the public sphere, which belongs to men by tradition. Women lack the psychic strength to give utterance to areas of life about which they have been trained to be silent.

I wanted to write. I wanted to discover through writing the meaning of my life and to let others know how I felt. I needed a mentor, someone to encourage me, to stroke, to guide, to support my dreams, and to help put them into effect. My immediate role models were loving, generous women who made excellent *Vereniki* and sewed fine stitches in quilts, but understood little of my longing to give myself away on paper. Writing was a frill, a luxury—not important for frugal, practical people. Further, it was unseemly for women to move into any field that might put them into competition with men or where they might judge masculine fields of endeavor.

As I began to write, both fear of success and fear of failure haunted me. Fear crouched close every time I opened my typewriter. *How do you think you can write with authority? You're not an authority in any matter except familial concerns.* Desperately I wanted the opportunity to gain insight and comprehension which would make me an authority. Fiction writer Tillie Olsen puts it this way: "How much it takes to become a writer. Bent (far more common than we assume), circumstances, time, development of craft—but beyond that: how much conviction as to the importance of what one has to say, one's right to say it. And the will, the measureless store of belief in oneself to be able to come to, cleave to, find the form for one's own life comprehensions." And she adds, "Difficult for any male not born into a class that breeds such confidence. Almost impossible for a girl, a woman."

If fear sat on one side, guilt moved in close on the other. *Shouldn't you be baking another batch of cookies for the children? What will the family say if they get hot dogs again tonight?* Writing can seldom be a first for women if they are wives and mothers. Women can be interrupted. I listened to a friend tell his wife he wasn't going to do any baby-sitting for her this summer because he planned to rewrite his thesis for publication. She turned down an assignment to teach vacation Bible school.

The wife of a famous scholar told me how her husband would on occasion invite his relatives for weekends she had reserved to work on a big writing project of her own and then go off to do his research, leaving her alone to entertain the guests. Women don't have a secretary, as many husbands have in their wives. Motherhood means constantly being interrupted by children, by husband, by the paperboy, by the telephone, and by the magazine salesman, so women are cooled out of the writing profession early. Many women never find out if they can write or do other creative tasks, for they don't fit into the jumble of dishes, chauffeuring, and entertaining. So they are eased out of writing early, unless they make peace between family concerns and writing.

Though for a while every time I sat down to write, a jury of solemn men in dark suits with large black thumb-indexed Bibles open to l Timothy watched me work, I slowly realized the barriers before me were not divine interdicts. The barriers were man-made, but they were also in me. I had to be persistent with my creativity.

Futurist Elise Boulding in *The Underside of History* says a person needs to define herself as a creator, as a futurist who will change society. "Be firm against injustice but persistent enough in your own creativity without being contentious." With the help of editors, friends, and children, I moved toward the barrier once again. Bumping, blundering, blustering, battering, bluffing, and blessing, I crossed over.

In the succeeding years I learned many things about writing, about religious publications, about editors, and about writers, particularly women writers in the church, and about myself.

When I first started writing in the early sixties I sensed that editors believed there was a big difference between a male writer and a woman writer and their audiences. Women were expected to write only for their own sex; although men could write for women as well as men, women could not write for men. Fortunately some of this has changed.

In the late fifties, William Lederer in *Spare-time Article Writing for Money*, in a chapter on "The Women's Magazines," wrote: "The mental needs of men and women are not alike. For the men the driving factors in their lives are to get a job, keep it, get ahead in the world, be able to support a family, be respected in society. The hub of these desires is the man's job. He wants to be a factor in the community, have prestige and importance." On the other hand, Lederer said, women want to feel they are a wonderful wife, beautiful, good homemaker, well dressed, and a fine mother. His advice was write for your audience. Write important things for the men. Write fluffy, soapsudsy things for the women.

In the early sixties when my writing interest was developing, writers workshop leaders advocated that women write children's stories about boys to ensure maximum sales. If they wrote about girls, only girls would read them. If they wrote for boys, both boys and girls would buy their work. Between the lines I was hearing that a woman writer could never expect to write anything significant because she was expected to write for women. And for a while I almost believed that the reading public looked to men to write the important, thought-provoking articles, while women were relegated to fashions, cake-decorating, diaper styles, and chitchat.

The person in me who began writing had a wide-eyed, gentle view of life, a transparent faith, and a terrible need to write. Pushed by God. At first it was a toss-up whether the trembling hand that held the pen belonged to Mrs. Walter Wiebe, Mrs. Rev. Walter Wiebe, Mrs. Katie Wiebe, or someone else. But the writer risked calling herself the latter.

My personal moral support ended when my husband died. Also, it was hard to remain a Mrs. without a Mr. My father, who had had rough times in his youth, reminded me I was a "Funk who can smile through tears." Katie Funk Wiebe had a nicer cadence to it than the jerky Katie Wiebe. So that became my new penname.

As I continued to write, I soon found that not only is writing a male-controlled profession (few editors of church organs are women), but the demands of writing as a profession are strenuous. Women have to continue proving their seriousness about life, about their faith and their writing without letting up on home duties. Male leaders (ministers, missionaries, church leaders) can duck out of family responsibilities for kingdom work; mothers can't.

I noticed also that men were asked to write articles for the church press with no other credentials than that they were ministers or theologians. Some had no writing skills whatsoever, yet the church world accepted their tedious tomes.

I found also that women are rarely in the middle of church life, its agencies, and institutions. When my husband was alive I at least had a pipeline into sources of information through him, but after he died, even that was cut off. The hard problems of the church are frequently discussed over coffee or golf or the kind of sessions women are not invited to. Women frequently don't know what is actually happening in the whole picture, a situation that makes writing for the religious world difficult. At times I felt huge gaps in my awareness of church life, rendering me powerless and vulnerable. All of these factors caused me to doubt my own calling.

I learned as I talked to other women writers they have greater difficulty becoming writers because they have a greater fear of being displeasing as a writer and also a greater fear of success, especially of outdoing their husband. Women get in their own way. They lack the confidence to write decisively, authoritatively, because they lack the political authority of position and the psychological advantage of those of the male gender. How often I cautioned myself, "If I write this down, will I ever be able to live it down or live up to it?" For centuries women have been conditioned to be pleasing in appearance, in dress, in manner, and in relationships. It is then impossible to risk being hard-nosed or displeasing as a writer. As one novelist says, "One voice says, 'Be like Mother and be safe.' Another voice says, 'Be like Daddy and make your mark.'"

I found that to write I had to have the courage to be wrong—and also the courage to succeed. When courage departed, my typewriter remained covered for days. It came as a mild surprise that to write publicly made me a wide-open target for readers' potshots. Some hit fairly. I appreciated well-thought-through criticism, but some readers punched well below the belt, with each critical word wrapped in barbed wire and then signed with some Christian greeting. Some letters to the editor seemed to want to demean the writer rather than criticize the work. Yet Thomas Merton's words in *Seeds of Contemplation* were helpful: "If a writer is so cautious that you never write anything that cannot be criticized, you will never write anything that can be read. If you want to help other people, you have got to make up your mind to write things that some [readers] will condemn."

I learned also that criticism about the church and its life coming from a woman is not as acceptable as coming from a man. A man is expected to be an apologist for God; men are expected to speak up for a cause. When they do, they are considered forthright and bold, outspoken, fearless for the truth. When a woman speaks up, she is being shrewish and unchristian, denying the Bible, her faith, and her womanhood. Yet I came to accept that women as well as men should have the right to say, "This situation is without merit" or "This decision is worthwhile" without losing their femininity.

Writing is a lonely profession. Few people can write in the midst of a family reunion. E. W. Marten states that the author's ideas and vision, whatever he or she writes, have to be communicated in loneliness. "Only by a dredging of one's own consciousness can one get the kind of power with which to remake an experience, to formulate a concept and shed light that has not been shed before on conditions, ideas, and situations."

Writers need the comradeship of other writers who respect each other's vision. I lacked strong women-teacher-intellectual models. I needed someone to encourage, to stroke, to coach, to support my dreams and help me put them into effect. I needed someone to create space for me to develop my goals, and particularly, to give moral support in times of stress.

Without this model/mentor, I decided at a number of key turning points to quit writing. To cover my typewriter for the last time. It was too hard, including the hard work of retyping revisions. I was weary. But I stayed with it. Why? At the back of everything was a simple belief that I had something to say and that God wanted me to say it. No huge neon sign in the sky told me what to do, but as I watched what was happening in the lives of friends and acquaintances, I saw aspects of the Christian life not being spoken to. I became convinced that whoever controls the word controls the Word, and to remain a theologizing disciple of Christ, I had to continue to write.

Glenn H. Asquith related at a writers' workshop at Green Lake, Wisconsin, in 1966 that one day he had visited a woman in a mental hospital. After the visit he stood in the ward waiting for the attendant to come with the key to release him. As he stood at the door, waiting, he had a feeling someone was behind him. He looked around. It was not someone, but all the people in the ward. About thirty of them. And there they stood, waiting. One of them finally asked, "Sir, don't you have the key?"

He told us at that writers' workshop that lined up everywhere are thousands of people with joys and sorrows, puzzlements, and conditions they cannot possibly resolve alone, and they're saying to writers, "Haven't you got the key?" At the time my little key didn't fit many keyholes, but I decided to put it into the hole and start turning. The memory of what I committed myself to then keeps me going.

I have a basic faith in God and his Son Jesus Christ, which is sometimes quite simple—a sense of the existence of God in a dimension beyond the material world. I believe in sin and evil. I believe in God's grace, love, and forgiveness. At heart I am a theologian. I yearn to know exactly what I believe and to separate that from what others think I should believe. I am willing to change my mind about many matters. It has been helpful not to lock my mind into thinking patterns and say, "Nothing can change." I have changed a great deal in the past several decades. I expect to change some more.

I know that the day I am no longer seriously involved in a creative working tension with my beliefs to bring new light to ideas and situations, my vision will dim and my computer will remain unused. As a writer, one always has to be open to new insights, new perspectives to an idea, an argument, a definition, while hanging on to what is basic to the faith. The energy in writing comes in focusing one's vision ever more clearly for oneself and for others.

I have been asked, "What if my vision seems foggy? Do I wait to begin writing?" You must write out of your convictions of what you see as truth. If you wait and wait for better understanding, you may never write a word. If you have something to say, start saying it. Most writers have only one consuming idea, and they keep writing about it from different perspectives.

The obstacles to passing on vision through writing will not come from lack of skill or talent. Failure at writing is usually due to loss of vision. The real obstacles to writing come from within oneself as a person, not from without, not from circumstances, such as lack of opportunity. In writing, you deal first with yourself. In part this is a spiritual matter. Many people with a strong and clear vision write successfully because their words come from a depth of spirit, while others with more advanced skills and greater talent fail because their technically perfect papers are flat and empty.

I have written a column now for more than twenty-five years as well as hundreds of articles and several books. The columns have, in a sense, become a journal of my life and concerns. As I reread them I can easily trace my interests, my ups and downs, periods of growth and stagnation. Grappling with a problem in my own life by putting it into words has often helped me to find myself. I thank those who have let me think in public for these many years.

Someone once said that the exercise of writing pushes one into the exercise of being. A person can't write honestly without becoming more alive and more aware of other people. In other words, you can't keep on faking that you are interested in your subject matter. As a writer you stand at the center of your thoughts and feelings and are involved in a real relationship with the objective world through words. You are engaged with your own experiences through words.

But there's a difference between being honest and seeming to be honest. Writing honestly forces a person to grow. There is always the subtle pressure to write for God seekers in such a way that the gospel will be comfortable to them. We feel pushed to explain, to simplify, and to reduce Christian truths to formulas that can be grasped easily. So we writers hammer and mold and routinize the faith into a shape that can be easily handled, recognized, and advertised. We think we can capture the mystery of the cross in a paragraph or two and tame the awesome working of God with our words.

Novelist Thomas Wolfe described the writing process vividly when he said that to write, just put a piece of paper in the typewriter and start bleeding. One has to be willing to say, "These are the things I think about deep inside me." Certain kinds of writing require giving oneself away through words. They are an exercise in self-revelation.

Must a writer live a colorful life to be a writer? No. Everyone has as much experience as he or she can handle. Experience is not what happens to you but what you do with what you experience. My experiences as a child in northern Saskatchewan were probably no different from those of any other child of immigrant parents, but I saw them as grist for my mill.

One writer friend once told me he doubted whether there was any such thing as a talent for writing—only pressures, which writers must apply to themselves. I have found that the most published writers are not the ones with the greatest talent, but the ones who think of writing like any other job—teaching a lesson, planting a field, or working in an office. They keep spading up words because it's their job. They do it because like a sneeze, they can't help themselves.

To wait until the mood hits me or until I have caught up with other work means I never write a word. I believe with many others that writing is 99 percent perspiration and 1 percent inspiration. Most good writing is not mere accident or the result of high inspiration. Usually it comes by work—hard work and lots of it. Deadlines are unyielding slavemasters, and the act of writing is tedious and painstaking and sometimes so wearying you wish you had never started.

Writing is a voracious consumer of time. Minutes slip into hours and hours into evenings, days, and weekends, as you research, write, revise, honing each sentence to razor-sharp clarity. I know my words will be read without benefit of intonations, gestures, or extra phrases a speaker can add to clarify tangled thoughts. It's first time or never with the reader.

The ideas won't come. The gates of inspiration seem hopelessly closed. The great idea I started with falls apart into a crumbling mess and must be thrown back into the hopper for another try. Or, if an idea does emerge, it won't behave and instead of resembling sparkling crystal, it becomes a bowl of cold mashed potatoes gone sour.

A look at oneself through one's own words is not always pleasant. Deficiency of thought, vagueness of expression, and lack of sensitivity show up clearly and permanently. And so you soon learn humility.

These years of writing have taught me discipline, the joy of creating, a sense of stewardship of ideas and gifts—and given me countless new friends. To me a writer used to be an unusual person with a rare gift for words. I claim only a small vision and a small talent. Elizabeth O'Connor in *The Eighth Day of Creation* showed me that until I willingly named my gift and made myself responsible to God for it, I would always have an excuse to hang loose with an abstract commitment and no need to risk.

The pieces I'd like to rip from the record are not those in which I spoke out boldly, but those in which I waivered or tilted at windmills to stay out of the heat of the battle. I struggle always with the compulsion to speak out and with my own need to keep life evenly spaced and paced.

I think I see more mellowness, but also a greater sense of the responsibility of a word-maker. When readers show me one of my articles or books which has been well underlined, or when people respond with long letters, I stand humbled but also afraid. Never has so much been written by so many for so many to make money rather than to build the church of Jesus Christ. Where do I stand?

Ahead? To keep making wondrous the truth of God's love with as much skill as given to me. Bologna god no longer. Now a disciple of Christ.

CHAPTER 18

Seeing through new eyes

*What would we see if we had not been told
what to see. . .? Jesus, I believe, deliberately
planned to shake up the establishment.*
—Rachel Conrad Wahlberg

After nearly forty years we met to match stories about what had happened since we had gone to college together. We had ended at the same place ideologically with regard to the role of women, although my feminist consciousness was a little older than hers. She had made a detour into depression after her attempts to fit quietly, submissively, into the established structures of the Christian community had warred too violently with her longing for a freer, fuller life. She paid a high price for her readiness to submit. She had emerged, however, from despair, from enslavement to prescription drugs, like a phoenix from the ashes, stronger, more vibrant, more confident of her gifts and her role in life. She was now a counselor, seeing clients in her home office, enjoying a good marriage. Her spirit refreshed me.

One of her last statements about our Bible college days haunted me for days. Most of the young men who had been studying with us had gone on into church work and now functioned as pastors, church administrators, and missionaries. "But what have they done for us, Katie?" she cried out passionately. Who among them had taken a small step to free the women of the church? It lay within their power, but almost to a man, those with whom we had gone to school had remained silent, supporting the status quo.

Numerous women who married and became mothers during the baby boom years following World War II chart a painful, often unwelcome, pilgrimage into a different lifestyle. They didn't want to become feminists. They wanted to remain traditional devoted wives and mothers. The two viewpoints seemed opposed to one another. The war years and absence of men pulled the women out of the home into the factories, professions, and marketplace. When the military personnel returned, most of the men wanted the peace and security of a family to come home to at the close of each day. A wife in a frilly apron waiting for her man, with supper ready on the table, seemed to include the best of all dreams. Consequently, many of the women left their employment to return to full-time kitchen duties.

But society hadn't always functioned like this with the husband working outside the home and the women in it. Before industrialization, women were actively involved in a home production society alongside their husbands and had considerable power in the household economy in the production of food and goods. Both husband and wife worked out of the home. Only after the industrial revolution the men and the poorest women (mostly single) went to the factories to augment family incomes. Outside employment became a social stigma, an idea the post-World War II society accepted as a principle existing for all time.

As scholars have documented, consequently, particularly after World War II, women were pushed into consumerism, into an existence which limited them to the home and church. Remunerative work, intellectual activity, and leadership outside the home were frowned upon even though earlier, women had already made many advances in the professions, business, and even church ministries. But now a new conservatism took over and backed by Scripture proof texts, the movement to limit women's involvement in society was launched.

Women, surrounded by a host of new labor-saving devices, a smaller family, and boasting a better education than their mothers, felt a strange emptiness they couldn't identify. Betty Friedan in *The Feminine Mystique* first drew attention to the problem without a name: women's dissatisfaction with their empty, boring lives and an inability to explain why. Often isolated from adult companionship, without intellectual stimulation, they individually tried to come to terms with their dissatisfaction.

And if Christian women analyzed their discomfort, it seemed to be rebellion against God—for didn't the Bible say woman's place was in the home? They were asking for liberation which church and society said they didn't need and shouldn't want. They were in their God-appointed place if they were at home. Because one sphere, the public one, was made more important than the private one, women, the larger segment of society, never had the opportunity to make full public use of their gifts and talents; and the men, the smaller group, were never free to acknowledge their nurturing qualities in the private sphere.

Often as a young married woman, I thought part of me was living in a void, but I numbed myself to the emptiness because I knew I shouldn't feel that way. I had what every woman wanted: a good marriage, four lovely children, and sufficient material resources. I was doing what I had always dreamed of doing as a young woman, yet I didn't grasp that the mind, the imagination, the inner life, must also be satisfied or its hunger pains can lead to another kind of death by starvation. The deadliest aspect of this self-destruction was that women didn't dare discuss their inner turmoil with anyone. To do so was to reveal a liberal view of life—even worse, an unspiritual attitude—for during the turbulent sixties a conservative society reacted harshly toward anyone who marched to a different drummer.

I checked my body for signs of abuse. I found no welts or bruises. No broken bones. Nothing. Yet I felt abused, though aware it was wrong to feel this way if one wasn't physically oppressed. I did not know how to check the health of my spirit. And I didn't dare approach a minister, for intuitively I knew I could not expect understanding.

But I said nothing. In the early years of my writing career I promoted what the church openly espoused: strong male leadership and dominance in home, church, and society; women's involvement in the private world of home and women's church organizations and overseas missionary service. I used exclusive language—because I had grown up with it and had been taught it. I saw no objection to its use. Nothing showed on the surface. I was the only one who knew of the pain gnawing inside me when I thought of the large reservoir of women whose gifts remained unused simply because they were women. It didn't seem right.

Finally I couldn't silence the voice that told me that to describe women's role only in terms of limitations, rather than opportunities, was wrong. If something is evil and sinful, it should be spoken against.

I found myself reading the Bible with new interest. Did a section of Scripture that began with "brothers" apply to me if the church insisted all sections about women applied only to women? Could I consider myself "in" in "brother" sections even if men couldn't include themselves in the "women only" sections? Were there any "men only" sections? What kind of a sieve should I use to read Scripture?

I read everything I could find on women in church and society and built a considerable library. I attended some of the first conferences in the evangelical world on women's roles. At the first Evangelical Women's Caucus held in Washington, D.C., in 1974, attended by about 300 women, most unforgettable were the tears shed openly by many women. They had never dared to speak about their hurts in their search for ministry and found that here, often for the first time, they were not being judged, just welcomed as a sister.

By then the women's movement was in full swing, with those who were speaking up openly receiving a full dose of ridicule and trivialization, particularly from men, but also from women, who felt uncomfortable or threatened by these new voices. Writing on the topic became a monologue, not a discussion. I understood the whistleblower in a government science laboratory who said, "If you must sin, sin against God, not against bureaucracy. God will forgive. Bureaucracy never."

What was at the heart of the contradiction between faith and enforced submission of women? Was the contradiction in God and the Bible? Or in women and men who claimed to be Christian, yet opposed the full development of women in church and society, usually with the words, "What do they want? They have more opportunities to serve than they need."

Those who have traveled this same path know the confusion of ideas one has to stumble and sort through. How valid is experience? If men can lean on a spiritual calling to the ministry, can women also say, "I believe God has called me"? What actually does the Scripture say? How much is the issue clouded over by a socially ingrained bias, beginning first with the translators, then the commentators of Scripture? Are Christian feminists unbiblical? Have they yielded to secularism and the human rights movement, to narcissism? Have they flagrantly denied God's will for their lives—which is primarily to marry and bear children? If their critics accused the women, the women also condemned themselves and felt guilt intimately.

One evening I inadvertently watched the film "Tell Me Where It Hurts" on television. It is the story of a middle-aged woman who finally deals with the emptiness of her marriage to a man who sees her role as making his meals, sleeping with him, and bringing him a beer when he props himself before the television. That she might have needs of her own is incomprehensible to him. I turned off the television and wept. I had no husband now, and he had not been an uncaring husband when he was alive, but I wept for the many women who were hurting but had no place to turn.

The lack of understanding for women being pushed into identical molds throughout society overwhelmed me. A former friend met me after many years in the hall of the college where I teach. His first question was "Are you a secretary here?" "No," I said, "I teach here." Embarrassed, he tried to cover his error. Yet in his mind he had a fixed role for women who worked in institutions of higher learning.

I knew many women were unable to tell others where it hurt. Some tried. One pastor's wife introduced herself at a workshop by her given name. At once someone else exclaimed, "No, she's our pastor's wife." "Don't do that," said the woman. "I want to be myself, to have my own identity." Her identity was her husband's and she wanted to find a way to find out who she was. I met women who saw themselves as an appendage to their husband. "He received the call to a church and I went along," one told me. "When he conducted a workshop, I found a corner to wait while he had a great time in the public eye," said another. Another acquaintance mentioned she never invites couples unless her husband is home because "he is a more interesting person than I am." It is only too true that some professional men have nondescript wives who were probably bright women in college but who later subsided into the background like a small puppy—never offering strong opinions and concepts because they aren't expected to.

Everywhere I went women shared small confidences. "Every time we move I lose my identity," said one seminary student wife. "Maybe in a sense I also lose my husband's identity for me when we move." Another mentioned she had spent her emotional energy on two major moves, one baby, and a change of jobs for her husband. "I wanted to keep my marriage together and give my children a secure situation, but part of me wanted to go beyond that. I thought a lot about music. To fit it into the family schedule I practiced in the college chapel from six to seven a.m. It got earlier and darker. It was just too much."

The difficulty in the church during the height of the women's movement was that it was without models which showed people how men and women could function together in the church, serving one another with love, mutual submission, and understanding. Jesus' radical approach toward women in his earthly ministry seemed like some feminist hare-brained idea.

In my small living room, I grieved for hurting women who in high school had been encouraged to use their gifts and talents, whose personality and leadership qualities won them many opportunities for public service, but later on had had to deny their growing sense of calling to ministry unless it was to missionary service. I had heard several such young women give a short testimony on how God was working in their life. Their free personality and vulnerable faith drew an immediate positive response. So they nurtured this sense of calling by accepting all opportunities for service. They took the next logical step—seminary. They heard the church pleading for more full-time Christian workers, but found it didn't open its doors when they stepped forward. The church's invitation to service had many sub- and grandfather clauses which shut them out.

But I grieved also for those concerned that all women, single or married, remain in their narrow "God-appointed" place in the home whether they had children or no means of support but what they themselves earned. I grieved for women who saw no opening for themselves in church work and deliberately left it rather than hassle with the status quo. As I sat there, I grieved also for myself because I, too, had to find my way through this tangle.

I wanted integrity in my life, what Erik Erikson terms the arrival at that stage in life in which one can give a blessing to one's own life. One evening recently I sat at the dining-room table, finishing the novel *East of Eden* by John Steinbeck. The final chapter ends with the son Caleb, who symbolizes the ancient Cain, standing at his father Adam's deathbed with the servant Lee attempting a reconciliation between the two, for Caleb has been instrumental in causing Adam's favorite son Aron to be killed. Lee begs the older man to "Free him! Bless him!" As I read these words I found my eyes welling with tears as I at last understood myself through my identification with Caleb. Though I had not killed my brother, much of my lifelong insecurity was due to the fact that I felt unblessed as a daughter of the kingdom. I had been asking in numerous ways to be freed, for a blessing upon my ministry. I wanted women as well as men to have the freedom to cry out with Jabez to the God of Israel, "Oh that you would bless me and enlarge my territory! Let your hand be with me, and keep me from harm so that I will be free from pain" (1 Chronicles 4:10).

To say women are oppressed and need to be officially freed means many red flags get raised, for people associate oppression with beatings and thumbscrews. I understand better now than I could at first the extreme discomfort of men who see themselves as kind, generous leaders yet who are accused of sexism. Any type of prejudice is so subtle, it is difficult for the unaware to spot it in others, even more difficult in oneself. For example, most men aren't aware how easily they interrupt a woman at a committee meeting. Or how the suggestion of a woman is disregarded only to be heralded as a great new idea when a man repeats it several minutes later.

In the early years of the movement, some feminists were determined to bring the church "howling and wailing" into the twentieth century, not prepared for the long haul, nor aware of their own anger and bitterness. Many who thought they had found their answers were sometimes perplexed and outraged by their own inconsistencies. I recall my daughter Susan telling me she was going to a job-related conference in the East. "Who will take care of the children?" I asked innocently. "Why Roger, of course," she replied. "When he goes to a conference, I take care of them. When I go, he takes care of them." In my generation a husband baby-sat his wife's children at her request. This generation accepts that the children belong to the father also. With my head I knew this. With my heart, I said, "Taking care of children is a mother's task."

One of the main influences on my own thinking with regard to women's role was the civil rights movement, which in many aspects paralleled the women's movement. For several years I taught black literature, considering the history of the blacks in America as well as their poetry, fiction, and drama and ended in a study of systems of oppression and ways of responding.

Until this decade white male theologians wrote most of the books in religion and theology, thereby controlling the public meaning of the gospel through their translation of the Scriptures, their preaching, and teaching. Like the black movement, the women's movement first examined societal practices and also Bible interpretations to document the case of prejudice against them. Blacks were concerned that whites get a clear picture of the black experience during slavery, reconstruction, and jim crow days until the present. Women also told their story of pain and deprivation. They reexamined the Old and New Testament to reveal the low place women had had in those early societies, the double sex standard, and so forth. This information had always been there, but people had overlooked it. They saw what they wanted to see. Now they were asked to see it through different eyes, the eyes of women as they looked at the gospel accounts of Jesus' relationships with women.

The blacks next promoted the idea that "black is beautiful," so don't try to be like a white person. The women's movement followed suit. Whereas some women had secretly longed to be male to enjoy male privileges, and in fact, sometimes were rejected by fathers for not having been a son, now they were encouraged to enjoy being a woman. It wasn't unusual several decades ago to hear someone say of a particularly talented young woman, "Too bad she wasn't a man." Now women could openly enjoy being female.

And women were told it wasn't necessary to learn how to be a woman by reading books any more than men had to learn how to be a man by reading books. One friend, after a divorce, was shocked to find how many volumes she had accumulated that instructed her how to act and live as a woman, as if womanhood was an aberration of humanity that needed correcting, while maleness was the norm.

The women's movement also brought to public attention neglected biblical texts relating to women and reinterpreted familiar ones to challenge a patronizing attitude. A new look was taken at passages dealing with creation, especially the use of terms like "headship," and at the difficult Pauline passages that forbade women to enter the male world of leadership and preaching.

A third stage in both the black and feminist movements has been to use imaginative works to reinforce the message that God also uses women in diverse ways to glorify him. Bible women's stories have been retold in poetry, song, stories, and drama. Women also share their own story in small, trusted groups, giving an account of their call to ministry, their prayers for open doors, their experiences with criticism, unwelcome in some mixed settings. In such a setting I heard one ordained woman say that at her ordination her mother had stated her position against women's ordination openly. Another licensed woman mentioned how difficult affirmation was for the older generation, entrenched in an earlier theological tradition. Her mother's question had been, "Rita, what do I tell my peers?"

These early pioneers of the women's movement received the most severe criticism, but some of us who came later had to deal with it also. I found I upset some women if I mentioned they might have other options for their lives or that discipleship might include making choices between the good and the better. I heard that I set back the cause by speaking openly. I was told I must have many personal hang-ups. When I spoke in the community where one of my critics lived, she had asked her daughter what I looked like. She said she expected me to be dressed like a Communist Party woman—sexless, black suit, severe hairstyle. She was surprised to find me normal, feminine, human.

Often persons who agreed with biblical feminism were hesitant to speak out because it was a political battle, rather than a doctrinal one. As someone has said, the opposition to the women's movement was the strongest blend of sanctified culture ever developed. Discouraging were comments like, "All right, we've discussed the matter. Now let's get on with our work," not accepting responsibility for change. More encouraging were those men who suggested women become more political in the church, less strident, even if I didn't agree fully with the advice of one that we should go to men for advice and cry a little on their shoulder. I appreciated one friend who told me to be bolder. Men get knocked down when they offer their opinions. Women should be able to take the gaff of public life also. My response was, "I'd feel better if I were knocked down for my ideas and not because I was a woman."

I recognize now how difficult it is to acknowledge the significance of an experience that does not parallel our own or to accept suggestions for change coming from those who are powerless to change the system. Though we may openly reject experience as the least reliable indicator of truth, what we feel still strongly determines the direction we move in life.

Races, sexes, social classes must have been oppressed in Paul's time, or why did he utter that ringing statement of freedom in Galatians 3:28: "There is neither Jew nor Greek, slave nor free, male nor female, for you are all one in Christ Jesus"? Unity in equality was his dream, as it should be ours.

Both men and women need an enlarging vision overshadowed by love. Knowledge without love is not acceptable.

James H. Cone, black theologian, writes, "Through dreams we can see what is supposed to be when what is blinds us to what ought to be." Dreams come from leaders. It takes courage to reach into the depths of one's being and identify the vision of God and then create it for others. It takes courage to allow the glory and awesome mystery of the vision of the church as a growing, reconciling community of love to shine forth when followers are demanding pedestrian black and white answers that can be codified, computerized, and classified. A vision is never passed on with a club or sword, or through monotony, routinization, and heavy-handed moralizing. It comes as a grass-roots movement and spreads even as a glimmer of light brings hope to a dark room. And grows and grows. And nothing can hold it back.

I'll admit it's easier to serve God without his awakening vision. I wish at times I had never become involved in Bible study, in prayer, in thought about women's ministry. Then I could pull back at any time. Yet the best times of life are when we are caught up in a leader's dream and know our place in that dream, as each black knew his or her place in Martin Luther King's great dream for the blacks on the mountaintop.

Now several decades after I first became interested in the women's movement, change has occurred. Many people are more consciously using gender-inclusive language, even though at one time some said the issue was too trivial to even discuss. Women are interested in ministry, and slowly, slowly, moving into leadership positions in some denominations. More women studying at seminaries means professors have to change their language and their approach to teaching. It also means that with more women theologians, questioning of our theology is more possible and likely. More people are aware that if only men serve in church ministries, the church is just a male talent agency. In a global church and at a time when women are as well educated and as well equipped with spiritual gifts as men, both sexes are needed in ministry. We all lose if one group is left out. More women on church boards and committees means that the affective area will become more dominant, and that the shift to more creativity, more nurturance, will change the face of the church.

People who have functioned on boards and committees tell me that when women are present the level of communication shifts to a more personal, caring level. Having had experience as outsiders and as powerless persons, women can speak to matters sometimes omitted from agendas. Not conditioned to being as competitive as men, more women in decision-making situations may lessen the political maneuvering on some boards—unless, of course, the women think the only way to get ahead in kingdom work is to follow the tactics previously used.

The rapid development of women's retreats, seminars, and Bible studies to nurture women's spiritual formation will also influence church life. Women are getting experience in moderating public meetings, serving as worship leaders, song directors, workshop leaders, and committee members. They are learning to know one another, breaking down distrust and replacing it with understanding and appreciation. They are also slowly discovering they are wealthy and that money has power. "Pin money" is a term never heard today, even though the full impact of women's wealth hasn't hit yet.

Why choose ministry as a woman? Why at this stage in my own life am I still excited about being part of a spiritual ministry even if opportunities are limited? Church work has an appeal for both men and women, especially women who have been the backbone of the church for decades and have proven they can carry out extensive programs. Women experience a genuine call to service. When given the opportunity, they have a genuine spiritual ministry. One woman pastor said, "Women need creative pastors to give them opportunity to speak. They need someone to give them an opportunity to add to their experience." But the signals they receive about ministry are vague. They, like Esau, whose brother Jacob stole his birthright, are pleading, "Bless me too, my father!" The church cannot remain strong if only the smaller portion of its membership receives the official blessing.

More than three decades ago at the end of the daylong celebration of my husband's ordination to the ministry, I collected my children and headed home. As I took off my new black velvet hat that late afternoon, I noticed that the sweaty fingerprints of the visiting minister, who had laid his hands on my head in prayer, had left permanent indentations. Thereafter I wore the mark of ordination on my head, although I had made no public promises and received no formal instructions or blessing for my role as a minister's wife. Was there a gift of the Spirit labeled "minister's wife"? I was convinced there was, but I didn't know what size or shape it was then and I don't know the exact dimensions of it now.

Though unblessed, yet still blessed, I pray for convictions strong enough to carry me through disappointments, painful encounters, and hard decisions about relationships, actions, and much more in the years to come. In Sinclair Lewis's novel *Babbitt*, Babbitt says to his son Ted at the end of the novel: "I've never done a single thing I wanted to in my whole life! I don't know's I've accomplished anything except just get along. I figure out I've made about a quarter of an inch out of a possible hundred rods. Well, maybe you'll carry things further." I would like my tombstone to indicate I had made more than a quarter of an inch in my life.

Changing my mind about women's place in God's economy has been a painful and far-reaching decision. I found it easy to change my mind about stained-glass windows (I like them), about plainness (I weary of it), about older people (they're delightful), about grown-up children (they make good friends). But I was pushed to the brink when I received phone calls, some in anguish, as, for example, one from a young professional woman who felt wounded and perplexed by her findings about what the Bible actually taught about women as opposed to what she had been taught. She was reeling from the inequity and downright cruelty some women experienced. She wanted a mentor. Her cry told me something had to change.

But another kind of calls from women ahead of me in the journey also encourage me. One morning the phone rang as I was debating whether to crawl out of bed fifteen minutes early and get a running start on the day or to enjoy my bed's comfort for a few minutes longer. I got up to answer the phone. The voice of a distant friend responded asking for a bit of information she needed for a speech. We shared views briefly. She gave me a word of affirmation for what I was doing. And the day began. But thanks to her I could go to class not feeling like a shriveled cucumber, but the flag bearer at the front of the parade. God loved me. Ruth loved me. It was a great day.

Chaim Potok in his novel *Davita's Harp* tells the story of a young girl whose American father has rejected Christianity and whose mother has done the same for her Jewish heritage. Both witnessed innocent suffering at the hands of cruel oppressors—the mother during the Holocaust and the father at a mob lynching of a labor leader in America. Davita, their daughter, is taught the gospel, especially how to pray, by a Christian missionary aunt. She is also reintroduced to the Jewish faith by some family friends, but brings with her to it the Christian truth that everyone, including women, can pray to God. Once having accepted this truth, she refuses to give it up. So in the synagogue she stands near a gap in the curtain separating the men from the women and prays despite their murmuring about her strange behavior. But in the women's section here and there other women say "amen" to her words. She has opened the way for them.

I am grateful for those who helped me find the hole in the curtain today and to know I am blessed. I pray I may direct others to it as well.

CHAPTER 19

Tell me your story

*You know, I don't think there are any
storytellers. There are only stories, and each of
us gets to carry one of them for a little while.*
—Laura Simms at Fifth Annual
St. Louis Storytelling Festival

I chose to write most of my books, but I fell into the writing
of *Good Times with Old Times: How to Write Your Memoirs.*
The director of our college's continuing education program for
the plus-sixty group had asked me to teach a short writing
course. I agreed. But what should I emphasize? Why not personal experience writing? My twenty-six students caught my
baited hook unhesitatingly. And out of the class came the book
encouraging older people to recount their life story. And after
that I couldn't quit encouraging others through memoir-writ-
ing workshops to keep telling their stories. Or to stop telling
mine.

We should never have stopped telling stories.

"Tell me the old, old story of Jesus and his love," we sang
lustily as children. We liked this song and also the Bible stories
parents and Sunday school teachers told us. Then we grew up.
We decided the old stories of Jesus were not as important as the
material in the rest of the New Testament.

"Let's skip the story part of the lesson," said the adult Sunday school teacher. "We all know it well. Let's move on to the lesson we get from it." We skipped the story—about the little boy and his lunch, about Joseph and his brothers, about the healing of the blind man. We moved on. To a higher intellectual level—to the "lesson," and to creedal statements and interpretations of Scripture—often well worked out and presented by notable scholars.

The important thing was to know what we believed about the Bible, God, Jesus Christ, and the Holy Spirit, and about salvation, baptism, the church, evangelism, and missions. We had the idea this information couldn't come from stories about a businesswoman like Lydia starting a church by the river, or the resurrected Christ first revealing himself to a woman. We learned statements about what we believed, so that if an inquirer asked about our faith, we could say, "I believe this and this about God and his love."

We memorized statements of faith. We chewed the big words finely and then carefully distributed them in our speech—sanctification, incarnation, justification, eschatology, righteousness, and so forth. Jawbreakers, most of them. We hoped they encapsulated our faith into a neat package, making it simpler to explain the good news. "I believe in the atonement" had a more sophisticated ring than telling the story of one who died on the cross. We defended fiercely what we believed, down to the fine points, even if we didn't always know why.

I can still hear the preacher of several decades ago say, "Please pardon the personal illustration, but. . . ." At the time I never understood the hesitancy, for often I liked the story better than the sermon. I thought he demurred because it was bad manners to make one's private life a public affair. Missionaries could tell stories about their experiences, and were expected to, but when they preached, they, too, switched gears and the stories stopped. Somewhere the connection between the story and belief got lost, even though Jesus did most of his teaching to adults through story.

The linear account of God's dealings with humanity from Genesis to Revelation—what he has done, is doing, and will do—never becomes one unified account for many people because it is not told as one continuing story. The grandeur of the story of how God came to humanity through an event, or a series of events, misses them. Their strong meat is some aspect of the systems that have grown out of the stories: Does a human being have a bipartite or a tripartite nature? Did Judas have free choice if he had to be the traitor?

The story was lost and with it the power and glory of the good news, for in the story lies the essence of faith. We must listen to the story again. The stories of God's dealings with humanity from the beginning of time. And our own stories.

When the stories are distilled and packaged for popular consumption into theological systems, they do not capture the imagination of the listener. Modern story-theologians are saying we must find ways again of telling the stories of the Bible in such a way that readers identify with the characters and say, "Aha, that's my story, too," for we learn and act because of stories. Because motivations for actions, feelings, and reactions remain the same throughout time and only the setting changes, stories appeal to the emotions.

The ancient Israelites had a strong sense of their story in which they saw themselves as part of a covenant community. They didn't come before God seeking him only as individuals, but as an individual always conscious of being a member of a people who had a story that went back many generations. At important junctures in their history, the leaders recited their story to the Israelites, a story that began with Abraham, Isaac, Jacob, and Moses. The New Testament apostles, when preaching to crowds, began by showing their listeners how they were part of the Jewish story. They belonged to the story of Abraham, and on through one story after another, to David and

Christ. They were part of the flow, of the movement toward completion, not isolated scraps of being drifting with the current.

I found myself reacting (perhaps there is such a thing as middle-age rebellion) to my awareness that as a church we have not only lost contact with the Bible stories in favor of a systems approach, which includes the three-point sermon. (How often is the sermon a story?) But we have also lost contact with the story of Jesus and his love in the lives of modern believers. We prefer the systems statement "I believe in the incarnation" to a story of a modern incarnation.

We prefer to say, "God can forgive your sin," than to explain how he forgave ours, though the truer statement about our faith is always our personal story. What I experience about God shows up in my personal history. If you ask me to tell you about my God, I can't tell you without telling my story. You will see the God I really know and trust only as you learn to know my story. Here my true theology is revealed.

This dearth of personal and family history is due in part to the contemporary emphasis that life begins with our particular generation, when we were bride and groom, rather than with the awareness that each new couple is a member of a family, of a continuum.

The lack of emphasis on story is due also to the contemporary view that the Christian life begins with the individual. New Christians are encouraged to begin testimonies with "I was saved on August 17, 1987, and became a member of the family of God" without acknowledging that the people of God were already present long before this, and it was only through people witnessing to them and showing them how the faith life could be lived did they become a part of it.

It is also partly due to the present emphasis on instant pleasure resulting from the fear that the nuclear arms buildup may escalate even more and destroy the earth. Television allows us to amuse ourselves to death without reflecting on our own story. Someone has said if we do look at history, it comes in the form of the instant replay. Again and again we look at yet another view of a play, from this side, from that side, and then again from this side.

What a congregation or a denomination believes about God shows up in the stories its members tell about congregational life. If a congregation believes in forgiveness, its history will reveal accounts of reconciliation with factions inside the congregation or without. If a denomination believes in evangelism, missions, social justice, its stories will be about people making the mission of the church their mission.

Several years ago literary critic Alfred Kazin told a conference of English teachers that "the immigrant writes to make a home for himself on paper—to find a place, a ledge." I understood then why my immigrant parents had told us children stories around the old oak table in our small frame house in northern Saskatchewan. They were trying to make sense out of the difficult experiences of war, revolution, and famine just behind them. We heard funny stories about courting during the war, sad stories about sudden death during the revolution, and courageous ones about immigration to America without money and carrying with them only a Russian samovar, a flour sack filled with toasted rolls, six polka-dotted diapers and a few other items packed in a few suitcases, and a tin cradle. They were telling stories to find a home, for people tell stories to identify the secure place: "This much I know about myself . . . this part of my life is secure. I can talk about it. Now how do I match this experience with what I yet don't understand?"

This kind of storytelling or life review to integrate all of life is an important exercise for the aging, for a person's story is God's work in their life. The telling helps them put together the bits and pieces. Writing this book has done that for me. One pastor mentioned that he used to ask people to share their "spiritual pilgrimage" but then he just got "churchy" histories. Now he asks for depth moments of all kinds, the "hot spots," the "energy-laden points" of people's history, where God met them in the stuff of their own stories. He expects them to share intimate inner struggles of both personal and collective experiences. I like to think of them as the "Aha!" times. Harvey Cox in *Seduction of the Spirit* states that "religion should be the seedbed and spawning ground of stories. But today religion is not fulfilling its storytelling role. Like the society it inhabits, it has become top-heavy with . . . systems."

I am convinced that both the older person and his or her possible audience are the losers when story-telling isn't a welcome activity, for a knowledge of the past gives understanding of how change affects everyone and that we all face an uncertain future.

After a number of workshops on memoir writing, I sensed everyone has at least one story they want passed on—recorded for posterity. At one workshop an eighty-four-year-old woman said that the story she wanted to write about had to do with a childhood experience on an Oklahoma farm. A board had fallen into the well, the only source of drinking water, contaminating the water. How could it be retrieved? Her parents decided to lower their three-year-old daughter into the well in a large pail. A dry run of the proposed procedure on solid ground indicated that the pail tipped too easily, so her father fastened the pail handle securely. A first lowering resulted in failure. The board was too slippery for small hands. The second time she was lowered, she grasped the board and brought it up.

Why did she want this story remembered? She wasn't sure, but some memory of a feeling had stayed with her these many years. Was it her parents' desperation? Or their trust in her? Or possibly her fear? Having older people tell me their experiences convinces me that we remember best events in which we experienced strong emotions. To retell these stories helps us to come to terms with them.

At the English conference, Kazin spoke particularly about the immigrant child (and he was one): "Language is the salvation of the immigrant child who must reorder his or her existence by means from within." Immigrants have only language by which to pass on what is important to them. The past is gone, as are family heirlooms and other artifacts. The territory in the adopted land is new. They are guided by memories, a set of values, and hope for the future. The only way to pass on the values inherent in their past and to explain the reason for making a break with the past is through stories.

Most of us, however, are not immigrants. We have lived in this country sometimes for generations. Yet in times of fast change such as we are experiencing we are immigrants of another kind. Vocational and geographic mobility, technological advance, changing value systems, have turned us all into immigrants, sometimes without clear ideas of our place in God's economy. The new frontiers are emotional, psychological, technological, intellectual, and spiritual. We are all looking for that safe ledge as much as the landed immigrant from another country. We all need to tell stories as we confront change, as we have sought and found new freedoms, as we have cast off old bondages, and won new victories. Anyone who has felt excluded from history, such as minorities and women, will feel the need for storytelling sooner than those who are content in their role.

As I hear older people discuss the faith life informally, their questions are not so much academic or doctrinal, as practical. They don't seem as much concerned about whether the virgin birth is possible as whether faith can survive the moral darkness, whether the church is actually concerned about fighting sin and evil, whether the words of the celebrity, toothily saying, "The Lord guided me to success," can be trusted, whether faith in Christ actually makes a difference in time of personal sorrow and suffering.

Modern immigrants in this unbrave new world need the

courage which comes from the story told by the person who shares life experiences with God. Such stories of faith and joy, but also of hopelessness and despair, can unlock the listener's own dreams, of which today there is a real dearth. They give the hearers permission to risk their own dream, knowing that though success may not always follow, the reaching is important.

Language has no meaning until the reader or listener attaches it to his or her own experience. We hear or read stories with our own experiences of love, hate, jealousy, embarrassment in mind. I received letters from readers in response to *Good Times* asking, "How did you know what my growing up was like?" I didn't. I just knew about mine, but the more personal the sharing, the more universal the experience becomes. Emotions are the same today as three thousand years ago. Hope is always hope, love is always love, courage is always courage, faith is always faith. Circumstances change—houses are made of brick instead of wood, floors of tile or carpet instead of mud. Benches have been exchanged for chairs, hard rope beds for water beds, the horse and buggy for a high-powered vehicle. But something always remains the same—what a child feels when coming home to warmth and love, the first awareness of a person of the other sex, the disappointment at a gift, the first knowledge of powerlessness, corruption, or violence, the first awareness of God's grace and mercy. We are all searching for these same truths and don't know it until we find ourselves in someone else's story.

Stories show how someone caused values to become living truth in another time and setting. The listener can then link his or her own questions and hopes with the shared experience. Such identification with the emotions involved in the story provide insight into the Christian life and open the way to a more mature faith. Without the story, preaching and admonishing seem just so much pressure to conform to group beliefs.

My book *Good Times with Old Times* is an attempt to encourage such storytelling. Occasionally readers, as part of their last passage, send me a copy of their manuscript in which they try to tell friends and family what they have been, what they wanted life to mean. They want to show that they were pilgrims, not just tourists through life. As they write their story they draw the loose ends together as best they can, in something of the manner that women used to make "grief quilts," patchwork quilts of pieces from all the various garments a deceased child had worn, helped to bring closure to remembering the child's life. Such a retelling gives both God and humanity their due. It is an act of construction, of creating meaning.

A return to an emphasis on stories, however, may create two problems. As John Ruth points out in *Mennonite Identity and Literary Art*, if there is no true story of cross-bearing for God present in a personal or congregational history, the "essential emptiness of the story will reveal itself soon enough." Which is possibly the main reason we stick to a systems approach. To tell our own story of Jesus and his love might reveal a stark poverty of spirit.

Furthermore, people may come up with new understandings of the Bible stories if they reread them with a fresh approach, forcing those who are very sure of their interpretations to defend their systems, which then may result in a different kind of story. This has happened before in history, with Martin Luther as a prime example. He went to the Bible and discovered in a new reading salvation by faith for all believers. Minorities, women, and the oppressed, who read the Bible stories with the understanding they are included in them and need not live on the fringes, rejoice in the gospel in a new way.

An authentic story makes it impossible to pass off a string of words as the essence of the redeemed life. Above all, it passes on to one's children not an empty bucket, but shows them where to find the well.

CHAPTER 20

Let's celebrate!

*The living, the living—they praise you, as I
am doing today; fathers tell their children
about your faithfulness.*

—Isaiah 38:19

One of my favorite television shows is "The Homecoming,"
which spun off into "The Waltons," the story of a large family
that lived in legend-rich mountain country, poor but rich in the
joy of living. This first script tells the story of a Christmas Eve
when the father is delayed returning home from work a
distance away. The wife learns there has been a train accident—and that probably her husband is on that train. So she
sends John-boy to find his father. Many things happen. But finally the father comes home late, safe and sound, with a sack of
presents for his children, to a tear-jerking reunion.

Each time I see the film, this celebration of family love tugs
at my heartstrings. It brings to mind my young adult years
working in the city and traveling home for Christmas by
train—sixty miles as the crow flies—but three times that
distance by train. During the war years, the trains were jammed full of military personnel and students—but spirits rang
high. Like Dorothy in "The Wizard of Oz," we were going
home to love and warmth and nothing could have felt better.

We belonged at home, safe and secure, unthreatened by life's tidal waves. We never spoke of celebrating, but that's what we did with actions, words, and thoughts.

Celebration has a specific place in the scriptural pattern: when sin is followed by forgiveness, celebration follows. In our pragmatic approach to the Christian life, the last stage in this pattern is frequently dismissed as unnecessary or given but a passing wave of the hand. Yet the home of the prodigal son stood for celebration, as well as forgiveness. This emphasis becomes clearer in the New International Version because it uses the word "celebrate" rather than the King James term "be merry."

Upon coming to his senses, the son returns from the far country where he has squandered his father's gift to him and lived without constraints. He returns home to ask forgiveness. The father meets him, embraces and kisses him, places a ring on his finger and shoes on his feet, and orders a festival. The grain-fed calf, reserved for special company, is killed and the celebration begins with singing and dancing, for "My son was dead and is alive." The remarkable characteristic of this father is that he doesn't worry that the son may return to his former patterns of living. He celebrates at once.

The older son returns from the fields. He hears the festive sounds of music and dancing (which some commentators believe was not actually dancing but a form of dramatic choral singing in which the younger son's story was acted out). Disturbed, he refuses to enter the house, and tells his father so. The father replies that everything he owns has belonged to the son these many years. Their relationship should have been a continual celebration. But the older son had never learned to enjoy it. He had never learned to be free and real about the right things—to celebrate.

As a child the day was a special celebration for me when all the relatives from across the river came. Mother cooked a big meal. The day before she had sent one of us to the butcher shop to buy a dollar's worth of roast beef—about seven pounds. At the time hamburger was five cents, liver almost free. Mother had baked a huge chocolate cake with thick creamy frosting. Dad sometimes brought home special treats of chocolate bars and candy. Occasionally the photographer came to take a family photo. We spent the day talking and enjoying one another.

That basically defines celebration—a spirit of joy, unity, and freedom in which we think of the other person before ourselves. We do it with food, with gifts, with words, with songs and dance, with our presence. When we celebrate someone we tell that person, "You are important to me and therefore I am ready to be present to you. During this time I have only you to think of—no one else." In celebration we attribute worth to another. When we celebrate God, we attribute worth to him. We tell him how much we value him.

People in our congregations need to be affirmed and celebrated for their decisions and contributions out of recognition that God is with them and us. Paul Chapman in *Clusters* writes that "anyone who wants to understand a people of another time or place will find in their rituals and celebrations a telling evidence of who those people were: their beliefs, their values, their social relationships." Our celebrations are visible symbols by which we identify ourselves and transmit values to the young by what we affirm.

A friend tells the story of a former San Quentin prisoner, four times on death row for murder, who had come to his congregation asking, "Can God forgive one like me?" Later, at his baptism, the congregation had clapped, then shouted, as they affirmed his decision and their acceptance of him. Yes, celebration defines us. It reveals our values. Those who get drunk together say they belong together. Those who celebrate a birthday or a wedding say they belong together. Those who have forgiven one another say they belong together.

The spirit present during the celebration, however, attracts or repels. Real celebration means that the attention of the whole family, the whole congregation, or whoever may be celebrating, is focused in one direction, identifying with one another in affirmation of someone or some value. It draws them together. Those who celebrated the return of the wanderer said, "We are a family. You are a member of this family. We thought you were lost, but you have returned to us. We have gained as a family." He longed to hear those words.

But the older son said, "Brother, you may have come back, but you are not part of me. I refuse to allow you to come in if it means I stay out. I cannot affirm your worth to this family." He did not identify with the others in their welcome and affirmation of the prodigal.

Real celebration says, "You are loved, you are cherished," something much needed in families and congregations. In our midst are many people who have never been celebrated for themselves because they do not meet societal norms. I recall a woman getting up at singles retreat to state boldly: "I want my singleness celebrated." Many people have never had their name in print, except in an obituary, never had a balloon flown for them, never had their artwork displayed on someone's refrigerator door. They live alone, never have anniversaries, graduations, births, or weddings, never bother to celebrate birthdays, never receive a compliment for singing or speaking in public, never are congratulated for work in a committee. Yet they need to be celebrated for being a unique person made in the image of God.

Several years ago after a silver wedding celebration of my youngest sister and her husband, the extended family, many of whom had come from a distance, decided to visit me in Hillsboro, where I live. My home was too small to accommodate them all, so I reserved a room in a local restaurant. As I sat down, my brother stood up to say, "Today we are celebrating Katie Funk Wiebe Appreciation Day." Obviously everyone had known about this surprise event but me. They presented me with a corsage, a gift of china, and speeches ranging from the ridiculous to the sublime. They let me know I didn't have to celebrate a wedding anniversary to be loved. They loved me for who I was. I cherish that memory.

Celebration is all-encompassing. Some celebrations are prompted by group members having had similar experiences. School alumni return for homecoming because they share memories and recognize they are stewards of these memories. A true celebration takes everyone in and is therefore a great leveler of social caste. There is no real celebration if the poor are forced to sit in one section of the dining hall eating jelly sandwiches and the rich in another, enjoying barbecued steak, or the singles sit in one section and the marrieds in another. True celebration says that those gathered have no one to fear, nothing to feel guilty about, or nothing to be selfish about in this group. They are one in the spirit.

Celebration is something very wonderful, yet fragile, like a delicate piece of crystal—shimmeringly beautiful, but easily shattered if mistreated. It moves us into another dimension of life—one we're afraid of, for we don't know where it may lead us. It moves us into the realm of the intangible, almost the mysterious, where meaning comes through the symbolic—singing, presents, food, special words, decorations, banners, and especially poetry, storytelling, and body movement.

Therefore celebration is easily lost in a practical, consumer-oriented society in which we rush to and fro looking for a certain shade of cloth or the newest fad in toys. The spirit needed for celebration is easily crushed by the need for efficiency, orderliness, or even perfection. It belongs to the dimension of life that can't be measured, counted, weighed, or shaped. When we most want this spirit of joy, it disappears, yet unless planned for, it doesn't happen.

We avoid celebration because we think it takes time and creativity, and we're stolid, hardworking people without time for such froth and frivolity. We avoid it with busyness, but also with passivity, sitting before the television, stupefying ourselves nightly. We kill it by the attempt to substitute money for it. "Here, take this money and buy yourself something," a husband may tell a wife. "Or let's go eat in an expensive restaurant," she tells him. Celebration is lost in the congregation when the staff or committee says, "Let's just collect the money we need for this project and forget about celebration—too much work and expenditure of energy." It would be better to plan an evening of celebration if there is something to celebrate and forget the money. But there's nothing more deadening than celebrations that celebrate nothing.

Sometimes I watch people celebrating an anniversary or a birthday by eating out. They sit at their table silent, waiting for the event to be over so they go back to sameness. Celebration always leaves when community disappears but invites when it is present. Some Christian political prisoners in South America celebrated the Lord's Supper together secretly, without either wine or bread. Other prisoners, sympathetic to them, carried on a loud conversation so the guards wouldn't spot this circle of men passing nothing, yet passing everything to one another. Later, one of the prisoners, not a Christian, said, "You people have something special, which I would like to have." The writer of the article wrote, "Is this not an example of the liberating, identifying evangelism that Jesus called us to?"

Yet celebration needs neither money, food, or much time—only a spirit of thankfulness, a desire for unity, and a readiness to let go of time. Celebration is an open, free exhibition of love—that moves us beyond ourselves freeing us from having to be sensible, calculating, and discreet. The greatest nurturer of celebration is simply overcoming through forgiveness the barriers that separate us. And forgiveness is needed most often in the circle of intimates, not strangers. They don't need it. And they don't usually celebrate together either, unless it is something superficial.

True celebration expects no return, yet creates joy that

produces an extra surge of energy and strength when one returns to the normal routine. Its spirit carries us for weeks and months. I enjoy my elderly neighbor's attitude toward celebration. On the morning of the anniversary of her wedding many decades ago, she was tempted to yield to sadness. But as she thought about that day when she and her deceased husband were married, she remembered they had eaten cinnamon rolls at the reception. So out came the yeast and flour. When someone phoned to ask what she was doing, she invited them to join her for coffee and a roll. One friend told another. By evening the day that could have turned out dismally became a full-length celebration of life that continued throughout the week.

Few celebrations are complete without storytelling, a witness to our pilgrimage, explaining the unique pattern of our lives. Usually when we plan celebrations, particularly for a congregation, we include reports and proclamation, but forget to tell the story of the way we have come, to connect the present with the past, so that the young can see the working of God in our lives.

Though family reunions are popular today, they can be merely gatherings of related people studying genealogies instead of celebrations. What happens depends on so many variables. Several years ago our family gathered. Three generations came—we, who thought of ourselves as middle-aged, our children, and a few of their children. The older fourth generation declined the invitation to travel long distances in the middle of winter.

Sister No. 2 said family reunions are mostly food. True. But food brings people close together around tables, so that elbows which years ago poked each other roughly to gain living space now rubbed in affirmation. Around a cup of coffee, we looked each other in the eye and asked, "Who am I? Who are you?"

As the middle sister, I looked at those on both sides of me. Two older. Two younger. Were these once the children, who, decades ago, huddled night after night under heavy woolen comforters in the slant-ceiling bedroom in northern Saskatchewan to listen to the oldest sister tell us "continuing stories"?

Were these once the children who locked the door on themselves in the lean-to playhouse behind the garage to enter their own world of make-believe? I recall arguments deciding whose turn it was to operate the nail-studded control panel of our flying machine. The operator had the awesome privilege of explaining to those squatting on the floor what they were experiencing as the machine narrowly escaped colliding with a meteor or skimmed dense tropical forests infested with dangerous animals. What had time done to those children? What had we done with time?

Now here we were, each one trying to resurrect the best story out of the past. Out of memory's trunk came the pranks, the embarrassments, and the near disasters. One Christmas Eve our chimney caught fire, and we all lost our heads, but a passing inebriate celebrating the season kept his. He saw the flames belching from the chimney, staggered into the house, and poured salt into the cavernous hollow of our pot-bellied heater. The fire went out and we went on preparing for Christmas.

We discussed clothing fashions and cars we had owned. Someone once purchased a Whippet for $100. Another had owned a car with a rumble seat. A second-hand McLaughlin Buick made travel pleasant for our family for years.

We told each other again about the teachers we had liked and disliked. We racked our brains to remember names of classmates and boyfriends.

We compared notes on health. Thinning hair and arthritis came up frequently. One person looked almost like Kojak, another like Edith Bunker.

We discussed changes in the church, value systems, and service opportunities.

In larger gatherings the funny stories erupted regularly. In little groups, late at night over yet another cup of coffee, personal struggles and trials, bitter moments and sweet victories unfolded quietly. We stayed away from platitudes about faith.

We talked about ourselves, about our children, and the effect of heredity and environment. For a few days all generations looked in the same direction—toward the past. While our children listened, we acknowledged that the past lives on in our minds and bodies. It has been a part in making us what we are. We cannot cut ourselves off from our roots. To reject the past is to bind ourselves to it even more strongly.

So we filtered the early years, with their good and bad experiences, through our conversation, each person adding a detail the others had missed, hoping the young would see their future more clearly because of this.

We told each other we no longer saw ourselves as exclusive models for our children as we once might have done. We hadn't received a perfect heritage from our forebears. Neither would they. But each of them, like us, has the opportunity to redeem that heritage.

And so we separated to take up our individual tasks and look to the future. With a good feeling. One member of the younger generation said she sensed that though the older ones had been through tough, sometimes disappointing and almost impossible experiences, they had survived. "Great is thy faithfulness," we had sung together. Her generation would survive, too, in their brave new world.

The younger ones didn't know our songs and hymns, our childhood games and customs. But one thing remained the same. The power of God's grace to redeem the past—its misunderstandings, sins, and shortcomings. We were not celebrating perfect families, but God's continuing working in our lives. We celebrated that family still represents an opportunity for undeserved love, dependability in crisis, a resting spot, a reuniting. In that lies the glory of family power and of celebration.

My mother, nearly ninety at the time, told me that she and Father, feeling the walls of life slowly closing in upon them and their own vigor to keep them at a distance diminishing, sometimes "just stood and hung on to one another." That's the essence of family celebration. We come together to hang on to one another for a little while before the tempo of life picks up again or a change takes place.

Celebration rejoices at the abolition of division and separation. At the heart of the gospel is the good news that Christ has brought together what sin and evil separated. Any celebration, whether in a family, among friends, or in a congregation therefore becomes a political act, marked by freedom and responsibility to show others the walls have come down. At the Lord's table, we tell the world that rich and poor, male and female, black and white, from every nation celebrate with the symbols of Christ's death God's uniting act in the incarnation and redemption.

Steve Biko, South African leader, writes that "our task is not to bring about freedom; freedom is already coming. Our task is to prepare ourselves for freedom, to live now as those already set free." As Christians celebrate, we, too, reveal we are set free. Sin, forgiveness, celebration—that's the pattern. Let's celebrate!

The Author

"I think I should try writing something—but if I have nothing to say, there is no use writing that nothing down on paper." Those words of Katie Funk Wiebe, written shortly after high school, would not be recognized today by readers of her books, columns, articles, and devotional and curriculum materials. For over twenty years she has been an articulate voice in the Christian community, putting into words her thoughts on various topics.

Wiebe is associate professor of English at Tabor College, Hillsboro, Kansas, where she has taught since 1966. She holds the M.A. degree from Wichita State University and the B.A. degree from Tabor College, both in English. Since 1976, when the youngest of her four children left home, she has written nine books, has had chapters published in numerous books, and has written hundreds of articles covering a wide range of topics from reflections on Christian life and thought to writing memoirs and biography. She is also a frequent retreat and workshop leader.

Among the books she has written are *Alone: A Search for Joy; Good Times with Old Times; Our Lamps Were Lit: An Informal History of the Deaconess Hospital School of Nursing; Women Among the Brethren; Second Thoughts;* and *Who Are the Mennonite Brethren?*

She was born in northern Saskatchewan into a Russian Mennonite family. Her parents' love for storytelling emphasized for her its significance in value-formation. She is a member of the Hillsboro Mennonite Brethren Church, where she is involved in Sunday school teaching and the diaconate.

The first paragraph of this author sketch is adapted from an article by La Vonne Platt, "Katie Funk Wiebe: Writer of Vision," in *The Mennonite* of July 6, 1982.